Y0-BQV-948

TRANSFORMING VISION

Transforming Vision

Imagination and Will in Kierkegaardian Faith

M. JAMIE FERREIRA

CLARENDON PRESS · OXFORD

1991

Oxford University Press, Walton Street, Oxford OX2 6DP

Oxford New York Toronto
Delhi Bombay Calcutta Madras Karachi
Petaling Jaya Singapore Hong Kong Tokyo
Nairobi Dar es Salaam Cape Town
Melbourne Auckland

and associated companies in
Berlin Ibadan

Oxford is a trade mark of Oxford University Press

Published in the United States
by Oxford University Press, New York

British Library Cataloguing in Publication Data
Data available

Library of Congress Cataloging in Publication Data
Data available

ISBN 0-19-826331-7

Typeset by Joshua Associates Ltd., Oxford
Printed in Great Britain by
Bookcraft (Bath) Ltd.,
Midsomer Norton, Avon

Acknowledgements

My foremost intellectual debt of gratitude is due to Walter Jost, my friend and colleague at the university, for many hours of patient reading and supportive sharing as this manuscript developed; the anonymous readers selected by my editor, Hilary Feldman, also offered wise counsels. I want to acknowledge as well the kind permission of the following journals to draw on materials published by them: *The International Journal for Philosophy of Religion* ('Kierkegaardian Faith: The "Condition" and the Response', 28 (Oct. 1990), 63–79); *The International Philosophical Quarterly* ('Kierkegaardian Transitions: Paradox and Pathos', 31 (March 1991)); and *Faith and Philosophy* ('Seeing (Just) *is* Believing: Faith and Imagination' (forthcoming 1992)). Princeton University Press has also kindly granted permission to quote from the *Concluding Unscientific Postscript*.

Finally, and most importantly, I dedicate this work to George Bruch who has taught me the truth of Wittgenstein's saying 'The light work sheds is a beautiful light, which, however, only shines with real beauty if it is illuminated by yet another light'. He has offered that other light through years of patient love and friendship and *joie de vivre*.

Charlottesville, Virginia
1990

Contents

Introduction

Like many in the philosophical tradition preceding him, the Danish thinker, Søren Kierkegaard (1813–55) was deeply ambivalent towards imagination. The numerous negative assessments found throughout his writings were in a long line of those who saw imagination primarily in terms of make-believe, pretence, and wishful thinking. Names like Hume and Feuerbach come readily to mind when one thinks of those who quite vocally argued, especially with respect to religious belief, that the imaginative contribution at the heart of belief was deceptive. But one need not turn to such modern critics of religion for the inspiration behind negative assessments of imagination, for Kierkegaard's diatribes against imagination express a deep-seated mistrust which is found as early as the Hebraic association made between original sin and imagination. Richard Kearney's genealogy of imagination, *The Wake of Imagination: Toward a Postmodern Culture*, records this Hebraic suspicion of the creative power of humans, carried on through the Greek and medieval traditions, and reveals the ironic twist of its negativity in the post-modern era where the imagination is no longer seen as a threat precisely because it is no longer seen as genuinely creative.[1] The post-modern deconstructionist's general programme of demystification includes among its targets the pretensions of imagination to be a genuine creative centre of meaning, relegating it to an activity in which we are limited to playing around with fragments of meaning which we have not created.[2]

This emasculation of imagination, however, issues from a tradition which from its beginning also included positive assessments of imagination, and Kierkegaard, acknowledging that an 'advantage' can become a 'curse',[3] was as deeply aware of the positive creative potential of imagination as he was of its dangers. Indeed, one can see in his writings a striking preoccupation with imagination which expresses itself finally in a remarkable appreciation of the value and even necessity of imaginative

---

[1] Minneapolis, Minn., 1988.
[2] Ibid., Introduction: 'Imagination Now' and ch. 7: 'The Parodic Imagination', *passim*.
[3] *Either/Or*, trans. Walter Lowrie (Princeton, NJ, 1959), ii. 16.

activity for genuine self-development. It is this appreciation, I suggest, which most warrants a reconsideration of his thought in our day.

KIERKEGAARD AND IMAGINATION

The contrasting strands of the tradition confronted Kierkegaard in the form of the nineteenth-century's romantic adulation of imagination and its rationalist denigration of imagination. His response was to expose the limits of both positions. Indeed, attacking such a dual target at once required a finely tuned sensitivity to all the functions of imagination, and he expressed this sensitivity by adopting a variety of perspectives on imagination throughout his writings. The attack involved a very nuanced understanding of the concepts of possibility and actuality in relation to imagination, evaluating positively for some purposes and contexts what was evaluated negatively for others. For example, anticipating the radical question raised more than a century later by Milan Kundera's consideration of the paradoxical 'unbearable lightness of being',[4] Kierkegaard himself explored the realm of self-development through various perspectives on the value of lightness and heaviness as they relate to possibility and actuality. His varied presentations of imagination align it at times with possibility, at other times with actuality. Moreover, at times it is possibility which is seen as light—the aesthetic (objective, disinterested, intellectual) possibility which distracts and dissipates the self—in contrast to the (heavy) demand of actuality (reality)[5]; at other times actuality is seen as light—because delimited—in contrast to the (heavy) demand of interested, required, inclusive, inexhaustible possibility.[6] Kundera's conclusion that 'the lightness/weight opposition is the most mysterious, most ambiguous of all'[7] is but an echo of Kierkegaard's own realization.

Despite frequent references to the lightness of aesthetic possibility, his suggestion that 'possibility is the weightiest of categories'[8] expresses a fundamental commitment that is common to a variety of his accounts—

---

[4] *The Unbearable Lightness of Being*, trans. Michael Henry Heim (New York, 1984).

[5] *Either/Or*, ii. 256 and *Concluding Unscientific Postscript*, trans. David Swenson and Walter Lowrie (Princeton, NJ, 1968), 282–8, 302, 304, 376.

[6] *Postscript*, 287, 320–1; *Concept of Anxiety*, ed. and trans. Reidar Thomte (Princeton, NJ, 1980), 156–7. For more on this, see my 'Repetition, Concreteness, and Imagination', *International Journal for Philosophy of Religion*, 25 (1989), esp. 28–9.

[7] Kundera, *The Unbearable Lightness of Being*, 6.

[8] *Concept of Anxiety*, 156.

namely, a commitment to the indispensability of imagination to ethical and subjective development. And in this commitment we can find, I suggest, the heart of his continuing relevance to philosophy; indeed, he anticipates in important ways a number of contemporary visions which emphasize ethical or moral imagination.

There is no question but that Kierkegaard was aware of the many ways in which imagination can mislead us, and that negative evaluations of imagination are found throughout his writings. Some of the most striking are attributed to Anti-Climacus, who warns that 'in possibility you can go astray in all possible ways', hence the 'tendency to run wild in possibility'; it is imagination which enables one to pursue possibility until 'at last he cannot find his way back to himself'.[9] Imagination can so carry a man 'out into the infinite that it merely carries him away from himself and therewith prevents him from returning to himself. . . . he becomes in a way infinitized, but not in such a way that he becomes more and more himself, for he loses himself more and more'.[10]

In the Climacus writings, which concern us more directly, we find similar warnings against wandering into the 'fairyland of the imagination', and we are told of the threat posed by 'the medium of imagination' (and the 'sphere of the possible') in drawing us away from the medium of 'becoming' and the realm of the ethical, existence, action, and reality.[11] On the other hand, there is an abundance of comments throughout the Kierkegaard authorship which reveal a positive appreciation of other uses of imagination. I want to suggest, however, that whether or not individual negative expressions are outnumbered by individual positive expressions, an undeniable commitment to the value of imaginative activity is integral to Kierkegaard's various presentations of selfhood. Despite the fact that imagination can be used in ways prejudicial to self-development, carrying one away from the demand and stability of actuality, its use is nevertheless necessary, in his view, to any and all genuine development of the self.

Imagination, for Kierkegaard, is only properly imagination of 'otherness'. Although one can argue that Kierkegaard and Nietzsche are diametrically opposed concerning the evaluative hierarchy of self-development, Kierkegaard is in agreement with Nietzsche in so far as Nietzsche (reformulating his general evaluation of the near and the far) counsels that 'your true nature lies, not concealed deep within you, but

[9] *The Sickness unto Death*, trans. Walter Lowrie (Princeton, NJ, 1954), 170.
[10] Ibid. 164.
[11] *Postscript*, 320; 284–6, 288, 376, 302–4.

immeasurably high above you, or at least above that which you usually take yourself to be'.[12] This contrast between what is 'deep within' and what is 'high above' is embodied, as we shall see in detail, in the reference to the 'other self' which is common to several Kierkegaardian accounts of the paradox of change generating the necessity of ethical imagination.

Ethical imagination for Kierkegaard involves not only the 'other' as the ideal self, however, but the genuinely separate and concrete 'other'. This is implied in his emphasis on each self's concreteness, for as concrete selves we are necessarily embedded in a concrete context of social relations. This focus on the individual as concrete (implying the concreteness of the 'other') effectively highlights the function of imagination in individuating, particularizing, intensifying[13]—in short, concretizing rather than abstracting. In this way Kierkegaard avoids the problems with those Kantian moral programmes which see ethical imagination simply in its role as an abstract, universalizing imagination.[14]

In appreciating ethical imagination as concretizing or, more precisely, as seeing the universal *in* the concrete particular, Kierkegaard anticipates that appreciation of ethical imagination expressed in several recent philosophical proposals. Roberto M. Unger, for example, in *Passion: An Essay on Personality*, emphasizes the necessity of an 'imagination of otherness' to any 'revision of character' or 'moral invention'.[15] Indeed, Kierkegaard anticipates both Unger's appreciation of particularity and concreteness as expressed in his formulation of the problems of 'solidarity' and 'contextuality' and his suggestion that transcendence of any context from within requires an imagination of otherness.[16] The imagination does more than simply set the stage for change, however, for, in Unger's words, it 'probes reality by conceiving its transformative variations and *thereby* changes the quality of desire'.[17] We shall find the

[12] 'Schopenhauer as Educator', in *Untimely Meditations* (1873–6), trans. R. J. Hollingdale (Cambridge, 1983), 129.

[13] See Philip Wheelwright's discussion of various operations of imagination; the 'confrontative' and 'stylistic' ways are of particular relevance here, while what he terms 'compositive' and 'archetypal' have a bearing on other roles of imagination which we will consider later (*The Burning Fountain* (Bloomington, Ind. , rev. edn. 1968), esp. 32–55).

[14] Those problems are pointed to by a variety of proposals of a 'feminist ethics', including 'The Kohlberg-Gilligan Controversy and Moral Theory: The Generalized and the Concrete Other', by Seyla Benhabib, in *Women and Moral Theory*, eds. Eva F. Kittay and Diana T. Meyers (Totowa, NJ, 1987), 154–77. My own defence of Kierkegaard in this respect is found in 'Kierkegaardian Imagination and "the Feminine"', Presidential Address, Society for Philosophy of Religion, 2 March 1990, New Orleans, La.

[15] New York, 1984, 38, 145, 178, 191; 98–9. See also Kearney's *The Wake of Imagination*, Conclusion: 'After Imagination'.

[16] Unger, *Passion*, esp. 3–15; 41–2.   [17] Ibid. 148, my emphasis.

same insistence on the efficaciousness of ethical imagination in Kierkegaard's proposals.

The indispensability of 'imaginative identification' is stressed even more strongly in Richard Rorty's recent description of the 'ironist' alternative to 'liberal' culture.[18] Rorty writes that human solidarity is a goal to be *achieved*, rather than discovered, and it is achievable 'not by inquiry, but by imagination, the imaginative ability to see strange people as fellow sufferers'.[19] The 'identification with "humanity as such"' which he vehemently rejects is replaced by an 'imaginative identification with the details of others', the development of 'skill at recognizing and describing' the concreteness of the other.[20] His emphasis, again anticipated by Kierkegaard, is on imaginative concretizing as opposed to imaginative abstracting and universalizing.

Although the importance of ethical imagination to certain Kierkegaardian accounts has been noted, the precise way in which imagination functions in such change has not yet been analysed either in relation to paradox or to will.[21] The centrality and indispensability of imagination is, I shall be arguing, anchored in the importance of *paradoxical choice* in such accounts. It is the distinctive function of imagination to hold elements in tension,[22] and without this activity paradox can neither be perceived nor appropriated. The Kierkegaardian accounts of the ethical provide a stark reminder that development cannot occur except paradoxically, and this explains both the necessity of imagination and the limits of the relevance of theoretical reflection to the process.

Kierkegaard's focus on the paradoxical tension central to the ethical or subjective self is clearly revealed, as we shall see, in his insistence that the task of the existing individual is to remain in the great 'contradiction'—between finite and infinite, positive and negative, comic and pathetic. The task is not to erase the tension (even if we could), but to sustain it, at the highest pitch possible. In this enterprise theoretical reflection is

---

[18] *Contingency, Irony, and Solidarity* (Cambridge, 1989).

[19] Ibid. xvi.   [20] Ibid. 198, 190, 93.

[21] David J. Gouwens provides an excellent documentation of both negative and positive understandings of imagination, with sensitive reference to historical context, in his *Kierkegaard's Dialectic of the Imagination* (New York, 1989). However, he does not address the kind of relation I examine between leap, paradox, will, and imagination—for example, there is not even an index entry for 'paradox' (or 'will') in the book. Nor is this a focus of his fine article, 'Kierkegaard on the Ethical Imagination', *Journal of Religious Ethics*, 10 (Fall 1982), which is incorporated into the book.

[22] Mary Warnock's suggestion that to 'perceive the universal in the particular' is 'the very central function of the imagination' is a variation of this ('Religious Imagination', in *Religious Imagination*, ed. James P. Mackey (Edinburgh, 1986), 152).

ineffective, for through such reflection we can only either resolve or reject tension—we cannot live it. What Richard Rorty in our time recommends as the 'turn against theory and toward narrative' is premised on his claim that all we can hope to achieve with respect to the various perspectives we want to integrate into our lives (public/private, justice/self-creation, solidarity/autonomy, etc.) is 'accommodation, not synthesis'.[23] Although Rorty would no doubt shy away from an association with Kierkegaard, I think the comparison is illuminating in this formal respect—namely, they both turn away from theory in the admission that 'such opposites can be combined in a life, but not synthesized in a theory'; at the level of theory, some things remain 'equally valid yet forever incommensurable'.[24] That is, I suggest that Kierkegaard expresses a similar appreciation of the problem of incommensurability ingredient in existence, though for him it is expressed in the idiom of *paradox*. Whatever the differences between them, and there are many, they both affirm in their own way that we can *live together* what we cannot theoretically unite. Moreover, one could argue that despite Kierkegaard's affirmation of the validity of the religious dimension, his concomitant affirmation of the centrality of paradox may well be another way of saying, with Rorty, that we cannot 'hold all the sides of our life in a single vision, [or] describe them all with a single vocabulary'.[25]

Kierkegaard's most radical difference from the Rortyan programme, however, lies in the fact that he does not stop with the response of moral imagination. Since for him the ethical is insufficient, and, like the aesthetic, is 'transfigured' rather than left behind in the transition to a fuller development of subjectivity in Christianity, Kierkegaard's contribution to an understanding of ethical imagination is at the same time a contribution to an understanding of *religious* imagination, and it is the role of imagination in this transition to 'faith' which is the ultimate focus of this work.

KIERKEGAARD AND THE 'LEAP'

The metaphor of a 'leap of faith', which has been popularly used by many—sometimes in impassioned defence of faith and at other times as a paradigm example of the indefensibility (or irresponsible irrelevance) of

---

[23] Rorty, *Contingency, Irony, and Solidarity*, xvi. 68.
[24] Ibid. 120.   [25] Ibid. xv-xvi.

such faith—is probably the element most widely recognized as a distinctive characteristic of a 'Kierkegaardian' account of the transition to religious faith. Both in popular and scholarly circles the Kierkegaardian
'leap' has usually been understood in terms of an act of 'will-power'.
Indeed, C. Stephen Evans has suggested in a recent article that a 'typical
picture' of 'Kierkegaard's view of Christian faith' is that 'it requires a
"leap of faith" [through which] assisted by divine grace, the believer
manages, through an heroic act of will, to get himself to believe what he
knows is absurd'.[26] Terence Penelhum, for example, seems to subscribe
to such a picture when he writes that 'In purely human terms this will
seem to be the sheer wilful acceptance of the logically impossible by an
act of will', for to 'make such a leap we require an act of will'.[27] Louis P.
Pojman similarly reads Kierkegaard as an example of a 'descriptive [and
'prescriptive'] volitionalist'—one who holds 'that we can [and sometimes
should] obtain beliefs and withhold beliefs directly upon performing an
act of will'.[28]

In such accounts, the 'leap' or 'decision' spoken of by Climacus in two
of Kierkegaard's major works is seen as a choice—either to set the understanding aside or to embrace the Absolute Paradox of God in Time—
which, although its character is not explored, is treated by commentators
as if it were an intentional, purposeful, deliberate, self-conscious, or
reflective 'act of will' or 'volition'[29] (on the side of the agent) through

---

[26] 'Does Kierkegaard Think Beliefs Can Be Directly Willed?', *International Journal for
Philosophy of Religion*, 26 (December 1989), 182. Evans, as we shall see in Chapter 6, is
also critical of such a picture.

[27] *God and Skepticism: A Study in Skepticism and Fideism* (Dordrecht, 1983), 82.

[28] *Religious Belief and the Will* (London, 1986), 143. He argues that 'among the non-
Catholic philosophers we have studied, Søren Kierkegaard is the most radically volitionalist, deeming every belief acquisition as a resolution of the will' (p. 146).

[29] The 'volitionalist' accounts to which I refer need not subscribe (though some may do
so) to the myth of 'volitions' criticized by Gilbert Ryle: namely, volition as a private mental
act which is the 'real' action, preceding and causing the overt behaviour (*The Concept of
Mind* (New York, 1949), 62–9). Since, like Ryle, I distinguish between 'voluntary' action
and 'intentional' action or action done 'on purpose' (p. 70), I also argue here (not against
the idea of a voluntary transition, but) against the understanding of the transition as an act
done 'on purpose' (an intentional choice among alternatives which are equally attractive);
such a model of decision (even if not subscribing to the strict notion of 'volition') is more
appropriate to decisions to do X than to decisions *that* X, the latter of which I take to
constitute the actual transition to faith. Thus I object to both ways of viewing the
transition—as neither is true to various accounts of conversion experiences nor true to the
Climacus account of the transition (which is reinforced by Kierkegaard's own journal
entries).

William Alston claims that though volitions are myths, sometimes actions are 'preceded
by a non-publicly observable decision, intention, or resolution to perform the act' ('The
Elucidation of Religious Statements', in *Process and Divinity*, eds. William L. Reese and

which one selects from a variety of alternative options. These options are
seen by the agent as equally 'real' possibilities, and the leap or decision is
seen as something we still have to do (to bridge a gap) *after* we have
appreciated the options. The force of such a concept of leap or decision is
to rule out the possibility of a non-intentional alignment with one or
another option, often to the extent of being seen as a choice against the
more attractive option(s). Even critiques of such 'volitionalist' interpretations have tended to assume the same model of decision in their
disapproval of it. Such an account of the decision or leap as intentional
(reflectively done 'on purpose') is, however, I suggest, at odds with, or
unable to do justice to, a number of other elements in the Climacus
account of the transition to faith. I want, therefore, to challenge the
relevance of that model of decision and to suggest a reconceptualization
of the transition which is at the heart of the popular reading of the
Kierkegaardian 'leap' of faith.[30]

Because the metaphor of a leap of faith is one which has been popularly used by many, this re-examination also has implications beyond
Kierkegaard scholarship. It bears importantly on an understanding of
transitions to faith in general (or, even more broadly, on conversion
experiences in general). I will be considering other accounts of the transition to faith—including autobiographical accounts—in the light of the
Kierkegaardian suggestions, and my hope is that an understanding of
conversions (religious and otherwise) will be enhanced by a mutual illumination.

Leap and Passion: The Mutual Correction

In a journal entry from 1842–3, Kierkegaard complained that 'Hegel
has never done justice to the category of transition',[31] and he obviously
tried to remedy Hegel's failure by focusing quite strikingly on the cate-

E. Freeman (LaSalle, Il., 1964), 436). My point is that whatever non-publicly observable
decision may occur in the case of the transition to faith, it conforms to the model of
decisions *that* X is the case.

[30] I want to make it clear that my reconceptualization, strictly speaking, concerns
Climacus's account of the transition to faith, but since this coincides with the popular
'Kierkegaardian' account I am, in effect, addressing interpretations of both views.
Moreover, although I am sensitive to the problems raised by the pseudonymous authorship,
I am focusing on the Climacus account of faith as it is reinforced and explicated by the
journals; this, I think, mitigates the problems of speaking of a 'Kierkegaardian faith'.

[31] *Soren Kierkegaard's Journals and Papers*, eds. and trans. Howard V. and Edna H.
Hong, assisted by Gregor Malantschuk (Bloomington, Ind. and London, 1967–78), i: IV C
80, n.d. [1842–3], 110.

gory of 'transition'. The prevalence of 'volitionalist' interpretations and critiques of them which both assume the same model of decision suggests that Kierkegaard's attempt to remedy Hegel's failure, even if successful, raises its own problems of interpretation. At the very least the terms of the current debate in the literature on Kierkegaard concerning the 'leap of faith' need to be re-examined.

At first glance at least, one of the elements which the volitionalist interpretation of the decision of faith seems at odds with or unable to do justice to is the striking claim by Climacus that faith is *a* 'passion'. He claims, as we shall see in more detail, more than that faith is an act made with passion—he claims it is itself *a* passion, *a* 'happy passion'.[32] The model of a passion, however, calls to mind something quite different from the model of decision noted above.

The dual characterization of faith as both leap and passion is seen by some commentators to constitute a 'problem' for Kierkegaard's account; for example, one claims that 'Volitions are acts, they are not simply passions',[33] so a resolution is possible only by appealing to different senses of faith. For others, the claim that faith is *a* passion is read simply as the claim that passion gives life to the decision, or passion is realized in making the decision, but the decision *qua* decision remains the same sort of selection among a plurality of equally real options. I suggest, however, that both interpretations are misleading (and in opposite ways), and that we need not either see the concepts of leap and passion as contradictory when applied to a single concept of faith or deny that they are, as they seem to be for Climacus, parallel concepts or categories at the same level and hence in tension with each other. Rather, I suggest that Climacus's understanding of faith, and Kierkegaard's contribution to an anatomy of faith, is able to be adequately appreciated only when the concepts of leap and passion are seen as parallel and as mutually and substantively correcting or qualifying each other, and thus that we cannot hope to make sense of Kierkegaard's notion of a leap if we fail to allow that the category of passion substantively qualifies what decision means in the case of faith.

In general I shall argue that the mutual correction implied in the correlation of the concepts of leap and passion should be read as an

---

[32] *Philosophical Fragments* and *Johannes Climacus*, Kierkegaard Writings, vii, eds. and trans. Howard V. Hong and Edna H. Hong (Princeton, 1985), 54, 61.

[33] Louis P. Pojman writes: 'There is a problem, too, in the relation between faith as an intuitive sense and faith as willing-to-believe. Intuitions happen; they are not acts. Volitions are acts, they are not simply passions' (*The Logic of Subjectivity: Kierkegaard's Philosophy of Religion* (University, Ala., 1984), 103).

attempt to do justice to an activity which, even at the level of human agency, is more dialectical than a unilateral choice among alternatives. The category of 'leap' or 'decision' used by Climacus is, as the correlative attribution of 'passion' would lead one to expect, far richer than the one-dimensional model too often assumed by those who attack it as well as by those who defend it. In particular I shall argue that the role of the category of passion in qualifying the leap (or, equivalently, the willing of the downfall of the understanding) can be fruitfully read as an attempt to highlight the activity of *imagination*—either in contrast to a simplistic notion of decision or as part of an enriched understanding of willing itself. I shall, in effect, be arguing against the view that for Kierkegaard the work of imagination in faith is simply to 'produce candidates for belief', after which 'the will decides which to believe'.[34]

I want to extend and develop the suggestion that imagination is crucial to Kierkegaard's accounts of selfhood by focusing on 'paradox' and 'willing' in faith. I will be arguing that the importance of imagination lies precisely in its relation to *paradox*: subjectivity, including the deeper subjectivity of faith, is constituted by paradox, and it is in its relation to paradox that the centrality of imagination to subjectivity and faith is anchored. Passion itself is a function of paradox—that is, passion is generated by paradox. Negative references to imagination notwithstanding, we shall find both implicitly and explicitly in Kierkegaard's thought just that appreciation of the value and necessity of imaginative activity which we should expect to find given his emphasis on paradox and passion.

My ultimate aim is to show how his understanding of the roles of imagination in the paradox and passion of subjectivity supports a reinterpretation of the category of 'decision' or 'leap' in the transition to faith. In the process I will explore the role of imaginative activity in transitions in terms of such notions as surrender, suspension, union, and engagement. I intend to highlight the possibility of a counterweight to a one-sidedly volitionalist view of transitions, including the transition to faith, which does not go to the extreme version of antivolitionalism contained in accounts which see the transition as something ineffable which simply happens to us.[35]

---

[34] This is a very common view; the formulation which I cite is from an explanation by Louis P. Pojman, in private correspondence (7 September 1987), of his reference to the imagination in *Religious Belief and the Will*, 73.

[35] This position is taken by David Wisdo in 'Kierkegaard on Belief, Faith, and Explanation' (*International Journal for Philosophy of Religion*, 21. 2 (1987), 95–114).

Climacus and Imagination: The Ladder and the Leap

It is a commonplace that the name Johannes Climacus, chosen by Kierke-gaard to be the pseudonymous author of the *Philosophical Fragments* and the *Concluding Unscientific Postscript*, refers back to a sixth-century ascetic and writer on the spiritual life, St John Climacus, the author of *The Heavenly Ladder* (or *Ladder of Divine Ascent*). This extraordinarily popular handbook on the ascetic and spiritual life detailed a ladder of thirty steps which a monk must ascend; each step represented the acquisition of a virtue or elimination of a vice, and the monk's discipline led him through an upward struggle against temptation, to the top step where he received the crown of glory from Christ.

The ladder for St John Climacus was clearly a metaphor for the ascent constituting the ascetic or spiritual life, but what Kierkegaard meant to suggest by the choice of the name Climacus is far from clear. Given his denunciations of monastic life in the *Postscript*,[36] one could argue that he was being ironic, intending to put down such an enterprise as the early Climacus's, such a recipe-like 'handbook' of the spiritual life. On the other hand, one could argue that such an ironic use need not be attributed to Kierkegaard, for his Climacus, like the early Climacus, indeed describes the spiritual life as a journey involving distinguishable stages, as a graduated ascent. Moreover, since Kierkegaard expresses through Climacus the possibility that one could know 'what Christianity is without being a Christian', and hence without knowing 'what it is to be a Chris-tian',[37] one could speculate that Climacus was intended to portray quite accurately what the Christian spiritual journey involved.[38] That is, Johannes Climacus could be seen as detailing (like the early Climacus) the process leading to the top of the ladder, a ladder which in his case took one from the ethical to the religious or from the ethico-religious to

---

[36] *Postscript*, 370–3, 440.

[37] Ibid. 332, 339.

[38] Thus, although it clearly would be a mistake to look to Climacus for an account of what it was 'to be a Christian', there is a sense in which it would not be the mistake C. Stephen Evans claims it is 'to look to Climacus for an account of what the Christian life is like' (*Kierkegaard's Fragments and Postscript: The Religious Philosophy of Johannes Climacus* (Atlantic Highlands, NJ, 1983), 23.) My position is in agreement with that suggested by Walter Lowrie's claim that the pseudonyms 'said the same things' (though in different ways and saying more as well) as Kierkegaard's non-pseudonymous works (Introduction to *Training in Christianity and the Edifying Discourse which 'Accompanied' It*, trans. Walter Lowrie (Princeton, NJ, 1944), xx), as well as with Louis Pojman's claim that 'What distinguishes Climacus from Kierkegaard is simply perspective. . . . both agree on how one becomes a Christian and on the content of Christianity' (*The Logic of Subjectivity*, 90).

religiousness proper; he would be straightforwardly providing reliable guidance concerning the character of the journey and goal—including what it is not, what it would take to make the ascent, as well as inappropriate steps or attitudes to avoid.

But much more, I think, could be implied in the adoption of the name Climacus than its reference to the author of the 'heavenly ladder', and that more lies in the suggestion that the ladder was one of the metaphors used in the medieval Church for imagination. Richard Kearney has proposed that St Bonaventure (1217–74), among others, used (in addition to the metaphor of a mirror) the metaphor of a ladder through which to speak of imagination.[39] It is clear that Bonaventure held a Greek view of imagination as a transitional faculty mediating between the senses and reason in the hierarchy of the mind's powers, and that he used the metaphor (spatial-vertical imagery) of an 'ascent' of 'six steps' in the mind's journey to (literally, into) God.[40] Kearney suggests that Bonaventure's use of the metaphor of the ladder is informed not only by the Greek but also by the biblical tradition—in particular, that his allusion to the image of Jacob's ladder[41] connecting earth and heaven implies that Bonaventure saw the imagination itself as a ladder:

As a transitional faculty of imaging, *imaginatio* is, of course, analogous to 'Jacob's ladder' (although Christ remains the true example of the ladder model). For just as Jacob dreamt of a ladder stretched between heaven and earth with angels descending and ascending, so too images may point towards sacred truths by mediating between the lower senses and the higher faculties of reason.[42]

In this way, just as imagination mediates between the earth of the senses and the heaven of the higher powers of the soul, so too it is a ladder through which we can make a spiritual ascent.[43]

[39] *The Wake of Imagination*, 127. Although Kearney has a section on Kierkegaard (pp. 201–11), he does not make any association between him and the medieval metaphor of the ladder as mediational imagination.

[40] *The Works of Bonaventure: Cardinal, Seraphic Doctor, and Saint*, trans. José de Vinck, i: *Mystical Opuscula* (Paterson, NJ, 1960), *The Journey of the Mind to God*, ch. 1, sect. 6, p. 11.

[41] This particular image of Jacob's ladder is repeated by Bonaventure at least twice: once in the *Journey of the Mind to God*, ch. 1, sect. 9, p. 13, and once in *The Life of St. Francis (Legenda Maior)*, ch. 13 (*Bonaventure*, Classics of Western Spirituality, trans. Ewert Cousins (New York, 1978), 303). A different, but related, use of the metaphor is found in the reference to 'Christ our Ladder' and 'Christ [as] the ladder', (*Journey of the Mind to God*, ch. 1, sect. 3, p. 10, and ch. 7, sect. 1, p. 56); reference is even made to how 'the created universe itself is a ladder leading us toward God' (ch. 1, sect. 2, p. 9).

[42] Kearney, *The Wake of Imagination*, 127.

[43] Although Bonaventure only explicitly places imagination as a rung on the ladder of

The term 'ladder' could, then, be used to speak metaphorically either of the spiritual life or of imagination or, more to the point, to speak metaphorically of the spiritual life as both an ascent and as an activity requiring imagination. It is my contention throughout this book that the Kierkegaardian Climacus's understanding of the transition to Christianity not only assumes (as did the early Climacus) that the transition is an ascent, but also crucially appreciates the importance of imaginative activity in the transition. The metaphor of a ladder (bearing both the early Climacus and the Bonaventure readings) would be an extremely congenial one to such an understanding; whether or not Kierkegaard explicitly intended this added dimension to the choice of Climacus as author, that authorship could become doubly meaningful for us.

The centrality of imagination to Kierkegaard's Climacus account is, I shall argue, revealed in the conjunction of his insistence that faith is a 'passion', with his understanding of passion in terms of paradoxical tension. Because it is imagination alone which can maintain elements in paradoxical tension, his calling a 'leap' a 'passion' would mean that the activity of the 'leap' centrally involves imaginative activity (and so cannot be seen as a simple volitional activity). In other words, in so far as the transition to faith is seen in terms of 'passion' as well as 'leap', the implicit category of paradox—of tension between opposites—qualifies the category of leap by bringing in imaginative activity. Allusion to the metaphor of ladder would be one way of reinforcing the importance of imaginative activity in coming to faith, and in this sense it might be said that the metaphor of a ladder imaginatively qualifies the metaphor of a leap.

Like all good metaphors, however, that of the ladder involves an interaction of many associations, and the very suggestion that the ladder (of imagination) qualifies the leap reveals additional possibilities for understanding the character of the transition or how the attribution of the term 'passion' (and the implied imaginative activity) qualifies the attribution of the term 'leap'. For example, people tend to think of a leap which exhibits a radical discontinuity as the paradigmatic qualitative transition, but a qualitative transition can be suggested by the metaphor of a ladder as well. What is interesting about a ladder is that it effects a

the soul rather than the ladder itself, his persistent tripartite divisions do make it quite plausible to take the allusion to Jacob's ladder to imply that the transitional faculty (imagination) between the senses and the entire group of higher powers is seen metaphorically as a ladder mediating between earth and heaven. Kearney rightly notes, however, Bonaventure's view of the limits of imagination.

qualitative transition while it obviates in some sense the need for a 'leap'; that is, the metaphor of ladder suggests not only the qualitative (hence discontinuous) character of an ascent, but also the concomitant continuity. Consider this first point. Although a ladder can be used to effect a horizontal bridge between parallel and qualitatively similar domains, the distinctive character of a ladder includes the vertical dimension, one that suggests a creative and qualitative achievement lacking to a mere horizontal bridge.[44] This qualitative discontinuity is clearly intended in the metaphors used by St John Climacus and Bonaventure: the crown of glory marks a qualitatively different logical space, and the realm of reason is qualitatively distinguished from that of the senses. A ladder, then, is an appropriate metaphor for qualitative transition. Second, a ladder can be seen as a way of facilitating a transition to a qualitatively different domain without requiring the absolute discontinuity of a simple 'leap' across a gap, for a ladder necessarily maintains continuity in an important way (i.e., it requires and touches the ground throughout the process of transition, even if one chooses to throw it away on reaching the goal). In these ways a ladder can provide a peculiarly apt metaphor for a transition understood as a qualitative ascent which nevertheless allows for continuity in the face of discontinuity.

The tension between continuity and discontinuity is an important one for my purposes and is expressed in a variety of levels. The very concept of metaphor itself embodies both the perspectives of continuity and discontinuity, for metaphor is both continuous with and discontinuous with literal uses of language.[45] The particular metaphor of the ladder with which I am concerned likewise embodies not only the perspective of discontinuity (in qualitative ascent), but also and at the same time the perspective of continuity. That the ladder has also been used as a metaphor for imagination suggests that imaginative activity might similarly be seen to embody these two perspectives. For example, one could see the concretizing function of imagination as an expression of continuity with the sensual and the abstracting function as an expression of discontinuity with it; one could even argue that abstracting is itself an activity which implies both continuity and discontinuity. The tension between these two perspectives is, I will propose throughout this book, expressed in the dual ascription of 'leap' and 'passion' to the same

---

[44] See George Lakoff and Mark Johnson's discussion of the positive character of 'UP' metaphors, in *Metaphors We Live By* (Chicago, 1980), 14–19.

[45] Eva F. Kittay explicitly notes this in *Metaphor: Its Cognitive Force and Linguistic Structure* (Oxford, 1987), 17.

phenomenon of transition. Popular readings of the transition to faith have emphasized, indeed over-emphasized, the discontinuity involved. I want to be sure that justice is done to the perspective of continuity involved, and to that end I shall be highlighting the way in which passion is used by Kierkegaard to qualify the discontinuity, particularly through the emphasis on interest and engagement. Imaginative activity is as necessary to maintaining continuity as to generating discontinuity, and imagination is necessary as well to maintaining those perspectives in tension. If, as I will be arguing is the case, the account in the *Philosophical Fragments* and the *Concluding Unscientific Postscript* of faith as both a leap and a passion highlights the role of imagination in the transition and embodies the simultaneous perspectives of discontinuity and continuity in the ascent, the authorship of 'Climacus' would seem to be a perfect vehicle for such an understanding of coming to faith.

Transitions and Imagination

My immediate task in the first chapter is to examine the concepts of 'leap' and 'passion' in the *Philosophical Fragments* and the *Concluding Unscientific Postscript*, to suggest that the two concepts mutually correct and qualify each other, and to show that the ends Kierkegaard wants to guarantee (or conversely, the things he wants to rule out) leave room for the mixed idiom of leap and passion to be understood as an attempt to express the activity of imagination in the *transition* to faith. I use the term 'transition' in a quite specific sense here—for while the overall acquisition of faith may well be a complex process in which there is room for choices or decisions in an everyday sense (either by way of pre-paration or confirmation), I am concerned to illuminate the transition to faith in the strict sense of the qualitative shift whose discreteness and decisiveness is highlighted by the use of terms like 'the decision' or 'the leap' of faith to indicate what is seen by the agent as 'the' moment of embrace or acceptance. I argue both that the qualitativeness and freedom of the transition are what is at stake in the concept of the leap and that the notions of a shift in perspective and a critical threshold show that such a transition need not be constituted (or *directly* achieved) by an intentional or purposeful volition or decision. This constitutes a negative argument in support of the possibility of a broader interpretation of the leap or decision which is the transition to faith. Examining the generic concept of a passion, and introducing the relation between passion and imagination, I argue that developing the concept of passion, limited only by the minimal requirements of the concept of leap, allows the possibility of a formulation of the transition to faith in which imaginative activity comes into its own.

I lay the groundwork for such a formulation in terms of *ethical* imagination in Chapter 3 and I explore it in terms of *religious* imagination in Chapters 4 and 5. Those whose main concern is in the light this study might shed on conversions to faith or transitions in general should feel free to go directly to those chapters. For those whose interest lies primarily in whether this project illuminates the category of transition in Kierkegaard in particular, I examine in Chapter 2 some of the Kierkegaardian texts which suggest a broadened concept of 'willing' and 'decision', as well as ties between these concepts and imaginative activity. These reveal a rejection of the dualisms implied in a purely volitionalist account of transitions; the consequent broadening of the concepts of 'will' and 'decision' reinvests the concept of will with some of the richness of the classical heritage in which will is seen as rational appetite, desire, or attraction. In addition, I address another antivolitionalist strategy, an appeal to ineffability, arguing that such an alternative to a volitionalist account goes to an equally unacceptable extreme. In particular, I argue that it is premised on a set of false dichotomies and that acknowledging the 'condition' for faith and faith itself as a divine *gift*, as Climacus clearly does, nevertheless allows a describable locus of human activity in the transition to faith (and not merely in the preparation for or consequent commitment to faith). That activity which constitutes the actual transition can then, in principle, be seen as an exercise of imaginative activity transcending a dualism between knowledge and will.

In Chapter 3 I approach the question of the transition to faith and its relation to imagination from the wider perspective of various Kierkegaardian accounts of choice and transition in the task of subjectivity or the ethical. I argue that the roles of imagination integral to those accounts imply a view of choice in which imagination is a constitutive element; such choice then provides a model of a transition as an imaginative, reorienting, transforming shift in perspective. Such a model also has affinities to a variety of accounts of the imaginative activity involved in *metaphor*, and I will explore the ways in which these two approaches to characterizing a transition complement and qualify each other. This understanding of choice grounds and informs my reconceptualization of the transition to faith in the following chapters.

In Chapters 4 and 5 I explore a formulation of the transition to faith which highlights religious imagination from a variety of perspectives. I detail in the Climacus accounts a model of 'surrender', composed of moments of imaginative *suspension* and imaginative *engagement*. Such a model expresses two central functions of imagination. In Chapter 4 I examine the role of imagination in a leap, particularly as that is formulated by Climacus as a setting aside of the understanding in the face of the Paradox. Referring to the activity of holding elements in tension, which I see as a distinctive function of imagination, I consider the special character of the suspension involved in the 'captivity' of the understanding and the 'letting go' of which he speaks. Another kind of suspension, that involved in the synthesis and extension constituting an imaginative revisioning, is then examined, first in relation to romantic (Coleridgean) notions of imaginative activity, and then in relation to independent accounts of conversion (to and from faith). I consider these in the light of the relevance of paradoxical change and transparency introduced in Kierkegaard's accounts of the ethical and subjectivity (Chapter 3) as well as in the light of several accounts of leap and volition in non-religious contexts.

In Chapter 5 I analyse how the concept of passion, which underlies Kierkegaard's evaluation of subjectivity, expresses itself in terms of 'interest' or imaginative engagement and involvement (the 'how' he so emphasizes). Exploring analogies with the surrender in aesthetic engagement and in the experience of love to highlight the imaginative activity involved, I suggest that engagement is best understood as an imaginative activity rather than the direct result of a decision. The realization of passion, in other words, is an exercise of imaginative engagement which illuminates the category of 'surrender', and hence illuminates what is involved in transitions. Moreover, I argue that the emphasis on the 'how' (in contrast to the 'what') is an emphasis on the relevance of engagement which need not imply immunity to criticism, but rather focuses on an activity which can facilitate critical appraisal.

In all these ways, then, I am in effect re-evaluating the Climacus account of the transition to faith, as it is reinforced by Kierkegaard's journal entries. Both implicitly and explicitly, I suggest, they call attention to the importance of imagination in such a way as to challenge all those classical divisions of the self which exclude or ignore imaginative activity, as well as those which one-sidedly limit imaginative activity to the negative ways in which thinking can be 'wishful'. They call attention, in particular, to the ways in which imagination informs paradoxical choice, and the ways in which a momentary transition can be understood as an imaginative, reorienting, transforming shift in perspective. Once sensitized to Kierkegaard's contribution our analyses of contemporary accounts of religious belief and the ongoing debate over volitionalist accounts of the transition to faith may look quite different. We will be able to pick out and look with suspicion on certain of the illegitimate dichotomies we are presented with in accounts of religious faith in general and Kierkegaardian faith in particular.

1

Mutual Correctives:
The Leap and Passion of Faith

The concept of a 'leap' is introduced in the *Philosophical Fragments* when Climacus, characterizing a demonstration of the existence of the god, claims that 'the existence itself emerges from the demonstration by a leap'.[1] That is, as long as one continues the process of demonstration, the existence is not revealed; rather, 'I have to let go of it [the demonstration]' (p. 42). Moreover, 'this letting go, even that is surely something; it is, after all, *meine Zuthat* [my contribution]. . . . it is a *leap*' (p. 43). Although he is here speaking of the leap involved in generic demonstrations of existence, the concept of leap is explicitly extended to that of religious, including Christian, faith in the *Postscript*, where references to both the categories of 'leap' and 'decision' are made.[2] The concept of that 'passion' whose name is finally seen to be 'faith' is also introduced in the *Fragments*, and the concept of passion is given detailed attention in the *Postscript*. In what follows I want to examine how in those works the concept of a 'leap' correlates with the concept of a 'passion'.

My immediate task in this chapter is to show that the ends Kierkegaard wants to guarantee (or conversely, the things he wants to rule out) leave room for the mixed idiom of leap and passion to be understood as an attempt (through the mutual correction implied in the dual attribution) to express the activity of imagination in the transition to faith. I do this by arguing: (1) that the qualitativeness and freedom of the transition are what is at stake for Climacus in the concept of the leap and that they do not require an intentional volition or decision, and (2) that Climacus's categorization of faith as a 'happy passion' implies the role of imagination in the transition and supports an attempt to understand the transition to faith by comparison and contrast with our transitions to other passions, like fear, anger, love, hope, etc.

---

[1] *Fragments*, 43. Succeeding parenthetical page references will be to this work unless otherwise indicated in the text.

[2] *Postscript*, 15, 86–97, 105, 231, 262, 306, 333, 340, 343.

The 'Leap' as 'Decisive'

The best known references to the 'leap' occur in Climacus's discussion of
Lessing, where its status as an alternative to a quantitative move is made
clear. Although he insists on the ambiguity, even irony, in Lessing's
references to the leap and although Kierkegaard himself may employ
irony in his discussion, he nevertheless suggests significant areas of
agreement between Climacus and Lessing. Most importantly, Climacus
agrees with Lessing both that the move from historical to eternal truths
would require a 'leap' and that a 'leap' is a 'qualitative' rather than a
'quantitative' move. Rejecting Lessing's suggestion that contempor-
aneity would alter the 'leap' required, he nevertheless seems to give
Lessing the benefit of the doubt allowing that, on the (possible) reading
of Lessing according to which all historical truths are, as such, acci-
dental, he and Lessing agree on the 'root of the incommensurability that
subsists between an historical truth and an eternal decision'.[3] The heart
of their agreement lies in their common opposition to what Climacus
describes as 'an attempt to create a quantitative transition to a qualitative
decision'.[4] He claims that Lessing rightly saw that 'the leap, as being
decisive, is subject to a qualitative dialectic, and permits no approxi-
mating transition'.[5] The deliberate contrast between a quantitative transition and a qualitative decision suggests that the emphasis is on the
qualitativeness of the transition and gives reason to read other references
to 'decision' in faith as similarly stressing the qualitativeness of the
transition.[6] This reinforces the point of the *Fragments*'s discussion of the
'leap'—namely, that the conclusion is not the issue of a continuous
movement; it is not the gradual or cumulative product of, nor compelled
by, any reasoning process.

His conclusion is that, given the 'incommensurability that subsists
between an historical truth and an eternal decision', the 'transition by
which something historical and the relationship to it becomes decisive

---

[3] *Postscript*, 90.   [4] Ibid. 88.

[5] Ibid. 94. This same point is repeated constantly in *The Concept of Anxiety*, Part I.
Gregor Malantschuk claims that 'the most important information' on the theory of the leap
appears in the journals and papers, but that in the authorship proper the category of the leap
is found most extensively in *The Concept of Anxiety* (*Kierkegaard's Thought*, eds. and
trans. Howard V. Hong and Edna H. Hong (Princeton, NJ, 1971), 132, 257–272).

[6] See *Fragments*, 52, 93, 111.

for an eternal happiness, is *metabasis eis allo genos* [change into another kind], a leap, both for a contemporary and for a member of some later generation'.[7] The relation to Christian faith is later made explicit: 'there is no immediate transition from the introduction to the becoming a Christian, the transition rather constituting a qualitative leap'.[8] The question then is what constitutes such a 'qualitative' leap or decision.

In the discussion of Lessing, Climacus notes how easy it is to make fun of the notion of leap—as if 'you shut your eyes, you seize yourself by the neck . . . and then—then you stand on the other side . . . in the promised land of systematic philosophy'.[9] Climacus presents this as a caricature of a leap—and I suggest that he sees it as a caricature independently of the question of where one lands. He rejects *that* particular characteriz-ation—the 'will-power' kind of leap, the kind in which 'will', as Simone Weil writes, designates 'something suggestive of muscular effort'.[10] He rejects that as a caricature, while accepting that a qualitative transition or leap is nevertheless necessary and possible. But if the transition to 'faith' is not that caricatured activity, what kind is it?

The 'Happy Passion' and the Passions

Some guidance toward an appropriate characterization of the 'leap' is offered by Climacus's correlative attribution of the term 'passion'. The claim that faith is *a* 'passion' is led up to in the *Fragments* by several allusions to a 'passion' as yet unnamed (pp. 48, 49, 54), and made directly in the following account of the response to the 'paradox' of God-made-Man, the Eternal in Time: 'when the understanding and the paradox happily encounter each other in the moment, . . . when the understanding steps aside and the paradox gives itself . . . the third something, the something in which this occurs . . . is that happy passion to which we shall now give a name. . . . We shall call it *faith*' (p. 59). He repeats only a few pages later the reference to 'that happy passion which we call faith' (p. 61).

Calling faith a happy passion, then, implies at least some parallel between that particular passion and other passions, like fear, anger, and love. Indeed, Climacus introduces the happy passion of faith in terms of happy (vs. unhappy) love and repeatedly draws on an analogy between faith and love (an analogy which I will explore further in Chapter 5). It

---

[7] *Postscript*, 90.
[8] Ibid. 340. [9] Ibid. 91.
[10] *Waiting for God*, trans. Emma Craufurd (New York, 1951), 193.

would be reasonable, then, to expect that Kierkegaard intends us to learn something of what Climacus understands as the transition to faith by considering particular passions, as well as how we come to have a passion in general.

Climacus's explicit motivation in calling faith a 'passion' is to guarantee two ends related to his understanding of the leap. The first end is to distinguish it from the theoretical: he tells us that 'faith is not a knowledge' (p. 62), and this for several reasons. The most directly related reason is said to be that knowledge can be either of the eternal or of the historical, but not the 'absurdity that the eternal is the historical' (p. 62). That is, a 'paradox' which 'unites the contradictories' cannot be an object of knowledge (p. 61). Earlier he had indicated other reasons: one was that the god's existence could not (without begging the question) be demonstrated from 'his' works (p. 42); another was that, even if it could be demonstrated, the tentativeness and conditionality of a process of demonstration would be incompatible with commitment to the object of the demonstration, for I 'would never finish and also would be obliged continually to live *in suspenso* lest something so terrible happen that my fragment of demonstration would be ruined' (p. 42). Finally, because there is always an 'ambiguity of awareness' (p. 104), faith is not a 'simple consequence of awareness' (p. 93)—it is not an intuitive knowledge.

The second motivation in calling faith a 'passion' is to distinguish it from the volitional: he tells us that 'faith is not an act of will' because it depends on a precondition (which he calls the 'condition' (p. 62)) which we cannot achieve by willing. Terming it a 'passion' is one way of calling attention to its not being an act of will in an unconditioned (or radically self-sufficient) sense.

Climacus's explicit claims that the happy passion of faith is not an act of knowledge or will are in line with Roberto Unger's contemporary account of passion as best understood not through the traditions which see it in terms of an ambivalence to reason or collective authority, but as something which precedes the distinction between knowledge and will.[11] Unger's account posits another feature of the passions (namely, that 'the passions are neither free acts of will nor events that just happen to people'[12]) which raises an important question about Climacus's own understanding of passion—namely, his understanding of the activity

---

[11] *Passion: An Essay on Personality*, 114.
[12] Ibid. 165

and/or passivity of passion. That understanding must influence the way in which he understands the 'leap'.

To see how Climacus stands in relation to the position on passion expressed by Unger, I need to consider a number of other accounts of the passions. Although I can provide only a brief sketch here, these will at least suggest some alternatives to Unger's claim that they are 'neither free acts of will nor events that just happen to people' and introduce some ideas which can be fleshed out in the later chapters on passion as surrender and engagement.

Popular usage, captured in dictionary definitions, views a passion as an intense or overpowering feeling or emotion: the *Oxford English Dictionary*, for example, defines passion as 'any kind of feeling by which the mind is powerfully affected or moved; a vehement, commanding, or overpowering emotion'.[13] These definitions express the common (though inaccurate) equivalence between 'passion' and 'feeling' and 'emotion'. They also express the common association of all three with passivity, for they are fundamentally informed by a more primary definition offering the original sense of the term, namely, 'the fact or condition of being acted upon or affected by external agency'. Different dictionaries variously emphasize 'subjection', 'abandonment to emotion', being acted on by what is 'foreign to one's true nature', and all of them make the contrast with 'action' or 'acting'. One of the later definitions of passion in the *OED*, however, has a quite different emphasis: namely, passion as 'an eager outreaching of the mind towards something; an overmastering zeal or enthusiasm for a special object'. 'An eager outreaching' is obviously far from passive. Although the view of passion as passive has been the dominant popular one, this more active view of passion (or emotion) is reflected in psychological and philosophical analyses. The implications of calling faith a happy passion, then, will only be clear in the light of an appreciation of what is at stake in the debate over passive vs. active accounts of passion.

In his *Rhetoric* Aristotle treats the passions under the general rubric of 'the things men do of themselves, the acts of which they themselves are the authors'.[14] Acts done through both rational and irrational impulse then (through reason and through passions, like anger) are our free acts, for which we are responsible.[15] Book II illustrates the passions or 'emotions' ('for example: anger, pity, fear, and the like'), formally

---

[13] *Oxford English Dictionary* (Oxford, 2nd edn. 1989).
[14] *The Rhetoric of Aristotle*, trans. Lane Cooper (Englewood Cliffs, NJ, 1932), I:10, 56.
[15] Ibid. 56–7.

describing them as 'those states which are attended by pain and pleasure, and which, as they change, make a difference in our judgments'.[16] But Aristotle's point is not simply that they cause changes in judgements— rather they embody judgements. This is clear from his definitions of particular emotions: anger, for example, is an 'impulse attended by pain, to a revenge that shall be evident, and caused by an obvious, unjustified slight with respect to the individual or his friends'.[17] Likewise, fear is 'a pain or disturbance arising from a mental image of impending evil of a destructive or painful sort'.[18] In other words, the emotions or passions of anger and fear are not simply feelings or bodily reactions—they are in part constituted by particular kinds of judgements and it is the judge-ments, not the bodily responses, which distinguish the passions from each other. Whatever the physiological changes one experiences, one could not experience the passion (emotion) of anger if one did not judge oneself to be slighted unjustifiedly, for example, nor could one experi-ence fear if one did not judge that danger was impending.

Aristotle's contribution to an understanding of emotion (or the passions) was to show that the cognitive dimension was essential to emotion—the judgement that danger is impending is not just concurrent with the emotion of fear, but essential to it.[19] The cognitive construal is built into the definition of the emotion—the distinctive character of a particular emotion is a function of the particular kind of judgements involved. Such an account, then, both implies an important distinction between a 'feeling' and a passion (or emotion), and precludes any simple passivity of passion.

The recent writings of Robert C. Solomon retrieve this Aristotelian emphasis by subjecting the 'myth of the passions'—the model of a passion as simply passive reaction—to lengthy and articulate attack. In *The Passions* Solomon argues a general case against the view of passions as things which (disruptively) happen to us, and proposes instead a model of a passion as something which we freely and responsibly *do*.[20] A passion, on this view, is a judgement or set of judgements which we freely adopt and which constitute an interpretation of the way things are. In the more recent *About Love: Reinventing Romance for Our Times* Solomon elaborates this understanding of passion with respect to the passion of romantic love, and there expresses the continuing emphasis on freedom

---

[16] *The Rhetoric of Aristotle*, 2:1, 92.
[17] Ibid. 2:2, 93.   [18] Ibid. 2:5, 107.
[19] William W. Fortenbaugh, *Aristotle on Emotion* (New York, 1975), 11–12; ch. 1 passim.   [20] *The Passions* (Notre Dame, Ind., 1983).

and responsibility in terms of the 'decision' or 'choice' involved: 'falling in love', he says, 'is a decision', or a series of them.[21] Solomon's rejection of the passivity of passion is clearly informed by an Aristotelian-like view of the role of judgements in passions. A passion, to repeat, is not a feeling (which is transient and episodic) but rather a set of judgements we make—it constitutes a dispositional interpretation of the way things are. As in Aristotle, we are the 'author' of the act. But as we shall later see in more detail, Solomon emphasizes the 'decision' or 'choice' involved:[22] 'falling in love is a decision', and just as we *decide* to fall in love, so we *make* ourselves angry. Solomon carries the rejection of passivity to the point of requiring a 'decision'; although interpretation remains central to the experience of the passion, his emphasis is on the claim that we *decide to interpret* our world or ourself in a particular way. Solomon concurs, then, with Aristotle and Unger in denying that passions are 'events that just happen to people', but he seems to adopt the view equally denied by Unger, that passions are 'free acts of will', and, moreover, he seems to equate 'free acts of will' with 'decisions' (of the sort we make when, to use Solomon's example, we decide to stay later at a party).

Volitionalist accounts of faith need not be understood, therefore, as ignoring the relevance of the claim that faith is a happy passion; instead, they can be seen as reading passion in Solomon's terms—i.e., formally paralleling the decision to stay later at a party with the decision which constitutes the transition to faith. I suggest that in their efforts to reject passivity, however, both accounts tend to an extreme. A closer look at Solomon's account of love will reveal that extreme.

Solomon does well to remind us that we are free and responsible for our passions, but the reminder is nearly as misleading as the view it seeks to correct. Admittedly, a passion is not something over which we have no control—we are not mere victims—but it is equally not something which we decide to have or not have in the same way we decide to have steak rather than cheese soufflé for dinner. A passion is not a compelled reaction, unavoidably dictated by things external to us—but neither is it a unilateral activity. It is precisely a *response*—which means that there is something affecting us to which we respond and, hence, features which contour (though they do not compel) our response. Although the data in any given case do not unambiguously dictate a response, we cannot responsibly put *any* interpretation we would like on the data before us—

---

[21] *About Love: Reinventing Romance for Our Times* (New York, 1988), 127 ff.
[22] Ibid. 127–9.

Solomon does not seem to take seriously enough this implication of his appeal to 'interpretation' or 'judgement'.

In the same way that love is not simply passive, it is not simply a decision—certainly not a decision of the sort we make when, to use his example, we decide to stay later at a party.[23] Decisions *to* stay later or *to* do X are not decisions in the same sense in which we decide *that* it would be profitable to stay later or *that* X is the more attractive option. To say that 'falling in love is a decision' and then to illustrate 'decision' with the decision to stay later at a party is, at best, misleading, for a decision to stay later at a party is a decision which may prepare the ground for the experience of falling in love without constituting the experience of falling in love. The experience of falling in love is on Solomon's own terms an activity constituted in part by an interpretation or set of judgements—but we cannot decide to have a particular interpretation of a situation in the way we can decide to perform an action which may be a necessary preliminary to having such an interpretation. The emphasis on the freedom of and responsibility for passions which is paramount in Solomon's work seems to undermine the point of affirming that passions are, at least in part, constituted by 'interpretation'. It also ignores the role of interest and attraction and evaluation *in* a decision, not merely prior to it or following it. A view of passion which tells us that we *decide* to be angry, to fall in love, etc., without discriminating between different ways in which things are decided, fails to appreciate sufficiently the role of interest and attraction (the contouring elements implied in the notion of 'response') and, equally important, it fails to do justice to what is implied in the claim that a passion is an interpretation. Although Solomon's account does a service by correctly rejecting the myth of passivity and reminding us of the cognitive dimension of a passion, it muddies the waters by its indiscriminate use of the term 'decision' and its unnuanced affirmation of activeness.

How, then, does Climacus's understanding of passion and the activity or passivity involved stand in relation to these various accounts of what a passion is? If one simply accepted an understanding of passion as a passive reaction, such as that suggested in the first dictionary definitions above, one might be inclined to argue that by calling faith a happy passion Climacus meant to suggest the simple passiveness of faith. Given the model of passion as a passive happening-to-us, a reaction over which we have no control (except with respect to expressing or not expressing it

---

[23] *About love*, 127.

in correlative behaviour), one could assume that the intention of calling faith a passion is in part to counteract the active connotations of the leap involved. Speaking of faith in terms of both leap and passion might then be meant simply to point first to the active, then to the passive, senses or moments of faith.

Such a reading, however, would fail to do justice to the fact that the attributions of 'leap' and 'passion' are not directed by him to distinct, successive moments of the phenomenon of faith—rather they both refer to the transition to faith (although the word 'passion' also applies, of course, to the sustained struggle throughout time). That is, the transition which is called a leap is also said to achieve a passion or, conversely, the 'onset' of the passion is co-extensive with the leap—'the something in which this [transition] occurs' is the happy passion of faith (p. 59), where 'this' which occurs is effectively the same transition referred to as a 'leap'. At the very least, then, one has to acknowledge that the phenomenon of the transition to faith would have to be said to be both active and passive at the same time, and so could not be understood either simply in terms of passivity or simply in terms of an act of will-power.

In other words, even on a passive view of passion, the attribution of the term 'passion' to faith would preclude a simple volitionalist account of the transition. But the situation is even more complicated than that because, while Climacus does indeed see the understanding of passion as the hermeneutical principle in light of which we are to understand the leap or the decision involved in reaching faith, he does *not* see a passion as simply passive, but rather as a descriptively more complex phenomenon. The category of passion is intended to qualify the active character of a leap or decision, but *not* by the simple strategy of opposing passive to active. My argument against volitionalism, then, is not premised on accepting an account of passion as merely passive. In what follows I will begin to make the case, to be developed throughout the remaining chapters, that Climacus's achievement is to incorporate the insights of a classical Aristotelian account of the passions, without going to the extreme reached by some contemporary rejections of the view that passions are passive, and that in so doing he offers an account of faith in which the transition is neither one-sidedly volitionalist nor an ineffable something which simply happens to us.

A number of elements in the Climacus account seem to be in line with the Aristotelian approach to the passions as non-passive and cognitive. For example, Climacus seems to make a distinction similar to that between passion (emotion) and feeling when he insists that the 'how' of

passion does not refer to 'demeanor, expression, or the like'.[24] De-
meanour and expression are, like feeling, more transient, episodic, or
superficial than the 'sustained' relationship of inward appropriation with
which he contrasts them. Moreover, Climacus emphasizes the responsible freedom of the act of faith—we are seen as authors of the passion,
rather than victims of it, for it is precisely the need for freedom (and the
ascription of responsibility) which precludes the relevance, as Climacus
sees it, of rational justification. I suggest, however, that although
Climacus's account rejects passivity in these ways, it need not assume
Solomon's alternative to such passivity; although Climacus could say (as
Unger would not) that passions are 'free acts of will', that need not mean
that he would thereby see them as intentional decisions. One argument in
support of this suggestion is found in Climacus's treatment of the
distinction between active and passive in general, and I turn now to an
assessment of its import.

It is both significant and undeniable that Climacus sees the possibility
of a tension between active and passive which does not constitute a
dualism or dichotomy between active and passive. He reveals this in his
description of 'offence' in the face of the Absolute Paradox, for 'offence'
(which is the analogue to unhappy love) is a phenomenon in which
activeness does not preclude passiveness. We must, he notes, distinguish
between 'suffering offense and active offense', yet we must nevertheless
not forget:

Suffering offense is always active to the extent that it cannot altogether allow
itself to be annihilated (for offense is always an act, not an event), and active
offense is always weak enough to be incapable of tearing itself loose from the
cross to which it is nailed or to pull out the arrow with which it is wounded.[25]

Offence, he concludes in the footnote, 'takes affront, therefore passively,
even though so actively that it itself takes affront'. Offence then
illustrates Climacus's understanding of the character of an 'act' as
contrasted with an 'event'—an act can be passive at the same time as it
remains active. It is not a case of either/or, here, but rather both/and in
tension. This could support the suggestion that Climacus sees the
obverse of offence—i.e., the transition to faith, the acceptance of the
Paradox—as similarly transcending the dualism between active and
passive. Harking back to the idiom of Solomon's account of the passions,
this understanding reveals a sensitivity to the possibility that the

---

[24] *Postscript*, 181.
[25] *Fragments*, 50, and note.

phenomenon of qualitative transition is something which is neither simply passive nor constituted by a decision (like the decision to stay later at a party).

Finally, I suggest that both the non-passive and cognitive dimensions of the Aristotelian account of the passions are indicated in the Climacus account because the happy passion of faith is precisely distinguished from 'offence' (i.e., the unhappy relation to the Paradox of the God-Man) by virtue of the interpretation involved in each case. I will argue this in more detail, for example, in relation to the discernment of patterns, in later chapters.

I conclude, then, that Climacus's claim that faith is the 'happy passion' in which we embrace the Absolute Paradox is, at the very least, *able* both to do justice to Solomon's salutary warnings against the passive reading of passion and to accommodate his positive proposal that passions are ways of looking at the world (interpretations or judgements). We can, however, understand the happy passion of faith as being characterized by particular judgements, by a particular interpretation, without having to say that one decides to have that particular interpretation of life in the way one can decide to stay later at a party. Both of Solomon's aims—the rejection of the passive reading of passion and the emphasis on the free, responsible, creative interpretation—can be safeguarded without requiring the conclusion that experiencing a passion is a simple matter of choice. Similarly, Climacus's emphasis on passion can be informed by a rejection of the passive reading of passion and an appreciation of the importance of free and responsible activity in faith without requiring that we read the transition to faith as a leap which is only and one-sidedly active, the result of will-power.

It is interesting to note here how congenial such an account is with that offered by another contemporary critic of Solomon. Robert C. Roberts, criticizing Solomon's view of 'constitutive judgements' as central to passions, offers an alternative account of passions as 'construals'.[26] Roberts rejects, as I do, the extreme volitionalism of Solomon's account and, although he rejects the necessity of 'judgements',[27] he nevertheless emphasizes the importance of what I have called the Aristotelian cognitive dimension of passions (as involving interpretations, with

---

[26] See 'Solomon on the Control of Emotions', *Philosophy and Phenomenological Research*, 44 (March 1984), 395–404.

[27] Roberts elaborates the claims made in 'Solomon on the Control of Emotions' and marshalls a strong case (with many allies) 'against making judgment essential to emotion' in 'What an Emotion Is: A Sketch', *The Philosophical Review*, 97 (April 1988), 195–201.

cognitive content). Indeed, Roberts makes clear that 'emotions always involve some assessment of one's situation' (which will involve 'reflection').[28] Passions, in so far as they are emotions, are, for Roberts, construals or mental events or states in which 'one thing is grasped in terms of something else'; they are 'nonvisual analog[s] of seeing-as'.[29] Moreover, Roberts adds the significant qualifications that these construals are 'serious' and 'concern-based' (for example, one must be concerned 'about being in the condition one construes oneself to be in'),[30] and that such construing is 'closely related to imagining'.[31] What he stresses as important about the latter claim is that, like imagining, such construing 'has both an active and passive side to it'—it is 'an experience, something that comes to me; something I *do* no doubt, but also something that *happens* to me'.[32]

The following chapters will provide further warrant for the claim that Climacus's understanding of passion appreciates the role of interpretation and imagination, and is sensitive to both active and passive dimensions at the same time, emphasizing freedom and responsibility as well as the role of interest and engagement. In so far as that is true, the attribution of the term passion to the activity of faith would still qualify the parallel attribution of the term leap, but with this proviso: it holds the concept of leap in tension with a concept of passion which does not mean simple passivity, but rather involves interpretation (or construal), yet is

[28] 'Some Remarks on the Concept of Passion' ('Passion and Reflection'), in *International Kierkegaard Commentary: Two Ages*, ed. Robert L. Perkins (Macon, Ga., 1984), 90.

[29] 'What an Emotion Is: A Sketch', 190; 'Solomon on the Control of Emotions', 399. There is a growing literature on the topic of 'seeing-as' which takes its point of origin from Ludwig Wittgenstein's *Philosophical Investigations*, trans. G. E. M. Anscombe (New York, 3rd edn. 1958), esp. 193–214. One of those discussions of 'seeing-as' argues, as does Roberts, that seeing A as X is quite distinct from believing that A is X (Hidé Ishiguro, 'Imagination' Part II, *Proceedings of the Aristotelian Society*, Supplement XLI (1967), 55).

[30] 'What An Emotion Is: A Sketch', 184, 188.

[31] 'Solomon on the Control of Emotions', 399.

[32] Ibid. 402. Roberts claims that we can sometimes simply choose to construe X as Y ('directly, without any situational fostering on our part' (p. 402)), but he also seems to deny this when he admits that when we seek to control an emotion (by 'seeking to reconstrue a situation') we are still at the '*mercy*' of emotions, for 'when he has done all that he can do, something is left to be accomplished, and that is that the emotion *come* or *go*' (p. 403). Moreover, his example of the visual analogue (even as he presents it) does not support this claim for direct control—and this is congruent with my own experience that in cases which are more subtle than that of the duck/rabbit, I cannot always 'shift back and forth at will between the construals of the figures' ('What an Emotion Is: A Sketch', 193). Other philosophical discussions also note the limits of direct control of 'seeing-as' and imagining (Ishiguro, 'Imagination', 53, and P. F. Strawson, 'Imagination and Perception', in *Kant on Pure Reason*, ed. R. C. S. Walker (Oxford, 1982), 97).

no more a direct act of will or decision by fiat than is any responsible interpretation.

Passion and Imagination

I want now to consider the happy passion of faith from another perspective provided by Climacus in the *Concluding Unscientific Post-script*. Although he does not speak of faith there as *a* passion, he does elaborate on the experience of passion in a way which gives us a fuller picture.[33] He speaks of passion in two ways. The more familiar way presents passion in terms of the 'how' as opposed to the 'what', or in terms of subjective appropriation as opposed to objective assessment.[34] The second way, which I will focus on here, directly implies the relevance of imaginative activity. He writes, for example, that it 'is only momentarily that the particular individual is able to realize existentially a unity of the infinite and the finite which transcends existence. This unity is realized in the moment of passion'.[35]

Passion, in other words, is generated in the experience or activity of holding or being two elements (infinite and finite) in a tension-in-unity. The centrality of the element of tension to the concept of passion is emphasized repeatedly: passion is precisely what occurs when a person comes 'nearest to being in two places at the same time' (p. 178). The reason that the 'unity is realized [only] in the moment of passion' is that no existing person can 'be in two places at the same time—he cannot be an identity of subject and object' (p. 178). The unity is not an identity, but a sustained tension: 'When he is nearest to being in two places at the same time he is in passion; but passion is momentary, and passion is also the highest expression of subjectivity' (p. 178).[36]

---

[33] Neither this difference between 'passion' and 'a passion' nor the following 'two ways' noted in the text correspond to the two Climacus uses of 'passion' referred to by Roberts— namely, passion as interest and passion as emotion ('Some Remarks on the Concept of Passion', 88). Kierkegaard does exploit the close connection between the two uses (as Roberts notes, 'an interest is a disposition to emotions', and emotion is one of the chief ways that passion as interest is manifested (pp. 88, 90))—however, he refers to both uses in the context of 'passion' as well as 'a passion'.

[34] *Postscript*, 181; ch. 2 *passim*.

[35] Ibid. 176. Succeeding parenthetical page references will be to this work unless otherwise indicated in the text.

[36] It should be obvious even from this that Climacus is not advocating the exclusion of the objective, for though we cannot be an 'identity' of subject and object, neither can we simply be in one place or the other—we must remain in two places at the same time.

Climacus later reflects on 'how one might bring a man into a state of passion', hypothesizing somewhat playfully:

> If I could get him seated on a horse and the horse made to take fright and gallop wildly, or better still, for the sake of bringing the passion out, if I could take a man who wanted to arrive at a certain place as quickly as possible, and hence already had some passion, and could set him astride a horse that can scarcely walk. . . . Or if a driver were otherwise not especially inclined toward passion, if someone hitched a team of horses to a wagon for him, one of them a Pegasus and the other a worn-out jade, and told him to drive, I think one might succeed. (p. 276)

This passage begins to develop a more concrete understanding of passion, and the progression of examples is revealing. The first example seems a straightforward case of the passion of fear or anxiety. The second is more complicated in that it points to the passion experienced in a situation in which two elements (one of which is itself already a passion) are in tension. The third develops this sense of tension—passion is generated in the experience of the tension between the Pegasus and the worn-out jade, paralleling the tension referred to earlier between the infinite and finite in an individual.

The importance of tension to this account of passion is clear, and I suggest that the relation of imagination to passion lies precisely in the importance of this kind of tension, for a distinctive role of imagination is that of holding elements in tension. Imagination holds together for us elements which in some way do not sit well together except under such pressure—either because they are not yet actually together or because, as in the case of infinite and finite, they are intrinsically opposed or antithetical and hence in a paradoxical tension. One would then expect that imagination would be centrally involved in any account of passion which emphasizes tension (or paradox) in this way, and we find exactly that to be the case in another of his references to passion. He writes: 'In passion the existing subject is rendered infinite in the eternity of the imaginative representation, and yet he is at the same time most definitely himself' (p. 176). He thus makes explicit the connection between passion and imagination in terms of the paradoxical tension which generates passion. I will consider in detail in Chapter 3 what it means for the imagination to render infinite a finite subject—the point for the moment is that 'imaginative representation' is not only the means of rendering infinite the finite subject, but it does so in such a way as to maintain that finitude of the subject in tension with its infinity.

The suggestion that the exercise of imagination is integral to passion (since passion is an imaginative activity, generated by the imaginative exercise of holding elements in tension), then, is effectively the suggestion that imagination is integral to the happy passion which Climacus calls faith. Moreover, the ascription of the term 'passion' to faith necessarily says something crucial about the character of the transition to faith since whatever understanding Climacus holds about how we come to have (or change) passions will bear on his understanding of the transition to faith. It should be clear, then, that faith cannot be understood as a leap except as it does justice to what is distinctive about the realization of a passion, and it cannot be understood as a happy passion except as qualified by what is distinctive about a leap. The overriding motivation informing this dual description of faith is, I suggest, the desire to guarantee the qualitativeness and freedom of the transition while appreciating its character as response. It is the attribution of passion, moreover, which reveals the importance of imaginative activity to the transition. This means that any 'decision' in which the 'happy passion' of faith is realized is either (1) an achievement of imaginative activity or, at the very least, (2) involves imaginative activity in a way in which much of what we ordinarily call decision need not, or (3) involves imaginative activity in a way which we do not normally appreciate as part of all decision.

THE CONTOURS OF DECISION

'The leap', Kierkegaard explains, 'is neither more nor less than the most decisive protest possible against the inverse procedure of the Method'.[37] The negative contours of the leap are clear—the transformation, however it is achieved, cannot be understood as one in which something 'flops over' by 'immanental necessity'.[38] What is ruled out, therefore, is a transition that is either quantitative or necessary, but that leaves room for the leap to be understood as *no more than* is needed to rule those out, and it is not immediately obvious what is thereby ruled in. The discussion in the *Postscript* shows that passion is not a directly or immediately willed achievement and in the *Fragments* faith is given bounds by contrasting it with knowledge, simple awareness, and unconditioned

---

[37] *Postscript*, 96.
[38] *Journals*, iii. VII² B 261: 22, n.d. [1846–7], 21. This is also what is at issue in the rejection of the Hegelian view that it is 'possible for the one standpoint necessarily to determine itself into the other', *Postscript*, 262.

willing. All of this leaves room for the leap of faith to be understood as an act of conditioned willing or an act resulting indirectly from willing, but it is not clear how such an act should be interpreted. The qualification by 'passion' suggests that, in so far as it is a decision at all, it should be more along the lines of a decision *that* something is the case than a decision *to* do something; even the latter kind of decision, however, can range over a wide spectrum, from compelled to arbitrary, and the more interesting questions concern the intermediate cases. What Kierkegaard means by decision and leap can be determined only by determining more precisely what is most at stake for him. To determine whether those ends can be guaranteed only by reference to an intentional decision to do something or a self-conscious selection among perceived alternatives we need to see more precisely his view of the contours (or *sine qua non* requirements) of the transition achieved in faith.

Decision as Qualitative Transition

Clearly, a plausible reading of transition in the Climacus account has to do justice to the *Postscript*'s emphasis on the crucial requirement that the transition be 'qualitative'—it is a 'breach of continuity', a 'breach of immanence'.[39] The 'leap' is the 'qualitative transition from non-belief to belief'; in particular, the transition 'from the introduction to the becoming a Christian' is not 'immediate', but is rather a 'qualitative leap'.[40]

It is crucial to realize at the outset that a 'qualitative' transition does not necessarily have to be brought about by a direct decision. *Gestalt* shifts, for example, are qualitative transitions which are not, at least initially, brought about by a direct decision. In what follows I suggest how the concept of a *Gestalt* shift can provide one perspective on the transition (or leap) in a conversion experience.[41]

In a situation where a *Gestalt* shift can occur, initially we can see only one possibility (for example a duck figure); at some point, after concentrated attention or perhaps after coaching or guidance, another alternative (a rabbit figure) comes into focus for us. Seeing the rabbit

---

[39] *Postscript*, 88, 94, 262, 306, 340.

[40] Ibid. 15; 340.

[41] Only after my writing was nearly finished did I come across Garrett Green's fine book, *Imagining God: Theology & the Religious Imagination* (New York, 1989) in which he too considers *Gestalt* shifts in relation to faith. Green, however, makes no reference to Kierkegaard in this respect.

figure for the first time is not the *direct or immediate* result of a decision or volition, although it may take much preliminary effort (and hence be an indirect result). It is not a choice in any standard sense because initially we see only the one possibility; at the outset we *recognize* no other equally real alternatives from among which to choose. We can decide or choose to *look for* the rabbit figure which we are told is there and cannot yet see, but we cannot decide or choose to see (recognize) it. We can directly do what will in all probability lead us to see the figure, but we cannot directly make ourselves see it. Recognizing it, then, is a qualitative transition which is not achievable by fiat; it is not the direct result of willing, nor is it the necessary result of the effort to look for it.

A *Gestalt* shift is a transition which occurs when a 'critical threshold' has been reached: just as in the case of an explosive, the material does not explode by degrees but gradually gets hotter until the qualitative change occurs, so too a new quality may emerge only at a critical threshold. Kierkegaard himself connects leaps with such critical thresholds when he speaks of 'the leap by which water turns to ice, the leap by which I understand an author, and the leap which is the transition from good to evil'.[42] These examples are cited in reference to the question 'Is this leap then entirely homogeneous?' and are admittedly presented in a context of examples which illustrate a 'qualitative difference between leaps'. But interestingly the example of a qualitatively different kind of leap is 'The paradox. Christ's entry into the world'. That is, the qualitatively different (non-homogeneous) leap is the one made by God coming into Time, *not by us*. On *our* side a transition may be sufficiently a leap (i.e., a qualitative transition) even if 'homogeneous' in contrast to the leap (made by God) of divinity into the world. Since a critical threshold and a qualitative shift occur even in the homogeneous leaps he illustrates by the examples of the leap by which water turns to ice and the leap by which I understand an author, I suggest that the category of critical threshold sheds light on the kind of activity he thinks we engage in when, for example, 'The thought of God emerges with a leap' or when there is 'the leap of sin-consciousness'.[43]

The emergence of a qualitatively different awareness at a critical threshold is a function of what precedes it, without, however, coming 'by degrees' with increases of evidence or attentive effort. The transition leads to a qualitatively different conclusion (in this sense it might be

[42] *Journals*, iii. V C 1, n.d. [1844], 17.
[43] Ibid. iii. V C 7, n.d., [1844], 19.

considered discontinuous with what preceded it), but it cannot occur unless much preliminary material is registered and so is a culmination of the preceding (in this sense it might be considered continuous with it). It is, so to speak, a creative culmination rather than a mechanical accumulation. Such a shift in perspective is an example of a qualitative transition which is distinguishable from a quantitative process as well as from a momentary, separable act of will or decision which fills a gap.

The contrast which is crucial to Climacus is clearly between a qualitative and a quantitative achievement, and the example of a *Gestalt* shift shows that a qualitative transition need not be made through a direct, instantaneous, intentional choice (a choice by fiat). That point remains valid even though there are admittedly some disanalogies between a *Gestalt* shift and the kind of transition I am exploring. I will consider these disanalogies in Chapter 3 and there introduce another perspective on the transition—the perspective provided by the category of 'metaphor'—which, I shall argue, compensates for the limits of the *Gestalt*-shift example and must be held in tension with the perspective provided by *Gestalt* shifts. As will become apparent when we consider how metaphor involves holding two perspectives in tension, the very exercise of our understanding the transition of which Climacus speaks is itself an imaginative and metaphoric exercise.

Decision as Free Transition

In addition to the qualitativeness of the transition, Climacus emphasizes the freedom of our religious response in faith and we need to consider the bearing of that requirement on our understanding of the transition. Any plausible reading of the transition has to do justice to the biblical notion of responsible freedom to which he is committed.[44] Faith involves will in the sense of obedience: 'how else', he writes, 'explain the passage in the New Testament which says that he who does not have faith shall be punished' or the Christian definition that 'Sin is not to believe' or the injunction to 'enter by the narrow gate'.[45] However, Kierkegaard has not

[44] Albrecht Dihle's respected study, *The Theory of Will in Classical Antiquity*, Sather Classical Lectures, vol. 48 (Berkeley, CA., 1982) details the contrast between the Greek and biblical notions of freedom (as an exercise of intellect vs. obedience); see especially chs. 1 and 4. Dihle makes a suggestive correlation between the articulation of a volitionalist account of freedom and the view of the inscrutability of the universe which results from a belief in a creator who can interfere with the laws of the universe and who rules 'solely according to His will and pleasure' (pp. 70–2).

[45] *Journals*, ii. I A 36, 25 November 1834, 3; iv. X¹ A 348, n.d. [1849], 109; ii. XI¹ A 24, n.d. [1854], 76–7.

only a biblical commitment, but a philosophical stance on freedom which also needs to be accounted for in any reading of the transition to faith and which must contour our understanding of his view of the biblical requirement. 'The most tremendous thing', Kierkegaard writes, 'conceded to man is—choice, freedom', and 'freedom means to be capable'.[46] But what freedom requires is never, for Kierkegaard, a matter of *liberum arbitrium* (freedom of indifference)[47]—such freedom, Kierkegaard and his pseudonyms agree, does not exist. Thus, freedom at every stage of the process of acquiring faith is an interested, contextualized freedom.[48] We learn from his journals that human freedom is compatible with absolute divine governance and omnipotence and that 'constraint' is compatible with freedom;[49] we learn that the choice he means to guarantee is not 'abstract freedom of choice', 'bare and naked', 'content-less', achieved through a 'perfectly disinterested will'.[50] We learn, in addition, that he distinguishes between 'freedom of choice' and 'true freedom' and that the latter is compatible with there being, in some meaningful sense, 'no *choice*'.[51] This complex understanding of freedom and choice illuminates (and qualifies) his biblical commitment to faith as obedience, and opens the way to a more subtle understanding of the necessary conditions for a *free* qualitative transition.

Let me explore this by considering Kierkegaard's musings, in his papers and journals, on the person of Climacus. These, I suggest, genuinely raise the question of the relation between will, imagination, cognition, and passion, and they not only reveal that his emphasis on will is an emphasis on freedom rather than direct volition, but they also illustrate his view of a free acceptance as one which is neither compelled nor necessary. He asks, for example: 'To what extent does the imagination play a role in logical thought, to what extent the will; to what extent is the conclusion a resolution?'[52] The importance of freedom is apparent in the contrast implied in the question: 'To doubt, what is it. a determination of the will or a necessity of cognition'.[53] Moreover, although his remarks on doubt bring in the relation of 'will', the import is

---

[46] *Journals*, ii. X² A 428, n.d. [1850], 69; V B 56:2, n.d. [1844], 62.

[47] *Concept of Anxiety*, 49, 112, 200; *Journals*, ii. V B 56:2, n.d. [1844], 61–2; also see the journal entries referred to in n. 49 below.

[48] This shall be explored more in Chapter 5.

[49] *Journals*, ii. VII¹ A 181, n.d. [1846], 62–3; I A 5, 19 August 1834, 56; X² A 428, n.d. [1850], 68; X³ A 618, n.d. [1850], 70–2.

[50] Ibid. ii. X⁴ A 175, n.d. [1851], 73; X² A 243, n.d. [1849], 67; III A 48, n.d. [1840], 59; IV C 39, n.d. [1842–3], 59.

[51] Ibid. ii. X⁴ A 177, n.d. [1851], 74; X² A 428, n.d. [1850], 68.

[52] *Johannes Climacus*, 234.   [53] Ibid. 250.

not immediately obvious. For example, he suggests that 'in order to doubt one must will it—the factor of willing must be taken away if one is to stop—consequently one must will to stop it';[54] yet Climacus's similar-sounding claim in the later *Fragments* that doubt is terminated 'not by knowledge but by will' (p. 84) is followed almost immediately with the comment that both belief and doubt are 'passions', in particular, they are 'opposite passions'. Thus will is subsumed under the rubric of passion.[55] What is meant by saying that doubt is halted 'by the categorical imperative of the will'[56] is qualified by the fact that the *Fragments* uses as interchangeable the claim that doubt is terminated by 'will' and the claim that the termination of doubt (that is, through belief) is a 'passion'. Moreover, the view that doubt can only be terminated by will is contrasted with the 'stupid opinion that one doubts by way of necessity' (p. 82). The crucial thing at stake, then, in the references to willing seems to be the *freedom* of both doubt and the termination of doubt, just as earlier he had written: 'If I am going to emerge from doubt in freedom, I must have entered doubt in freedom. (Act of will.),'[57] so in the *Fragments* he writes that doubt is terminated 'only in freedom, by an act of will' (p. 82).

The repeated contrasts between cognition and will, and between cognition and passion, are used in the service of emphasizing the free character of the act. The claim in the *Fragments* that 'belief is not a knowledge but an act of freedom, an expression of will' (p. 83) reinforces this very point—what is rejected is compulsion or necessity. We can take 'act of freedom' and 'expression of will' as appositives (as in the earlier claim that doubt can be terminated only 'in freedom, by an act of will' (p. 82)) and read the latter in terms of the former. Support for such a reading is found in the *Postscript* where the requirement is 'subjective acceptance', and what is ruled out is that the conclusion follows as a 'matter of course' (p. 116). But ruling out necessary or compelled conclusions is not the same as claiming that a conclusion or 'acceptance' is effected by deliberate self-conscious decision. In such cases, the idiom of will can well be used simply to highlight the freedom of the acceptance, and the freedom of the acceptance is understood by contrast with a necessary or passive or compelled reaction.

[54] *Johannes Climacus*, 259.
[55] James Collins likewise claims that 'the will is regarded by Kierkegaard as a major natural passion', and that Kierkegaard includes 'under the broad term "will" . . . not only the power of resolution itself but also the operations of intellect and the passions' (*The Mind of Kierkegaard* (Princeton, NJ, 1983), 262; 75).
[56] *Johannes Climacus*, 233–4.   [57] Ibid. 265.

Such an understanding of freedom is congruent with the implications of my earlier consideration of a *Gestalt* shift. The qualitative change which occurs in a *Gestalt* shift, for example, can be free in the sense that it is not compelled (either physically or rationally) without being self-consciously intentional and without having an explicit acknowledgement of a variety of options. A free transition need not be achieved by a deliberate decision or direct act of will; a free transition need not be effected by fiat. Qualitative changes can also be free without being arbitrary since freedom does not require a total absence of constraint, though of course it is incompatible with compulsion. Thus, there is a meaningful sense in which such a transitional shift in perspective can be considered free as long as it is not necessary or compelled.

A free act need not be an act done 'on purpose', as it were, with explicit acknowledgement of a variety of plausible options. As important, lack of compulsion is not the same as lack of constraint—an uncompelled activity might nevertheless be subject to some constraint. A response can be free even while it is a response to something. Thus, if willing is correlated with free activity, it need not be seen as contrasted with other activities (like imagination or cognition) unless the latter are seen as activities which compel acceptances. Indeed, Kierkegaard's self-questionings about the role of imagination and cognition are very understandable as an expression of questioning about the degree of compulsion effected by each. In any case, the rejection of the category of necessity, which Kierkegaard so emphatically insists on, can, in principle, be maintained without turning either to intentional or to arbitrary decision. As long as these points are admitted, the requirement of a decision or leap of faith could, in principle, be fulfilled by an account of willing which was understood more in terms of 'active recognition' or 'acceptance' than in terms of decision by fiat. Thus, the qualitative and free transition which is at stake for Climacus could, in principle, be achieved in ways which have little to do with the emasculated model of decision as a discrete, direct act of will in contrast to other activities.

It might be objected that Kierkegaard's emphasis on the freedom of faith as obedience (for which blame and reward are appropriate) is not adequately accounted for by such a compatibilist notion of freedom (as non-compelled). At the very least, his distinction between freedom of choice and 'true freedom' gives one reason to wonder about such an objection, but even if one conceded that objection, one could still argue that it may be sufficient for the responsibility he seeks to guarantee (the obedience or rejection he needs to account for) that there are deliberate, by fiat, choices by which we prepare ourselves for the transition (or confirm it after the fact)—even if the actual acceptance or transition is not directly achieved by such a choice. In other words, in so far as freedom requires the possibility of more than non-compelled choice, the freedom of faith in obedience can be guaranteed by reference to relatively unproblematically free choices by which we cultivate or stifle the transition to faith, choices by which we enhance or diminish our chances to see a new vision.

I would still maintain, however, that in so far as an appeal to will or decision in the Climacus account needs to be accounted for in the actual moment of transition, it can be accounted for by reference to our free activity in an acceptance or recognition which is neither compelled nor necessary. That is, if we take into account the implications of Kierkegaard's complex understanding of true freedom in relation to 'freedom of choice' we can meaningfully allow that not only are our choices preparatory to the transition (our choices to look, to attend in particular ways) our free activity, but that the actual shift in perspective which occurs is free as well. The example of a *Gestalt* shift, in spite of being limited in application, none the less shows that both the freedom and qualitative character of a transition can be achieved without requiring a direct decision along the lines of a decision to do something (or a discrete direct act of will to fill a gap). The notion of a *Gestalt* shift of perspective and the category of a critical threshold, as well as the recognition that a free transition is compatible with constraint (though incompatible with compulsion or necessity) and does not require a deliberate, intentional act of will, broaden the possibilities for understanding a qualitative and free transition in general. This provides a negative argument in support of the possibility of a broader interpretation of the 'leap' or 'decision' which is the transition to faith. The bearing of the description of faith as a passion, highlighting as it does the relevance of imaginative activity, yields some indication of positive content to the transition. In Chapter 3 I will specify the content of the transition by approaching the question of the transition to faith and its relation to imagination from the wider perspective of various Kierkegaardian accounts of choice and transition in the task of subjectivity; I will argue that the role of imagination revealed in those accounts of 'choice' supports a reinterpretation of the category of 'decision' in the transition to faith. But first, to open the way more fully for that interpretation, I turn briefly to consider some suggestions in the Kierkegaardian texts of a broadened concept of 'willing'.

2

Pathos-filled Transitions: Will and Imagination

Among the references to a leap in his familiar discussion of Lessing, Climacus makes the suggestive, perhaps even surprising, comment that Mendelssohn 'has indicated quite correctly the lyrical culmination of thought in the leap'.[1] The term 'lyrical' strikingly evokes a creative, non-mechanical, and non-volitional transition—one might say an imaginative one. In what follows I will explore some of the Kierkegaardian texts which reinforce such an understanding of a leap by revealing a broadening of the concepts of 'will' and 'decision'. I will argue that the ways in which willing or decision is tied to imagination in these texts imply a rejection of the dualisms assumed in a purely volitionalist account of transitions (or conversely, that the way in which such treatments of willing or decision imply a rejection of such dualisms ties them to imagination). All of this is intended to make room for a non-volitionalist understanding of the leap in the acquisition of faith without, however, going to the opposite extreme of seeing it as an ineffable something which happens to us. I want to argue for the importance of a describable human activity in the acquisition of faith, an activity, however, which is better understood on the model of imaginative transition than an act of will-power.

CLASSIFICATIONS OF EXISTENCE AND IMPLICATIONS FOR WILLING

One of the ways in which a broadened concept of will and its tie with imagination is suggested is found in the presentation of two separate sets of classifications of existence, one by Climacus and one by Anti-Climacus. Although these classifications are proposed by different pseudonyms, I suggest that they make the same point, by different

---

[1] *Postscript*, 95.

means, and contribute to a fuller picture of imaginative activity in willing.

Prior to his description of the subjective thinker as one whose task is 'to understand the greatest oppositions together',[2] Climacus makes a tripartite classification of 'all the factors' of existence, dividing them into 'thought', 'imagination', and 'feeling': 'In existence all the factors must be co-present. In existence thought is by no means higher than imagination and feeling, but coordinate' (p. 310).[3] The importance and value of imagination is revealed in his claim that the 'task' is to give them all 'equal status': the ideal is to unify them 'in simultaneity', rather than to establish a hierarchy (p. 311). To lose imagination is 'quite as bad' as to lose reason (p. 311), for imagination and passion are what 'pierce the illusions of probability' (p. 409). The role of imagination, integral to the poetic, must be affirmed and preserved 'as long as a human being makes claim to a human form of existence' (p. 311). The claims that the triad of 'all the factors' of existence includes imagination on a par with thought and feeling, and that a 'human form of existence' requires imagination, show beyond a doubt the indispensability and importance of imaginative activity. They are just the claims one would expect him to make about imagination given his characterization of the task of becoming subjective as one of understanding 'the greatest oppositions together', for of the triad of 'all the factors' of existence it is imagination which is most suited to holding oppositions together.

The importance of imagination, revealed in the designation of imagination as one of the three coequal factors of existence (thought, imagination, and feeling), is affirmed as well in another classification in which Anti-Climacus claims that imagination is not one faculty among many, but the faculty *instar omnium*, the qualifier of all our faculties:

What feeling, knowledge, or will a man has, depends in the last resort upon what imagination he has, that is to say, upon how these things are reflected, i.e., it depends upon imagination. . . . Imagination is the possibility of all reflection, and the intensity of this medium is the possibility of the intensity of the self.[4]

In other words, we cannot speak of any of the faculties or activities of the self (feeling, knowing, and willing) except in terms of imagination. Hence, an emphasis on the importance of imagination is equally achieved in both classifications, although by different means. In these

---

[2] *Postscript*, 316. Remaining parenthetical page references are to this work.
[3] See his remark in *Journals*, i. V A 20, n.d. [1844], 19.
[4] *Sickness unto Death*, 163–4.

classifications we find just that acknowledgement of the importance of imaginative activity which we would expect to find in accounts which, as we shall see in more detail in Chapter 3, emphasize categories of 'paradox', 'passion', and the 'infinite'.

In addition to revealing his positive assessment of imagination, these classifications also have implications for a broadened understanding of the 'will'. In the first classification noted above (in which imagination is made coequal to thought and feeling) Kierkegaard accounts for '*all* the factors' of existence without bringing in a separate category of 'will' at all. This is noteworthy because even sensitive and perceptive commentaries on imagination in the Climacus texts repeatedly and inexplicably read 'will' into the description of the factors of existence, although the text refers here only to *Taenkning*, *Phantasie*, and *Følelse*.[5] The implication of the text is that will informs or is to be predicated of all our activities (thought, feeling, and imagination)—that is, that willing is not seen by Climacus as an activity on a par with thought or feeling or imagination. The result is that this classification puts in question contrasts between will and other activities or faculties—thus imagination (and thought and feeling) are not seen as counterparts to, or prolegomena to, or consequences of willing, but rather as activities of which 'will' can be predicated. The implication is that a reference to 'will' could then plausibly be understood as a remark on the *freedom* of any of these activities.

Although in the second classification will is contrasted with knowledge and feeling, the point is that we cannot speak of willing as such, but only of willing qualified by imagination.[6] Both classifications thus acknowledge the activity of imagination in such a way as to put in question contrasts between will and other activities or faculties (especially between will and imagination).

Moreover, if we compare both tripartite classifications we can see that the place of the will in one is taken by imagination in the other. Thus in spite of occasions when 'will' is contrasted with other activities of the self, both these classifications imply that 'will' is not so easily contrastable: either because 'all the factors' of existence can be accounted for and understood without reference to a distinct category of 'will', or alternatively, because 'willing' cannot be understood except in terms of

[5] David Gouwens does this, for example, in his *Kierkegaard's Dialectic of the Imagination*, 115, 141; this is not in keeping with the Danish text (*Samlede Vaerker* (Gyldendal, 1963), Bind 10, 48).

[6] Presumably this applies as well to *Journals*, iii: IV C78, n.d. [1842–3], 694.

imagination. This conclusion is supported by the self-questioning way in which some of Kierkegaard's formulations of the contrast between will and other activities (imagination, cognition) are expressed—suggesting that the character of the relation between them is genuinely open to question.[7] One could argue on the basis of these classifications, then, that Kierkegaard is in effect, though not necessarily fully self-consciously, contributing to a broadened concept of 'will', and hence of 'decision'.

DECISIONS AND INFERENTIAL CULMINATIONS

Another indication of a broadened concept of will and decision can be clarified by drawing out the suggestion made above that a reference to 'will' could be understood as a remark on the freedom of any of our activities. That suggestion reaffirms my initial discussion of freedom in Chapter 1, where I noted a variety of elements which suggest that the idiom of will is meant to emphasize freedom. To repeat my earlier example, Climacus contrasts the view that doubt can only be terminated by will with the 'stupid opinion that one doubts by way of necessity'.[8] He often uses the phrases 'freedom' and 'act of will' as appositives, as when he writes 'I must have entered doubt in freedom. (Act of will.)', or that doubt is terminated 'only in freedom, by an act of will'.[9] As appositives, the force of 'will' can be read as that of 'free' activity. The claim in the *Fragments* that 'belief is not a knowledge but an act of freedom, an expression of will'[10] reinforces this very point—what is rejected is rational compulsion or necessity. The same point is made in the *Postscript* where the requirement is 'subjective acceptance', and what is ruled out is that the conclusion follows as a 'matter of course'.[11]

Conclusions which do not follow as a 'matter of course' are those which Kierkegaard elsewhere refers to as 'leaps'—he repeatedly refers to the 'leap of inference in induction and analogy', claiming that in such cases 'the conclusion can be reached only by a LEAP' (his emphasis) and 'all other conclusions are essentially tautological'.[12] But to speak of a leap or act of will in an inductive inference is clearly to speak of a broad-

---

[7] *Johannes Climacus*, 234, 256.
[8] *Fragments*, 82.
[9] *Johannes Climacus*, 265; *Fragments*, 82.
[10] *Fragments*, 83.   [11] *Postscript*, 116.
[12] *Journals*, iii. V C 7, n.d. [1844], 19; V A 74, n.d. [1844], 16.

ened concept of will. A conclusion that-*p*-is-true may well be spoken of as a decision, but it is clearly quite different from, for example, a 'decision *to* go to the store'. Judge William's conclusion that 'only ['in this way'] does existence become beautiful'[13] may be a decision, but it cannot be read on the model of a 'decision to go to the store': both decisions can be 'free', but the two are very different and the implicit use of a monolithic model of decision only obscures the character of the transition involved in each case. The former is a decision which is constituted by a reorienting shift of perspective—it is surely distinguishable (as Kierkegaard explicitly requires) from an immanental determination or necessary 'flopping over', but it is also distinguishable from a deliberate, self-conscious act of 'will-power' in the face of equally plausible alternatives. By thus extending the category of leap to all non-tautological conclusions, Kierkegaard broadens the possibilities for understanding the free and qualitative transition to faith.

Moreover, this broadening of the category of leap implies a relationship between imagination and willing. An inductive or analogical inference is a leap because it is a non-mechanical extension—it involves a creative extrapolation or stretching of terms, an extension beyond what is actually given. The claim that there is a 'leap of inference' in 'analogy' is suggestive because he elsewhere notes that analogies 'awaken the mind to an understanding'[14]—that is, both the creation and understanding of an analogy imply a use of imaginative extension. Such a view, I hinted earlier, would plausibly account for the (perhaps otherwise surprising) suggestion by Climacus that Mendelssohn 'has indicated quite correctly the lyrical culmination of thought in the leap'.[15] The transition is a culmination 'of thought' and the term 'lyrical', I repeat, quite strikingly evokes the creative, imaginative quality of the transition.

PATHOS-FILLED TRANSITIONS

By way of elaboration of the preceding, the character of the leap or decision of faith can be illuminated by reference to Kierkegaard's obsessive musings in the journals on the notion of qualitative transition,

---

[13] *Either/Or*, ii. 182.
[14] *Fragments*, 26. See John Coulson's use of the term 'analogical leap' in his discussion of imagination and analogical descriptions, in *Religion and Imagination: 'in aid of a grammar of assent'* (Oxford, 1981), 29.
[15] *Postscript*, 95.

change, and motion integral to what he calls his 'theory of the leap'.[16] There a broadening of the concepts of will and decision is indicated by the association he makes between transitions (leaps) and pathos.

In general, qualitative transitions or leaps are central to any account of development of the self—'does not the whole of life', he asks, 'rest in that?'[17] In particular, he asserts a relation between passion and some kinds of transition when he contrasts a 'dialectical transition' with a 'pathos-filled transition'.[18] The latter, he notes, is the kind of transition at issue in *Fear and Trembling*, for pathos is 'the substance of the leap'.[19] For our purposes here, what is important is his claim that 'A pathos-filled transition can be achieved by every one if he wills it, because the transition to the infinite, which consists in pathos, takes only courage'.[20] But 'willing' a transition which 'consists in pathos' or whose 'substance' is pathos, is 'willing' in a richer or more extended sense than that normally thought to be involved in an ordinary decision to do something. In so far as the reference to pathos invokes the relevance of imagination in passion, the pathos-filled transition can be said to consist in an imaginative leap or shift—something that may indeed take courage.

That such a transition is not achieved through intentional decision is clear too from his striking claim that 'In the final analysis what I call a transition of pathos Aristotle called an enthymeme'.[21] It was reading about enthymeme in Aristotle's *Rhetoric*, Kierkegaard reveals, which led to his shock of recognition: the enthymeme of which Aristotle spoke seemed to him remarkably like a 'pathos-filled transition', a 'willing' which took courage, the kind of 'leap' he was himself concerned to explicate (in the effort to remedy Hegel's inadequate treatment of transition). But Aristotle's enthymeme was, after all (as would have been clear to Kierkegaard), in Aristotle's own words a 'syllogism', a 'rhetorical proof'—although it was not a 'scientific demonstration' or 'logical syllogism', it was a syllogism, a persuasive argument, none the less.[22] The difference between enthymeme and scientific demonstration for Aristotle lay in the character of the premises, not in its persuasive potential. The subject-matter of enthymemes is, almost exclusively, 'what is to be chosen or avoided in human conduct' and such arguments address the

---

[16] *Journals*, iii. V C 12, n.d. [1844], 20.
[17] Ibid. i. IV C 87, n.d. [1842–3], 110.
[18] Ibid. iii. IV C 12, n.d. [1842–3], V C 1 n.d. [1844], 15 and 18.
[19] Ibid. iii. V B 49:14, n.d. [1844], 16.
[20] Ibid. iii. IV C 12, n.d. [1842–3], 15.
[21] Ibid. iii. VI A 33, n.d. [1845], 20.
[22] *Rhetoric*, I:1, 5.

objects toward which people aim, including goods of various sorts as well as 'release from evil'.[23] An enthymeme is rhetorical—that is, it is geared to its audience, recognizing that, as Aristotle says, ' "persuasive" means persuasive to a person'.[24] Making due allowance for the context dependency of evidence, the transition in an enthymeme is nevertheless 'to conclude from certain assumptions that something else follows from those assumptions (something distinct from them, yet dependent upon their existing) either universally or as a rule'.[25] Aristotle notes that 'the function of all persuasive utterance is realized in some decision',[26] but the enthymematic transition is achieved when the hearer is persuaded that-(realizes that-, recognizes that-) p-is-the-case. Admittedly, to refuse to act accordingly is to prevent the function of the enthymeme from being realized, but the transition itself is more like the decision-that-p than a decision-to-do X.

Finally, the references to pathos as the 'substance' of the transition are crucial, for they serve to bring back in focus the role of imagination in the transition. They echo the *Postscript* explanation that in our paradoxical state of being both comic and pathetic, the pathetic element is due to the fact that the 'striving is infinite'.[27] But it is imagination alone which can do anything 'infinitely'. Imagination is thus integral to 'willing' a pathos-filled transition, a transition to the infinite which takes courage.

WILLING AND PASSION

A broadened concept of willing is also suggested by the claim in the *Fragments* that the understanding 'will[s] its own downfall'.[28] The understanding is inherently motivated, not externally moved, by its 'passion' to think what cannot be thought[29]—it, after all, wills its *own* downfall. Climacus thus refuses to dichotomize either will and passion or will and understanding. Willing its own downfall just is the expression of passion—and a willing which can only be done in passion is, obviously, clearly different from much of what we normally call will or decision. Repeated references to the 'paradoxical passion' hint,[30] as we have seen, at the relation of imagination to passion, and hence qualify the kind of willing which is exercised in the transition to faith. Such a qualification

[23] Ibid. 2:21, 150; I:1-10 *passim*; I:10, 59.
[24] Ibid. I:2, 11.
[25] Ibid. I:2, 10.
[26] Ibid. II:18, 141.
[27] *Postscript*, 84.
[28] *Fragments*, 47.
[29] Ibid. 37, 44.
[30] Ibid. 44, 47.

of 'willing' leaves room for a reading of the understanding's 'stepping aside' in the face of the Absolute Paradox,[31] the 'letting go' which constitutes embracing the paradox, in terms other than ordinary decision. That is, the passion of thought impels its own letting go, and the paradoxical letting go effects the acquisition of faith. This non-standard character of the 'decision' by which one becomes a Christian is also apparent when Climacus describes it by using both the idiom of a wonder which 'happened' and the idiom of 'decision', implying that both are equally appropriate.[32]

Moreover, it should be remembered that there may well be an asymmetry between a willing which stifles a stepping aside and a willing which constitutes such a stepping aside. Although the passion of thought impels its own letting go or stepping aside, it does not guarantee it—we can take offence or refuse to embrace the paradox. The inner dynamic can be stifled. But even if a deliberate act of will may be necessary to stifle it, that does not show that the same kind of act of will is required to affirm the momentum towards downfall. The kinds of willing involved in each movement may be asymmetrical: it is possible that we can stifle by deliberate decision what we cannot create by deliberate decision. Since it is conceptually possible to distinguish between the kind of willing which stifles the understanding's stepping aside and the kind of willing which *is* that stepping aside, the deliberateness and purposefulness of a stifling cannot automatically be imported into the category of willing which constitutes a stepping aside.

WILLING AND THE VALIDITY OF THE SOCRATIC

The non-standard character of the 'decision' involved in the acquisition of faith, and its relation to imagination, is, in addition, suggested by the way Climacus in the *Fragments* uses the term 'will' even in his description of the activity required in the Socratic model of gaining truth or knowledge. It should be noted first that Climacus's formulation of the contrast between the Socratic and non-Socratic positions has been used in support of a 'volitionalist' reading of faith. Climacus explains the non-Socratic alternative in the *Fragments* by contrasting willing 'within the condition' with willing before the condition is given: willing, he concedes, is 'efficacious only within the condition', only 'once the

---

[31] *Fragments*, 59.   [32] *Postscript*, 333.

condition is given', but once it is given, 'I possess the condition and now can will it'.[33] Since he says that faith is not an act of will because one cannot will the condition, one might infer that once the condition is given a self-conscious and deliberate decision still needs to be made. But although Climacus contrasts the Socratic and non-Socratic alternatives in terms of the source and temporal conferral of the 'condition', the character of the 'condition' seems to be the same in both cases, and this, I will argue in what follows, does not support a 'volitionalist' model of the decision of faith.

Climacus describes the non-Socratic alternative as one in which the teacher must bring to the learner the truth as well as 'the condition for understanding it', 'for if the learner were himself the condition for understanding the truth, then he merely needs to recollect, because the condition for understanding the truth is like being able to ask about it— the condition and the question contain the conditioned and the answer' (p. 14). In this passage Climacus is describing the character of the condition which, on the non-Socratic (Christian) alternative, the learner needs to be given and which, on the Socratic model, he already has; interestingly, the contrast between the Socratic and non-Socratic situations does not seem to involve the character of the condition as such. The condition, which 'is like being able to ask about' the truth, seems to be the same on either alternative: namely, a question which contains its answer.[34]

How does this understanding of the condition relate to the contrast between willing before and after the condition? The relevant passage, which I have already cited in part, is the following:

All human willing is efficacious only within the condition. For example, if I have the courage to will it, I will understand the Socratic—that is, understand myself, because from the Socratic point of view I possess the condition and now can will it. But if I do not possess the condition . . . then all my willing is of no avail, even though, once the condition is given, that which was valid for the Socratic is again valid. (pp. 62–3).

The important implication to be drawn is that *once* we assume the presence of the condition (regardless of its genesis) there is parity in the learners' situations. Receiving the condition and the truth would renew

---

[33] *Fragments*, 62, 63. Succeeding parenthetical references will be to this work until otherwise noted.

[34] This also explains Climacus's claim that when one has 'put on the condition', he, '*by doing so*, has become immersed in the truth' (*Fragments*, 18, emphasis mine).

Socratic validity because even when the condition is given by the Teacher, the character of the condition seems to be the same as when the condition is possessed eternally—it is a question containing an answer. Once I possess the condition my 'willing' is efficacious *in the way it was* for the Socratic learner: once I possess the condition I too, like him, 'can will it'.

This is important in terms of supporting a broadened notion of 'will' because it means that even on the Socratic model 'willing' is relevant. From this we can discover something significant about the learner's activity in the case where Socratic validity is renewed.

Consider again the initial Socratic situation. We know that although the Socratic learner has the condition for understanding the truth, and in one sense 'has' the relevant understanding, he still has to 'do something' to realize that understanding. Socratic validity allows a distinction between possessing the truth in ignorance and realizing the truth, and between knowing and knowing that you know (p. 65). All is not accomplished simply in virtue of having the condition within and having the occasion of the teacher—a free active response is required on the part of the learner. Thus the Socratic situation is such that one can have an understanding of the truth as part of the condition—as the answer contained in the question—and yet need free activity or response in the transition to a realization of that understanding. Climacus's suggestion that Socratic validity is *renewed* once the condition is given at least allows the possibility that the acquisition of faith would similarly involve a free active transition. But is that transition necessarily an intentional decision?

The kind of free active transition involved in the case of Christian faith—where Socratic validity is *renewed*—can be clarified by continuing the analysis of the transition in the Socratic model: in particular, the possibility of a free qualitative transition which is not a deliberate intentional decision begins to be apparent when we notice more precisely how Climacus describes the Socratic learner's activity in terms of 'will'. If 'once the condition is given' what 'was valid for the Socratic is again valid', and 'from the Socratic point of view I possess the condition and now can will it' (p. 63), this implies that even on the Socratic model I can still be said to need to 'will' something in order to understand the truth even though I already have the truth (even though, that is, I possess the question which contains the answer). But on the Socratic model what is required is 'recollection'—not decision or volition. Climacus apparently has no difficulty using the term 'will' or 'willing' to refer to the free activity of 'recollection' required for coming to knowledge on the Socratic model, yet such a coming to realize what one already knows is not readily seen as the result of a decision. 'Willing' within the Socratic model is better seen as having to do with notions of active attending and concentrating, recognition, and shift in perspective, rather than of intentional decision. The situation in which Socratic validity is renewed need not, therefore, imply a decision since the original Socratic transition did not—the term 'will' is used broadly enough by Climacus to cover the free activity exercised by the Socratic learner.[35]

As in the case of a *Gestalt* shift, the disciplined effort of 'attending' can be thought of as an act of will, but it is not at all the direct willing of the acceptance of a conclusion. The *attending* is active and free, yet the recognition we have is not achievable by fiat. William James, in his *Principles of Psychology* (1890), pointed to the importance of attention, seeing '*effort of attention*' as '*the essential phenomenon of will*', and concluding that '*the essential achievement of the will, in short, when it is most "voluntary", is to* ATTEND *to a difficult object and hold it fast before the mind*'.[36] Rollo May offers a contemporary reminder of James's explicit identification of 'belief', 'attention', and 'will', suggesting that James's contribution was to show that 'The effort which goes into the exercise of will is really effort of attention; the strain in willing is the effort to keep the consciousness clear, i.e., the strain of keeping the attention focussed'.[37]

The role of such attending in the active and free transition to a realization of what one potentially has fits well with Kierkegaard's claim that the transition from possibility to actuality 'takes place in freedom'[38]—that it is a free transition, rather than a necessary unfolding, suggests that the transition can be a qualitative change. He sees such a transition as qualitatively different from Hegel's kind of transition—this explains why he immediately follows his complaint about Hegel's treatment of the category of transition ('Hegel has never done justice to the category of transition') with the suggestion that 'It would be significant to compare it with the Aristotelian teaching about *kinesis*'.[39] This Aristotelian teaching, with which Kierkegaard agrees, is expressed

---

[35] See my 'Kierkegaardian Faith: The "Condition" and the Response,' *The International Journal for Philosophy of Religion*, 28 (Oct. 1990), 63–79.

[36] New York, 1950, ii. 562, 561.

[37] Rollo May, *Love and Will* (New York, 1969), 220.

[38] *Fragments*, 75.

[39] *Journals*, i. IV C 80, n.d. [1842–3], 110.

in the recognition that *kinesis* (change) is of three kinds: namely, with respect to *quality* as well as quantity and place.[40]

A clarification is in order, however, for my suggestion about this qualitative transition from possibility to actuality does not reduce the transition to Christianity to the transition which occurs in the religion of immanence (religiousness A). The two situations remain radically different because, whatever the character of the transition as such, on the Christian alternative the condition must be *given*. We cannot generate the possibility from within—the possibility itself must be restored to us. I am merely taking quite seriously the Climacus suggestion that 'once the condition is given', the situation is Socratically valid again, drawing out the implication that the qualitatively free transitions in both cases may be formally parallel.

WILLING AND THE 'GIFT' OF FAITH

Showing that the transitions may be formally parallel means showing that there is no intentional 'will-power' decision involved in the transition, and this is one way of undermining a volitionalist interpretation of the leap. But the arguments against the relevance of such a 'will-power' decision might seem to suggest that the alternative is a reading of the transition as something which is simply done to us, something ineffable which happens to us. For example, one critique of volitionalist interpretations of the leap of faith argues that one cannot appeal to a 'decision' to explain faith because one cannot appeal to *any* human activity—faith is a 'wonder' and a 'miracle' which as such is not susceptible to 'explanation'.[41] Another critique of Kierkegaardian faith concludes that 'it is not really the man's, but an act of God's grace in the man'.[42] I want now to suggest that taking the renewal of Socratic validity seriously also serves to reveal the limits of that kind of interpretation as well. By claiming that the transition to faith is ineffable and/or an act of God's grace in us, such criticisms of volitionalism go to an opposite and equally untenable extreme, and they do so, I shall argue, because they

---

[40] *Journals*, i. IV C 47, n.d. [1842–3], 110.

[41] David Wisdo, 'Kierkegaard on Belief, Faith, and Explanation', 95–114.

[42] Terence Penelhum, *God and Skepticism*, 83. Penelhum sees this as what Kierkegaard means when he 'both speaks of it as though it is a human act of will, a leap, and says that it is not an act of will'. But Kierkegaard's claim that it is not an act of will does not mean there is a sense in which it is not the man's act, but rather that it is not an unconditioned act (we cannot create the necessary condition by willing it).

make two assumptions which are not shared by Climacus (or Kierkegaard).

The claim that the acquisition of faith is ineffable and/or God's act of
grace in us attempts to do justice to Climacus's commitment to faith as a
'gift', not achievable by human fiat or unconditioned human activity of
any kind. But it makes the mistake of assuming: (1) that because faith is
not the result of unconditioned human activity it cannot require human
activity, and (2) that its character as 'gift' is exclusive of its involving any
describable human activity. To say that faith is a wonder or miracle is
not, however, in itself to preclude its being a free, though conditioned,
activity capable of description. At the very least we could note that
Climacus describes the gaining of faith as follows: 'until the wonder
happened (if we wish to express it in this manner) that he became a
Christian, or until he chose to become a Christian'.[43] Since Climacus
himself treats the two descriptions as equivalent, one cannot use the
claim that faith is a wonder to refute the claim that it is a choice of some
kind.

Equally important, that an activity is a divine gift need not negate its
character as genuine human activity. Such a dichotomy is illegitimate,
and this has been recognized recently by several authors. The illegitimacy
of the dichotomy is an implication of Kathryn Tanner's philosophically
sophisticated and theologically sensitive analysis of the relation between
divine creative agency and the efficacy of creatures in *God and Creation
in Christian Theology: Tyranny or Empowerment?*[44] Tanner addresses
the theologically pressing and much-debated question of the relation
between divine and human agency, and argues persuasively against any
theological position which 'refuses to the creature the ability to act or
produce effects by its own proper power, in order to ensure the
sovereignty of divine agency'.[45] 'The theologian', Tanner insists,

talks of an ordered nexus of created causes and effects in a relation of total and
immediate dependence upon divine agency. Two different orders of efficacy
become evident: along a 'horizontal' plane, an order of created causes and
effects; along a 'vertical' plane, the order whereby God founds the former.[46]

If to be free means to be 'master . . . of that which conditions choice on
the created level', then '[f]reedom or contingency of such a sort says

---

[43] *Postscript*, 333.
[44] *God and Creation in Christian Theology: Tyranny or Empowerment?* (Oxford,
1988), esp. ch. 3.
[45] Ibid. 86.   [46] Ibid. 89–90.

nothing about a creature's freedom or contingency with respect to the divine agent who creatively founds the whole entire created beings and their effects and their mode of relation'.[47] In those cases where there is a theological commitment to the insufficiency of created causes for created effects, it may be theologically appropriate to say that 'God effects what is discontinuous with our prior sinful inclinations or what exceeds altogether the created capabilities of human beings', but even then such statements about the 'infusion of a divine power' must still 'avoid implying a distinction within the created order between what is and is not the direct effect of divine agency.'[48] Tanner's case is illustrated with respect to a broad range of figures from Biel, Molina, and Banez to Barth and Rahner. The only reference to Kierkegaard occurs in a quotation used as a chapter head: Tanner quotes his journal entry that 'the art of using power is to make free'—something which only 'omnipotence' can do.[49] Tanner's citation of the passage is significant because it suggests that Kierkegaard rightly understood what Tanner is arguing—namely, that the theologian must 'maintain a direct rather than inverse proportion between what the creature has, on the one hand, and the extent and influence of God's agency, on the other'.[50] Climacus's repeated reminder that 'a man can do nothing of himself'[51] makes the same point, undermining any useful contrast between human activity and God's graceful gift.

In so far as the choice we make is to will the downfall of the understanding, it is clear that Climacus thinks it is something *we* do (indeed, as we saw, for Climacus everything we do is really God's gift). It is something we could not do without an enabling condition, but it is not something efficaciously imposed on us; not only is it not against our will, it is not without our activity. The point, then, is that we are significantly active and if it is *our* willing, it should be describable in some way. The real question is not whether it is an 'act of will' or a 'gift'[52]—the real

---

[47] *God and Creation in Christian Theology*, 90.

[48] Ibid. 100–1.

[49] Ibid. 81 (Tanner cites the Alexander Dru selection and translation; the standard Hong reference is ii. VII¹ A 181, n.d. [1846], 62–3).

[50] Ibid. 85.

[51] *Postscript*, 434–5. This reminder does not, of course, deny that there is a distinction between those acts (like faith) which exceed our fallen capacities and those (like breathing) which do not.

[52] Although he realizes that for Kierkegaard 'every instance of free will regarding the good can be seen as a gift of grace', Louis Pojman nevertheless seems to assume this dichotomy when he interprets Climacus's requirement of a 'condition' as implying that faith 'is not an act of the will, but a gift' (*The Logic of Subjectivity*, 92).

question is only whether such 'willing' is best understood on the model of deliberate decision or on some other model.

My analysis of the Socratic model in the preceding section illustrated the possibility of a transition which is neither totally passive nor the direct result of a deliberate decision—in particular, it illustrated the possibility of a free transition which is not a decision to realize the truth. The claim that Socratic validity is *renewed* once the condition is given may well support a parallel in the case of Christian faith.

The resort to ineffability or grace as a response to volitionalist interpretations of the acquisition of faith, the denial of any describable human activity in 'explanation' of the acquisition of faith, is thus based on two illegitimate dichotomies. One would, perhaps, be pressured into resorting to the inexplicability of the gift of the condition or faith, and denying any possible 'explanation', *if* the only alternative were an account in which human activity unconditionally causally resulted in faith. But such a dichotomy is exhaustive only if a divine gift is seen as exclusive of human activity, or if the freedom of an act is seen as incompatible with its being a gift. Since the freedom of an act, in Climacus's view, is not incompatible with its being a gift, there is no a priori reason why he would reject the possibility of a description of an agent's free transition in which faith is (conditionally) brought about. Thus, there is no reason to see as exhaustive a dichotomy between a human transition and a transition through grace. Second, there is no need to accept as exhaustive a dichotomy between faith as decision and faith as ineffable (or God's act)—that is, there is no reason to see decision as the only relevant form of human activity.

The recognition that neither of these dichotomies is exhaustive would allow one to try to do justice to the point of Climacus's references to a capacity and to a decision or leap (namely, free, responsible activity) by developing an understanding of faith as constitutively involving free response, but along the lines suggested by the idea of renewed Socratic validity—that is, along the lines of 'attention', of a shift in perspective or an imaginative revisioning, rather than in terms of deliberate decision. The 'condition' is, after all, spoken of as the ability to 'envision the god'.[53] Moreover, Kierkegaard's retrospective account in his *Point of View for My Work as An Author*, adds to our appreciation of the possibility of a non-volitionalist account of transition. There he speaks of the teacher (whom he explicitly associates with Climacus) who attempts

---

[53] *Fragments*, 63.

to free the Christian who is trapped in an 'illusion' concerning what it is to be a Christian as 'bringing to light a text which is hidden under another text' and compelling him to take notice of things in such a way that 'possibly he may come to his senses and realize what is implied . . . '.[54] His whole authorship, he insists, 'opens the eyes to what it is to become a Christian' and he describes his own transition as a 'religious awakening' in which 'I came to understand myself in the most decisive sense', to 'recognize myself in a deeper sense'.[55] Such descriptions fit in perfectly with a reading of the transition in terms of a shift in perspective or a revisioning.

In summary, then, I have assembled in this and the preceding chapter some reminders about the category of transition, especially in the Climacus account: first, in Chapter 1, the reminder that what is at stake is a qualitative and free transition, and that this could be achieved in ways other than a 'will-power' type of decision or leap; here a set of reminders of some of the ways in which the Climacus account and the journals reject the reification involved in a volitionalist account of the leap, without thereby precluding the crucial importance of describable human activity in the transition. That describable activity, moreover, is revealed in terms of varied characterizations of decision and will through which Kierkegaard effectively rejects dualisms implied in a purely volitionalist account of the decision or leap—dualisms, for example, between will and other faculties or activities (like understanding and feeling and imagination), as well as between active and passive, in general.

If, then, we take the category of leap minimally to require qualitative and free change, and if we duly appreciate the non-standard characterizations of 'willing' found in the Climacus accounts, we are able to exploit the category of passion along the lines of its relation to imagination. That is, if we develop the category of passion as limited only by the minimal requirements of the category of leap or, conversely, if we develop the category of leap or decision so as to cultivate the potential implied by its concomitant characterization as a passion, we see the possibility of a different formulation of the transition to faith in the Climacus account—a formulation in which imaginative activity comes into its own. In what follows I lay the ground for that formulation by considering the roles of imagination in Kierkegaard's various accounts of selfhood, subjectivity, and the ethical.

---

[54] *The Point of View for My Work as An Author*, trans. Walter Lowrie and ed. Benjamin Nelson (New York, 1962), 40, 37.

[55] Ibid. 90, 83–4.

3

Choice and Paradox: Imagination in the Task of Subjectivity

Despite his clear sensitivity to the many ways imagination can mislead us and be prejudicial to self-development, an undeniable commitment to the value and necessity of imaginative activity is integral to Kierkegaard's various accounts of genuine selfhood and, I shall argue, supports a reinterpretation of the category of qualitative transition, hence of 'decision' and 'leap'. 'The task of becoming subjective', Climacus insists in the *Postscript*, 'may be presumed to be the highest task, and one that is proposed to every human being.'[1] That task, I suggest, crucially requires imagination precisely because it involves paradoxical tension, and it is a distinctive function of imagination to perceive and maintain such tension. In what follows I will indicate how several of Kierkegaard's accounts of the task of subjectivity highlight the paradoxical tension involved, and its relation to passion, and provide an increasingly explicit specification of the role or roles of imagination. In particular, I will be arguing that in so far as these accounts locate paradox in 'choice' (the transition to the ethical or subjectivity) they imply a view of 'choice' in which imagination is a constitutive element (rather than merely something which presents the options from which one then chooses). Such choice provides a model of an imaginative transition which is a reorienting, transforming shift in perspective. Moreover, such a model has affinities with the 'conceptual leap' which is said to characterize metaphorical activity, and I shall explore the way in which this complements and qualifies the model of *Gestalt* or paradigm shifts in perspective. The way is thus opened to highlighting the importance of imaginative activity in Kierkegaardian transitions in general, including the Climacus transition to faith.

---

[1] *Postscript*, 146; see also 141–2.

The paradoxical character of transition is a theme common to a variety of Kierkegaard's accounts of selfhood. In *Either/Or* Judge William introduces the transition to the ethical as a 'perilous transition' which does not 'annihilate' the aesthetical but rather 'transfigures' it.[2] The oddness of the transition is hinted at when he writes that 'the ethical is that whereby a man becomes what he becomes' (p. 229); becoming oneself is, moreover, described equivalently as choosing oneself absolutely, or repenting oneself (pp. 257, 181, 245, 252–3). In what follows I will argue that the transition is understood by Judge William as a locus of paradox, and I will explore the implications of that view.

Choice and the Paradox of Change

Choice both is the mark of, and constitutes the transition to, the ethical, for 'The act of choosing is essentially a proper and stringent expression of the ethical' (p. 170). In such choice, the person transforms himself; he 'becomes himself, quite the same self he was before, down to the least significant peculiarity, and yet he becomes another, for the choice permeates everything and transforms it' (p. 227). The 'perilous transition', then, is the choice—to choose is to change. Moreover, the 'choice' involved in such transformation is clearly a paradoxical performance, for 'choice performs at one and the same time the two dialectical movements: that which is chosen does not exist and comes into existence with the choice; that which is chosen exists, otherwise there would not be a choice' (p. 219).[3]

In this description of choice by which one becomes oneself, Kierkegaard brings into bold relief the radical realization that change (and choice) as such is paradoxical. The situation of change (and choice) is one in which elements are held in tension—the self becomes 'another' while becoming 'himself'. The point of saying 'he becomes another' is lost if he ceases to be at the same time the same self, for then 'he' would

---

[2] *Either/Or*, ii. 257–8. Succeeding parenthetical references are to this work until otherwise noted.

[3] Louis Dupré formulates this paradox in terms of freedom: 'A self which posits itself by choosing itself and which, on the other hand, could not choose itself without preexisting its own choice, must be a free self. Indeed, freedom becomes free only when it asserts itself and yet, how could it assert itself were it not already free' (*A Dubious Heritage: Studies in the Philosophy of Religion After Kant* (New York, 1977), 31).

not be becoming another—there would be a different person rather than a transformed person. Change, then, is a paradoxical activity, and one changes in one's choice. This realization, we will see later, is played out in detail in Climacus's understanding of change, but for the moment it is enough to note his similar view of the unchanging implied in the process of change (becoming, coming into existence): 'if that which comes into existence does not in itself remain unchanged in the change of coming into existence, then the coming into existence is not *this* coming into existence but another'.[4]

Change understood in this sense is like the paradoxical process of *renewal* of which Kierkegaard speaks (through the character of Constantin Constantius) in *Repetition*. What characterizes such change is precisely what characterizes 'repetition', for what characterizes repetition, in the sense in which Constantius explains that 'life is a repetition', is that 'actuality, which has been, now comes into existence'.[5] Renewal is what occurs when something which 'has been, now comes into existence', for 'that which is repeated has been—otherwise it could not be repeated—but the very fact that it has been makes the repetition into something new'.[6]

Renewing involves the paradox of 'has been, yet comes into existence' in the same way as it involves the 'unchanged in the change'—the given which is made new must remain or there is only something different, not something renewed; on the other hand, renewal is a creation rather than mere recovery. An appreciation of this paradox of renewal (either as old-yet-new or unchanging-in-change) informs Roberto Unger's contemporary description of the 'capacity to live your own life, and to master the effects of your deed upon your character, so that you can change without ceasing to be, in your own eyes, your self'.[7]

Still another formulation of this paradox is found in Judge William's reminder that I can only transform myself into something if 'already . . . I have this in myself' (pp. 265–6).[8] This is a reference to the paradox of

[4] *Fragments*, 73.

[5] *Repetition: A Venture in Experimenting Psychology*, Kierkegaard's Writings, vi, eds. and trans. Howard V. Hong and Edna H. Hong (Princeton, NJ, 1983), 149. See my 'Repetition, Concreteness, and Imagination', 13–34.   [6] *Repetition*, 149.

[7] *Passion: An Essay on Personality*, 109.

[8] William F. Lynch expresses this sentiment theologically: 'it is something in the present and in our actual humanity of the moment, some good taste of the self, as it is now, no matter how small the taste, that will help bridge the gap between the actual and the promise. In some form or other the kingdom of God must be already there, or else the mind will not take the step from the actual to the possible' (*Images of Faith: An Exploration of the Ironic Imagination* (Notre Dame, Ind., 1973), 130–1.

'not yet, but already', and the transition accomplished by choice is a paradoxical transformation in this sense as well. Highlighting the 'not yet, but already' character of the transition effectively highlights the fact that any transition from one world-view to another, from one set of orienting categories or values to another, cannot be made entirely from within either of the frameworks. A free transition to another perspective assumes an appreciation of both perspectives which has this 'not yet, but already' character; that is, it assumes the paradoxical possibility of sufficiently appreciating another context for it to attract us *before* its categories or values are accepted by or actualized in us.

One way of looking at the paradoxicalness of change which informs Kierkegaard's discussion of the transformation of self is found in contemporary philosophy, when Donald Davidson refers to the 'irrationality' involved in the phenomenon of 'self-criticism and self-improvement'.[9] He writes that in cases where we try to change our desires:

From the point of view of the changed desire, there is no reason for the change—the reason comes from an independent source, and is based on further, and partly contrary, considerations. The agent has reasons for changing his own habits and character, but those reasons come from a domain of values necessarily extrinsic to the content of the views or values to undergo change. The cause of the change, if it comes, can therefore not be a reason for what it causes'.[10]

Davidson's point is cited by Richard Rorty as illustrating his own thesis that the chief instrument of change is not argument but rather redescription.[11] Our task—namely, to 'make the best selves for ourselves that we can'—involves, he writes, appeal to 'continual redescription',[12] and our response to any given redescription is peculiar because such a redescription

does not pretend to have a better candidate for doing the same old things which we did when we spoke in the old way. Rather it suggests that we might want to stop doing those things and do something else. But it does not argue for this suggestion on the basis of antecedent criteria common to the old and the new language games. For just insofar as the new language is really new, there will be no such criteria.[13]

Suggesting that in such change the distinction between reasons and causes 'loses its utility',[14] Rorty echoes Davidson's claim that such shifts

---

[9] 'Paradoxes of Irrationality', in *Philosophical Essays on Freud*, eds. Richard Wollheim and James Hopkins (Cambridge, 1982), 289–305.   [10] Ibid. 305.
[11] Rorty, *Contingency, Irony, and Solidarity*, 7.   [12] Ibid. 80.
[13] Ibid. 9.   [14] Ibid. 48.

are irrational. His conclusion is that the shift is not the result of argument (nor the result of an act of will[15])—it is, rather, a response to the attractiveness of a tempting redescription.

Still another way of looking at the paradoxicalness of change is brought to light in Steven A. Edwards's discussion of paradoxes of motivation and learning. 'Paradox arises', he explains,

> when the parent or teacher attempts to appeal to the adolescent's lower-order motivation in order to help him forward to a higher-order motivation. If he tries to be honest for honesty's sake in the interest of approval, then he is not being honest simply for honesty's sake; and if he tries to be honest for honesty's sake without any ulterior motive, then *ex hypothesi*, this has no effect—he simply isn't *there* yet.[16]

The problem Edwards describes is precisely the paradox appreciated by Judge William: 'What motivation could not only appeal to an individual in B but also lead that individual up to A?', for 'In B one can say, "Do a for the sake of b", but this will only be one more case of activity in B; and in A one can propose, "Do b for the sake of a", but since the individual is not yet in A, such an appeal has no appeal—it does not mesh with his present priorities, the only priorities that are, in fact, available'.[17] The paradoxes inherent in 'enjoined spontaneity', in inducing voluntary change, or in teaching someone to be autonomous—these, Edwards concludes, are standard paradoxes in ethical motivation and are the source of many of the paradoxes of religion.

Such a sense of paradox is not the philosopher's invention, not a made-up problem whose resolution will exhibit philosophical cleverness—such paradox troubles us all at one time or another. Robert Penn Warren's memorable character Jack Burden may be more self-conscious than many, but he is not at all unusual in his sense of the quandary:

> Perhaps the only answer, I thought then, was that by the time we understand the pattern we are in, the definition we are making for ourselves, it is too late to break

---

[15] Ibid. 6.

[16] 'Paradox in Context: Impasse and Passage', American Academy of Religion paper (1985), 2.

[17] Ibid. Edwards elsewhere argues that although 'Aquinas removed the appearance of paradox almost completely from the *Summa*', substantive ethical paradox remains in his account: in particular that paradox which is 'common to all contexts in which the learner is held responsible for a level of behavior beyond his or her present known capacity.' He concludes: 'Paradox, it might be said, was as often multiplied as removed when Aquinas drew his distinctions' ('Structure and Change in Aquinas's Religious Ethics', *Journal of the American Academy of Religion* 54/2, 1986, 298, 300, 298).

out of the box. We can only live in terms of the definition, like the prisoner in the cage in which he cannot lie or stand or sit, hung up in justice to be viewed by the populace. Yet the definition we have made of ourselves is ourselves. To break out of it, we must make a new self. But how can the self make a new self when the selfness which it is, is the only substance from which the new self can be made?[18]

We need to be able to revise our definition of our self, redefine our self, while having no more than the resources of the self which is to be redefined. In other words, we need to be able to understand a radically alternative context sufficiently to feel its attractiveness while being in a context which is, *ex hypothesi*, incommensurable in some sense with that radical alternative. But how is it possible to transcend a given context in these ways from within it?[19] The answer Judge William gives, that I can only transform myself into something 'if already . . . I have this in myself', raises more questions than it answers. It points to what Climacus will call that 'being that nevertheless is a non-being' which is presupposed in every change[20]—it points, that is, to what he calls 'possibility'. The richness of that 'answer', however, is not obvious—it needs to be explored. In what follows I will be suggesting that the relevance of the elements in tension to which Judge William adverts ('self' and 'another' self) coincides with the relevance of the 'possibility' implied in the situation of 'already, but not yet', and that both of them reveal the role of imagination in choice.

It is a distinctive function of imagination to hold elements in tension, so in an account of change and choice, like Judge William's, which focuses on the tension within both, we would expect imagination to play an important role. We will see exactly that to be the case.

Judge William elaborates his account of paradoxical choosing or becoming oneself in terms which imply the role of imagination: 'This self which the individual knows is at once the actual self and the ideal self which the individual has outside himself as the picture in likeness to which he has to form himself and which, on the other hand, he never-theless has in him since it is the self'. (p. 263). It is only imagination which can enlarge the horizon of possibilities through presenting the ideal self as a 'picture' of what is not yet actualized. But it is crucial that this 'picture' not be thought of as a static presentation or 'image'—and here two major functions of imagination are brought to light. First, the activity of the self in changing is an *active picturing* of the actual and

[18] *All the King's Men* (San Diego, CA, 1976), 351.
[19] Unger, *Passion*, 8–11, 41–2.
[20] *Fragments*, 74.

ideal self together, at the same time, in tension. The 'picture' to which he refers is not a passively viewed *separate* possibility, but a *maintained tension*, because I can only transform myself into something if 'already . . . I have this in myself'. Because 'the self which the individual knows is at once the actual self and the ideal self' the awareness essential to transformation is both an active and paradoxical holding of elements in tension—as such it necessarily involves the activity of imagination.

Just as important, the presentation of the ideal self is not a static presentation for another reason—namely, because the picture is not of a *neutral* possibility. It is one 'in likeness to which he *has to form himself*', a possibility which is recognized or appreciated as a *demand*—and such a 'seeing-as' requires imagination. To see a possibility as a demand is to go beyond the given in a way that only imagination can; to see as a demand what could otherwise be seen (by you or others) as a neutral possibility is to explore it imaginatively (explore, as it were, the various possibilities within the possibility) and thus to hold different descriptions in tension. To appreciate a demand as such we need to see it in the light of something which provides a contrast—and that something can be thought of either as the neutral possibility or as the actual self. To see bindingness where there need not be bindingness, to see a demand in a possibility, is an imaginative extension.

The reason Judge William concludes that genuine choice does not occur in the aesthetic realm is that what makes choice as such ethical is precisely that the possibility is communicated *as a demand*. Since that can be achieved *only* through imaginative engagement, imaginative activity is integral to choice. It is the efficaciousness of this engagement which explains why Judge William claims that the awareness of actual and ideal together 'impregnates' and is 'fruitful'. When what is seen is not a neutral possibility laid out before one, but a possibility recognized and appreciated as a 'task', the relation between imagination and choice can no longer be the simplistic one in which imagination first lays out options and *then* we shut our eyes and hold our breath and 'will' one.

This role of imagination I have been focusing on in Judge William's account is supported from another vantage-point in Richard Kearney's study of the genealogy of imagination, *The Wake of Imagination*. Kearney calls attention to the role of imagination in such change as I have been describing when he suggests the relation between temporality and imagination. He writes that 'it is only by virtue of the synthesizing horizon of imagination that something can be experienced as necessarily the same through change'.[21] Talking about the temporalized self is another way of talking about elements held in tension in the changing self, the presence of the unchanging in the change. The temporalized self implies elements in tension which can only be appropriated imaginatively; the achievement of experiencing something as 'the same through change' is thus an achievement of imaginative activity.

Kearney argues that Heidegger saw imagination as crucial to Kant's theory precisely because Kant was the first to interpret being in terms of time.[22] Whether or not Heidegger was correct in his estimate of Kant, I suggest that Kierkegaard assuredly interprets being in terms of time, and the tie between imagination and the temporal reinforces the connection between imagination and the process of holding elements in tension which I have been suggesting is involved in change. Judge William's account of the paradoxical performance of choice includes in it both perspectives on the single phenomenon—experiencing oneself as 'the same through change' is the converse of holding the self outside in tension with the self within, and though neither temporal nor spatial metaphors can do justice to the paradoxical experience, they do contribute to the awareness of paradox which Judge William tries to evoke.

Choice, on the view I have been delineating in Judge William's account of the transition to the ethical, is not understood on the ordinary model of a selection among alternatives (a model which suits the choice of, say, a pint of milk rather than a half-pint)—it is instead a paradoxical engaging activity, a transforming which implies elements in tension and is played out, as we shall see in more detail later, through suspension and engagement. One could draw either of two conclusions: that such choice, at the very least, involves imaginative activity in a way in which much of what we ordinarily call choice does not or, alternatively, that such an account of choice highlights the imaginative activity which is involved in any choice in a way which we do not ordinarily recognize or appreciate. Judge William's account draws our attention to the variety of ways in which there is a correlation between the notions of choice, transformation, and practical reorientation, and to the relevance of imaginative activity to them. What becomes clear is that once imagination is seen not merely as the presenter of neutral possibilities, but also as the source of efficacious engagement with possibilities, one can no longer maintain a simple contrast between choice and imaginative activity.[23]

---

[21] *The Wake of Imagination*, 194.   [22] Ibid. 193.

[23] The view of a simple contrast between imagination and choice which I am rejecting might seem to be just the one supported by the following kind of remark: 'Everyman

Choice and Transparency

The character of 'choice'—the character of the transition to the ethical—and the role of imagination in it is further illuminated by the connection Judge William makes between 'choice' and 'transparency'. This connection reinforces the notion of transition as a transforming shift in perspective. While, on the one hand, he says that 'choice' is 'essentially a proper and stringent expression of the ethical' (p. 170), on the other hand, he says that 'transparency' is the mark of the ethical: 'being transparent'—'precisely this is what the ethical wills' (p. 258).[24] The 'principal difference' between the aesthetic and the ethical, 'the one on which everything hinges', is that 'the ethical individual is transparent to himself' (p. 262). Being ethical is described in terms of a kind of clarity: 'he who lives ethically has seen himself, knows himself, penetrates with his consciousness his whole concretion' (p. 263). The decisive transition which constitutes becoming oneself, repenting oneself, choosing self absolutely is the penetration of one's concreteness with consciousness, i.e., seeing oneself truly. The transition is accomplished by achieving true vision—i.e., knowing oneself in one's concreteness. The demand for transparency is not, however, a demand for the static revelation of what is already there so much as it is a demand for transforming what is there.[25] Such a transforming transition takes great courage, makes a qualitative difference, and will not happen of itself.

I am arguing, in other words, that the relation between choice and

possesses in a greater or less degree a talent which is called imagination, the power which is the first condition determining what a man will turn out to be; for the second condition is the will, which in the final resort is decisive' (*Training in Christianity*, 185). Although this emphasizes imagination in contrast to will, the context of this formulation suggests the role of imagination in presenting possibilities as neutral, non-engaging possibilities—i.e., a use of imagination to present 'unreality', since the picture 'lacks the reality of time and duration and of the earthly life with its difficulties and sufferings' and hence 'always looks so easy, so persuasive' (p. 186). Such a use of imagination is indeed insufficient for determining 'what a man will turn out to be'. 'Will', in this contrast, could refer to the aspect of imaginative engagement which I have pointed to in Judge William's understanding of a possibility appreciated as a demand. In other words, one can read this comment on imagination and will as a contrast between two ways of being imaginative rather than as a claim which precludes our interpretation of choice and transition as in crucial ways an imaginative achievement.

[24] The importance of transparency is stressed across the accounts—not only by Anti-Climacus, as we shall see, but also in *Concept of Anxiety,* 127 n.

[25] See Richard Rorty on the difference between conversion conceived of as 'self-discovery' vs. 'self-transformation' (Romanell Lectures, No. 1, 10–11 [unpubl.], University of Virginia, Jan. 1988).

transparency is not seen by Judge William as one of successive cause and effect. Transparency is not the result of choice—but rather the choice which transforms is accomplished *in and through* the deeper seeing. This is what I take him to mean when he writes that: 'Only when in his choice a man has assumed himself, is clad in himself, has so totally penetrated himself that every movement is attended by the conscious-ness of a responsibility for himself, only then has he chosen himself ethically' (p. 252). Such penetration or knowing, the achievement of transparency, is here said to be what we do 'in' the choice—it constitutes the choice. Similarly, he writes that 'when I choose myself repentantly I gather myself together in all my finite concretion' (p. 253). The transitional choice is effectively an imaginative penetration or imaginative gathering together, the achievement of a clear vision which itself transforms. The activity of penetrating one's concreteness with consciousness just is the activity of choosing self, transforming self—it constitutes the transition.

If that makes it sound like 'choosing' self is really a case of 'knowing' self, that is because in an important sense it is. Judge William acknow-ledges that his injunction to 'choose oneself' is equivalent to the *proper* understanding of the Greek injunction to 'know oneself'. He tells us that he 'deliberately preferred to use the expression "choose oneself" instead of "know oneself" ' to highlight the fact that this knowing is 'not a mere contemplation', but is 'a *reflection* upon himself *which itself is an action*' (p. 263, emphasis mine). That is, the requirement of choice is meant to emphasize a particular way of knowing oneself—namely, a knowing which, as the Greeks understood, is self-involving and efficacious.

Positing a choice which is a 'reflection' as well as positing a knowing which is not 'mere contemplation' but is 'in the highest degree fruitful' is a way of challenging the dualism between passive and active. One need not view choice as active in contrast to reflection. Choice need not be understood in terms of a deliberate decision preceding or following that reflection, but rather can be seen in terms of the descriptively more complex phenomenon of a reflection upon oneself which itself consti-tutes a change rather than simply setting the stage for subsequent change—that is, choice is the *transfiguring* move of an agent's 'reflection upon himself which itself is an action'.

Some light may be shed on this characterization of choice (as a reflec-tion which is itself an action) by looking at how Iris Murdoch, attempting in ethics to replace a model of 'choice' by a model of 'vision', plays out her suggestion that imagination similarly transcends the dualism between active and passive.[26] She argues that the activity of imagination is neither simply active nor simply passive: it is, like 'seeing', a kind of reflection and a kind of exploring at the same time. Imagination is, she writes, 'a type of reflection on people, events, etc., which builds detail, adds colour, conjures up possibilities in ways which go beyond what could be said to be strictly factual'.[27] It is at the same time a 'doing'—a 'sort of personal exploring' which, she says, is 'difficult not to see . . . as an exercise of will'.[28] A choice which is similarly seen by Judge William as both a reflection and a kind of doing could be understood then as constituted by the activity of imagination in achieving a shift of perspective, an increased vision, or transparency. On this reading Judge William's references to reflection are descriptions of what constitutes choice rather than descriptions of the preliminary to or consequence of choice, and they centrally involve imagination.

Such a view of the transition is also expressed in Judge William's conviction that if you go to 'that point where the necessity of choice is manifest' (by recognizing the contradiction in the aesthetic (p. 167)) and 'contemplate existence under ethical categories', 'you will see that only then does existence become beautiful, that only in this way can a man succeed in saving his soul and gaining the whole world, can succeed in using the world without abusing it' (p. 182). To *see* 'that only [in this way] does existence become beautiful' just *is* to be changed, though one is of course free either to try to undermine that recognition or to act according to it. Such an active seeing is precisely the transition (not the prolegomenon to or consequence of it). For example, to explore and penetrate oneself to the extent that one comes to see oneself now as bound together with another in a common future is what it means to bind oneself. A redefinition of self is both demanding and transforming.

In sum, choosing self is penetrating with consciousness one's concreteness—such penetration, seeking transparency, is an imaginative exploration of self. However, we should not be misled by the reference to transparency in terms of *self*, for the vision which transforms is as much a vision of world as of self. We are changed by coming to see ourselves in a given way (X')—but this means at the same time seeing a world in which we fit as X', hence a different world. Coming to see the world differently is coming to see ourselves differently, and vice versa. To see, for example, that only in a particular way does existence become beautiful is at the same time a development of self-understanding—to see the world in a

---

[26] 'The Darkness of Practical Reason', *Encounter*, 27 (July 1966).
[27] Ibid. 48.   [28] Ibid.

different way is to see oneself differently. Robert C. Solomon provides an excellent example of this mutual implication when he rightly reminds us that 'the exhilaration that accompanies falling in love is only half the discovery of one's lover; the other half is a (re)discovery of oneself'.[29] Self-understanding is achieved through seeing the world in a new light. With this qualification, then, we can conclude that the 'choice' of self is indeed a leap, but it is an imaginative leap of self-understanding more than it is an intentional decision.

To see oneself in any way other than simply the way one presently expresses oneself is an imaginative exercise. The role of imaginative activity implied in fulfilling the ethical requirement of transparency as Judge William presents it reinforces the role of imagination implied in his description of the fulfilment of the task of subjectivity through the paradoxical activity of 'choice'. In other words, Judge William's model of subjectivity implies the importance of imaginative activity both in terms of a paradoxical process of change and an achievement of transparency—in both cases 'choice' is a transition or transforming shift in perspective which cannot be understood except in terms of such imaginative activity.

IMAGINATION, PARADOX, AND THE INFINITE CONCRETE

What is implied about the activity of imagination in Judge William's account is made explicit in Climacus's description of the task of subjectivity, for he both elaborates on the presence of the paradoxical and introduces explicitly the role of 'imaginative representation'. The general character of the task is suggested by Climacus's claim that 'Existence involves a tremendous contradiction' and the 'business' of the subjective thinker is to remain in it rather than abstract himself from it.[30] The task of becoming subjective is one of fully affirming the concreteness of existence, and he understands this as the need 'to understand the greatest oppositions together' (p. 316): for example, 'at one and the same time to see the comic and the tragic in the same thing', 'at one and

---

[29] *About Love: Reinventing Romance for Our Times*, 149; Roberto Unger also writes that 'Each foray out into this world of dealings with other people is also a probing into the self: each variation upon our mutual jeopardy and dependence becomes the occasion for a refinement of the capacity to understand, to sustain, and to change what you are as an individual' (*Passion*, 108).

[30] *Postscript*, 313. Succeeding parenthetical references will be to this work until otherwise noted.

the same time to be crushed in spirit and yet free from care' (p. 317). It is the need 'to have one mood rich and full, and also to have the opposite mood, so that in giving the one mood its pathos and expression, the opposite mood is slipped in as an undertone', or 'to think one [thought] and simultaneously have the opposite in mind'—in both cases, 'uniting these opposites in existence' (p. 317). The task is to remain in concreteness rather than to abstract oneself from it, and the implications of concreteness are clear: 'In the same degree that the subjective thinker himself is concrete, his form will become concretely dialectical', for 'it must be as manifold as the opposites he holds in combination' (p. 319). That is, in abstraction things can be understood successively, but to understand himself the concrete individual has to hold opposites 'in combination', that is, not mediating or resolving them into a synthesis, but maintaining a tension between them. To exist in subjectivity is to 'perceive', to 'see', to 'think', opposites *together* (pp. 316–17)—this is a paradoxical task which cannot even be addressed (much less achieved) without a particular appeal to the activity of imagination in holding opposites in tension. The paradoxical task of the existing individual is also expressed by Climacus in other ways, for example, in terms of the realization of a unity of finite and infinite, or the attempt to be 'in two places at the same time' (pp. 176, 178). Moreover, the 'genuine subjective existing thinker is always as negative as he is positive, and *vice-versa*' ('his positiveness consists in the continuous realization of the inwardness through which he becomes conscious of the negative' (p. 78)), and he is at the same time both comic and pathetic (pp. 81, 84). Finite and infinite, positive and negative, comic and pathetic, the subjective thinker embodies paradox.

The connection of this paradoxical task with imagination is made explicit in the following comment on the momentary realization of the unity of finite and infinite which generates 'passion': 'In passion the existing subject is rendered infinite in the eternity of the *imaginative representation*, and yet he is at the same time most definitely himself' (p. 176, emphasis mine). The 'imaginative representation' renders infinite the finite subject, but in such a way as to *maintain* that finitude of the subject in tension with its infinity—imagination is, consequently, explicitly recognized as central to the task of subjectivity because it is the means of holding those opposites in tension.

The paradoxicalness of the task is made more specific as well: 'really to exist' means to 'interpenetrate one's existence with consciousness, at one and the same time eternal and as if far removed from existence, and yet also present in existence and in the process of becoming' (p. 273). Such an attempt to 'interpenetrate one's existence with consciousness', in fulfilment of the task of subjective existence, is explicitly characterized as paradoxical (at one and the same time 'as if' x and yet not x)—it is thus an imaginative exercise of holding elements in tension. Climacus in this way makes more specific the paradox implied in Judge William's description of the ethical man as one who 'knows himself, penetrates with his consciousness his whole concretion'.[31] Climacus's claim that 'the development of the subject consists precisely in his active inter-penetration of himself by reflection concerning his own existence, so that he really thinks what he thinks through making a reality of it' (p. 151), likewise carries on Judge William's understanding of such interpenetra-tion of one's existence with consciousness as a reflection which itself constitutes a change. The importance of seeing a possibility as a demand (i.e., imaginatively seeing-as) is also emphasized when he writes: 'I ask about possibility', not as an 'aesthetically and intellectually disinterested possibility', but rather as 'a conceived reality it is related as a possibility to my own reality, so that I may be able to realize it' (p. 287).

The emphasis on the attempt to 'interpenetrate one's existence with consciousness' also brings to the fore again the relevance of the imagination in a different way—this time in terms of the 'concrete'. Penetrating one's existence with consciousness is penetrating one's 'whole concretion', one's concreteness. What is concrete is what is non-finalized, in process: 'The empirical object is unfinished and the existing cognitive spirit is itself in process of becoming' (p. 169). In so far as one is existing, then, one is inexhaustible. What is finished is either exhausted or potentially exhaustible, whereas the open-endedness of what is always becoming is another way of speaking of inexhaustibility, unlimited-ness—the penetration of which requires the impulse of imagination because it continually goes beyond what is at any time actually given, to the 'not yet'.

Such inexhaustibility is also affirmed in the dialectical character of concreteness which we noted earlier as opposites in tension. Not only is imagination required to hold opposites in tension, but imagination is required for the exploration of our concreteness, for to say, as he does, that the concrete is expressible only in the 'concretely dialectical' is to say that the concrete can only be explored dialectically—and dialectical exploration is implicitly imaginative because implicitly unending. Con-

---

[31] *Either/Or*, ii. 263.

crete reality cannot be captured—only the expansiveness of imaginative appropriation can begin to do what theoretical classification in unable to do. The penetration of our concreteness, as the exploration of becoming, is a penetration which is inescapably imaginative because of the implicit future reference.

In addition, the relation between imagination and passion, by way of paradox, is brought out by Climacus. The paradoxical unity between finite and infinite can be realized 'only momentarily', and is 'realized in the moment of passion' (p. 176); 'when one is nearest to being in two places at the same time he is in passion; but passion is only momentary' (p. 178). Because the paradoxical interpenetration of one's consciousness is what constitutes existence, 'it is impossible to exist without passion' (p. 276). Finally, it is because existence is a paradoxical holding together that 'when existence is penetrated with reflection, it generates passion' (p. 313).

The formulation of subjectivity as the paradox of being rendered infinite while maintaining that infinity in tension with one's definite finitude is an elaboration of an earlier *Postscript* formulation of the task of subjectivity—namely, 'to strive to become what one already is' (p. 116). Climacus's description of this paradoxical task appears continuous with Judge William's formulation of ethical transformation through the perception of actual and ideal self in tension. The parallel emphasis on the role of the interpenetration (or penetration) of existence (or concretion) with consciousness is striking: coming to know is a mode of changing. Moreover, Climacus makes more explicit the role of imagination in the process. Finally, Climacus echoes Judge William's realization of the paradox inherent in change when he writes of the transition which constitutes making 'the absolute venture'. 'The individual', he writes, 'becomes infinite only by virtue of making the absolute venture', and 'in making the absolute venture he becomes another individual. Before he has made the venture he cannot understand it as anything else than madness. . . . And after the individual has made the venture he is no longer the same individual' (p. 379). One cannot help but recall here the earlier references to the paradox of change which I elaborated in terms of the 'irrationality' of self-improvement and change of value frameworks; the continuity with Judge William's position is striking.

PERSPECTIVAL SHIFTS: GESTALT AND METAPHOR

Climacus's description of the paradoxical task (or art) of existing—namely, holding contradictory elements in tension—calls to mind some formulations of metaphor found in recent accounts of its linguistic structure and cognitive status. Most obviously, the claims that 'metaphor results in the placing of an object in two perspectives simultaneously', and that what distinguishes metaphor is the 'tension' between the two components, whose 'juxtaposition results [in] a reconceptualization',[32] seem aptly to describe the situation to which Climacus calls our attention. In what follows I will argue that the category of transition (including the transition or leap of faith) can be fruitfully explored in terms of metaphorical activity, and that the perspective of metaphor can be used to complement the perspective of *Gestalt* shift and critical threshold discussed earlier to illuminate the character of a qualitative transition. While the description of the paradox of change seems, at first glance, to differ from the description of the paradoxical art of existing, I will argue that the relevance of metaphor applies equally to each. If, as one recent analysis of metaphor claims, the 'distinctive metaphorical move' is 'the perspectival shift' or 'jump' across semantic fields,[33] then metaphor may well provide a very helpful perspective on such qualitative transitions, including the transition to faith.

By using the perspective of metaphor to complement the perspective of *Gestalt* shift and critical threshold, I am, in effect, engaging in an activity which is itself metaphorical, imaginative, and ultimately paradoxical—namely, the metaphorical activity of putting the category of transition 'in two perspectives simultaneously'. I do this because I think that both perspectives are necessary (for either alone is misleading), and that together they shed light on the category of transition.

Transformation: The case of Gestalt shift

Before exploring the perspective provided by discussions of metaphor, however, I want to review for a moment the relevance of the concepts of *Gestalt* shift and critical threshold which I introduced in the first chapter. There I used those concepts to illustrate how a qualitative transition need not be created by an intentional decision or act of will-power, need not be

---

[32] Kittay, *Metaphor: Its Cognitive Force and Linguistic Structure*, 4, 28.
[33] Ibid. 313–14, 270.

done 'on purpose'. That negative argument allowed a broader range of possibilities for understanding a qualitative transition. I suggest now that the varied formulations of the paradox of (ethical and value) change which I have considered thus far in this chapter provide positive warrant for actually employing the concepts of *Gestalt* shift and critical threshold to illuminate the transition in question—both because those formulations all point to the same paradox which *writ large* is involved in the much-discussed question of change between incommensurable scientific frameworks or paradigms, and because that discussion, initiated by Thomas Kuhn, N. R. Hanson, and others, explicitly brings in the heuristic tool of *Gestalt* shift to explain such change. I shall, therefore, briefly consider what can be learned about transition from that discussion. Kuhn writes in the well-known and seminal work, *The Structure of Scientific Revolutions*:

The transition from a paradigm in crisis to a new one from which a new tradition of normal science can emerge is far from a cumulative process, one achieved by an articulation or extension of the old paradigm. Rather it is a reconstruction of the field from new fundamentals, a reconstruction that changes some of the field's most elementary theoretical generalizations as well as many of its paradigm methods and applications. During the transition period there will be a large but never complete overlap between the problems that can be solved by the old and by the new paradigm. But there will also be a decisive difference in the modes of solution. When the transition is complete, the profession will have changed its view of the field, its methods, and its goals.[34]

Some have noted, he continues, that this aspect of scientific advance— this qualitative transition—has similarities with 'a change in visual gestalt: the marks on paper that were first seen as a bird are now seen as an antelope, or vice versa.'[35] Expressing his agreement, he explains: 'Just because it is a transition between incommensurables, the transition between competing paradigms cannot be made a step at a time, forced by logic and neutral experience. Like the gestalt shift, it must occur all at once (though not necessarily in an instant) or not at all.'[36]

At the same time, however, as he exploits the parallel with *Gestalt* shift, Kuhn admits that there are respects in which the parallel 'can be misleading', for, first, '[s]cientists do not see something *as* something else; instead they simply see it', and second, 'the scientist does not preserve the gestalt subject's freedom to switch back and forth between

---

[34] Chicago, 2nd edn. enlarged, 1970, 84–5.
[35] Ibid. 85.   [36] Ibid. 150.

ways of seeing'.[37] 'Nevertheless', he concludes, 'the switch of gestalt, particularly because it is today so familiar, is a useful elementary prototype for what occurs in full-scale paradigm-shift.'[38]

Kuhn explicitly adverts to the way N. R. Hanson featured the role of *Gestalt* shifts in his understanding of scientific work and advance. Hanson used a number of standard examples of figure/ground illustrations which allow *Gestalt* shifts in perspective (convex/concave cube or staircase, old woman/young woman, bird/antelope, goblet/faces) to show how a different conceptual organization and different appropriations of context will produce different visual experiences in people, even when 'elements of their experiences are identical'.[39] What is particularly important, however, is Hanson's claim that the paradigm case of seeing is not the visual apprehension of 'colour patches', but 'things like seeing what time it is, seeing what key a piece of music is written in, and seeing whether a wound is septic'.[40] The shift in perspective, then, involves seeing 'that' certain things obtain and that certain other things would follow. Thus, he explicitly extends his suggestions and conclusions to more than visual imagery, but on his own terms they can be extended even further. Indeed, P. F. Strawson interestingly suggests the broader scope for discerning a *Gestalt* when he reminds us of the shift in perspective involved in 'seeing eternity in a grain of sand'. [41]

Although Hanson's point is to deny the traditional view that such different experiences, such shifts in perspective, are the result of *applying* different interpretations to the same visual experience, his emphasis on the role of 'seeing that' in such shifts of perspective allows us, I think, to understand what is happening in the shift as an experience which constitutes a new interpretation. We can speak of interpretation, that is, without buying into the myth of an uninterpreted epistemic 'given' or the myth that interpretation is a level of activity added to an otherwise already complete experience. When we see, as Judge William suggests we can, that 'only [in this way] does existence become beautiful', we see life differently, we discern a new *Gestalt*: we see, as it were, something dipping where before we saw it standing still, or something convex where before we saw something concave. As long as we remember that 'the construing is there', as Hanson says, 'in the seeing',[42] we can call the new seeing a new interpretation.

---

[37] Chicago, 85.   [38] Ibid.
[39] *Patterns of Discovery* (Cambridge, 1969), 18.   [40] Ibid. 16.
[41] 'Imagination and Perception', 95.
[42] Hanson, *Patterns of Discovery*, 23.

Returning then to Kuhn's suggestion that the transition to a radically alternative scientific framework or paradigm is illuminated by reference to the mechanism of a *Gestalt* shift, it is interesting to apply this to the transition to a radically alternative framework such as the transition to the ethical or to subjectivity. Such a transition, Kuhn argued, occurs 'all at once', 'though not necessarily in an instant', and it radically reconceptualizes or reconstructs one's world-view. In addition, what he calls 'the conversion experience' has another feature which is particularly relevant to my purposes here, and it is highlighted when he contrasts 'translation' with the transition of conversion. He writes:

To translate a theory or worldview into one's own language is not to make it one's own. For that one must go native, discover that one is thinking and working in, not simply translating out of, a language that was previously foreign. That transition is not, however, one that an individual may make or refrain from making by deliberation and choice, however good his reasons for wishing to do so. Instead, at some point in the process of learning to translate, he finds that the transition has occurred, that he has slipped into the new language without a decision having been made. Or else, like many of those who first encountered, say, relativity or quantum mechanics in their middle years, he finds himself fully persuaded of the new view but nevertheless unable to internalize it and be at home in the world it helps to shape. Intellectually such a man has made his choice, but the conversion required if it is to be effective eludes him.[43]

The similarity to which Kuhn points—a crucial one—is that the transition is (like a *Gestalt* switch) one which is qualitative yet not the result of choice or decision.

Kuhn reinforces this aspect of the transition in a way which calls to mind Climacus's own understanding when he concludes the previous passages as follows:

The conversion experience that I have likened to a gestalt switch remains, therefore, at the heart of the revolutionary process. Good reasons for choice provide motives for conversion and a climate in which it is more likely to occur. Translation may, in addition, provide points of entry for the neural programming that, however inscrutable at this time, must underlie conversion. But neither good reasons nor translation constitute conversion . . . .[44]

This conclusion about the relation between translation and transition echoes the position we noted at the outset in Climacus—in Kuhn's idiom, it is that the transition is possible because translation is possible,

---

[43] Kuhn, *The Structure of Scientific Revolutions*, 204.
[44] Ibid.

but it is not the same as translation; in Climacus's idiom it is that the transition is possible because one can know 'what Christianity is' before one is a Christian,[45] but the transition is not the same as that preliminary required knowing (the translation).

Thus, the primary relevance of *Gestalt* shifts to understanding transitions to alternative frameworks lies, for Kuhn, not only in the claim that both transitions are all-or-nothing (though not instantaneous) kinds of transition, but also in the claim that neither transition is the result of choice or decision (one 'finds that the transition has occurred'). I suggest that the qualitative transition to which Kierkegaard refers in various accounts can begin to be understood better when we keep in mind these important suggestions about the character of transitions to alternative frameworks in general.

The perspective of *Gestalt* shift can thus be useful in highlighting these possibilities for interpreting the various Kierkegaardian presentations of transition. These similarities notwithstanding, however, Kuhn, as I pointed out earlier, notes the limits of the *Gestalt* shift analogue in illuminating transitions to incommensurable or radically alternative scientific frameworks or world-views—for example, that there is not the same freedom to go back and forth as in the case of a visual *Gestalt* shift. Moreover, both Kuhn and Hanson point to the limits of the use of the category of 'seeing-as'. I suggest that for similar reasons the perspective of *Gestalt* shift is limited in its application to transitions to different value frameworks, and that the perspective of *Gestalt* shift needs to be complemented by another perspective, one which brings to the fore the decisive non-symmetrical character of the shift and its cognitive contribution. That perspective is provided by contemporary discussions of metaphor.

Transformation: The case of Metaphorical shift

The relevance of discussions of metaphor to an understanding of transitions to alternative frameworks is initially suggested, as I indicated earlier, by the similarity between some of Climacus's descriptions of the task of subjective self-development and some descriptions of metaphor—namely, those in both cases which, as we shall see, involve a tension. For example, Climacus's description of the subject as holding finite and infinite (positive and negative, comic and pathetic) in tension seems to fit

[45] *Postscript*, 332, 339.

easily with descriptions of metaphor as resulting in the placing of an object in 'two perspectives simultaneously' or the 'result of the tension between two terms in' or 'two interpretations of' an utterance.[46] While it may not be immediately obvious how shedding light on the phenomenon of holding two perspectives simultaneously can also shed light on the phenomenon of qualitative change which we considered earlier in terms of *Gestalt* shifts, I think metaphor can provide a fruitful point of reference in both cases. This is because the task of subjectivity and the phenomenon of change are really variations on the same theme. While there is a more radical sense of transition in formulations of the paradox of change than in formulations of the task of subjectivity, the difference is more one of emphasis or focus than of substance, for both are transforming, non-static activities and both achieve qualitative transitions. The plausibity of the suggestion that metaphor can provide an illuminating perspective for both is increased when it is seen that the same account of metaphor which speaks of it as resulting in holding 'two perspectives simultaneously' also speaks of the 'jump' across semantic fields, the 'linguistic realization of a leap of thought'.[47] In what follows I will explore how elements in accounts of metaphor relate to the transformation achieved in the paradox of change, and suggest how they provide a perspective which complements that of *Gestalt* shift in elucidating qualitative transitions.

Although metaphor is strictly speaking a trope or linguistic device, the Greek root of the word (*metapherein*) is more broad—it indicates a general process or activity of transference or carrying over. In the views we have considered, self-transformation is, at the very least, presented as a process in which something is carried over: the subject becomes different while remaining the same subject, the 'not yet' carries on the 'already in us'. To the extent that we can see similarities between the process or activity in metaphor and the process of change in the task of subjectivity, it would seem perfectly appropriate to discuss such change as a metaphoric activity.

Judge William's message is, as we have seen, not merely that the 'perilous' transition to the ethical involves becoming a new self while remaining the same self, but also that self-evaluation involves seeing self in the light of an 'other'. Self-development, self-improvement, transformation of self—all involve redescribing or redefining oneself in the

---

[46] Kittay, *Metaphor*, 4; Paul Ricoeur, 'Metaphor and Symbol', in *Interpretation Theory: Discourse and the Surplus of Meaning* (Fort Worth, TX, 1976), 50.

[47] Kittay, *Metaphor*, 270, 90.

light of an 'other self'. This message could be rephrased quite easily in the terms of the earlier descriptions of metaphor emphasizing *tension*: as resulting in putting 'an object in two perspectives simultaneously', or as the 'result of the tension between two terms in' or 'two interpretations of' an utterance. The latter account (by Paul Ricoeur) is developed in terms of 'the conflict between some prior categorization of reality and a new one just being born', or again, in terms of a 'tension between sameness and difference', and the imaginative 'seeing' which 'effects the shift in logical distance, the rapprochement' between far and near.[48]

Judge William's understanding of transformation could also be rephrased quite easily in the terms of another recent definition of metaphor as that 'whereby we speak of one thing in terms suggestive of another',[49] for the transforming shift occurs through seeing oneself in terms suggestive of an 'other' self. Thus, transformation is at the same time a process in which we put ourselves in two perspectives simultaneously and a process which requires us to redefine ourselves in terms suggestive of 'another self'. That simultaneous holding of ourselves in two perspectives, that redescription in terms of something else, can force a reconceptualization which effects a 'perspectival shift' or transformation. In an important sense we are how we (re)define ourselves—to (re)define ourselves is, therefore, to become different.

Another element found in recent theories of metaphor is the emphasis on 'interaction' or 'interanimation'. Max Black, for example, suggests that the 'crux' of the 'interaction' view of metaphor is:

In the context of a particular metaphorical statement, the two subjects 'interact' in the following ways: (a) the presence of the primary subject incites the hearer to select some of the secondary subject's properties; and (b) invites him to construct a parallel implication-complex that can fit the primary subject; and (c) reciprocally induces parallel changes in the secondary subject.[50]

Janet M. Soskice too argues for the importance of interaction in an account of metaphor, presenting it in terms of 'interanimation' (though as we shall see, she challenges Black's claim that there are two subjects). Dynamic tension—whether in the form of interaction or interanima-

---

[48] Ricoeur, 'Metaphor and Symbol', *Interpretation Theory*, 56; 'The Metaphorical Process as Cognition, Imagination, and Feeling', in *On Metaphor*, ed. Sheldon Sacks (Chicago, 1979), 146, 145.

[49] Janet M. Soskice, *Metaphor and Religious Language* (Oxford, 1985), 49.

[50] 'More on Metaphor', in *Metaphor and Thought*, ed. Andrew Ortony (Cambridge, 1979), 29.

tion—is likewise integral to the process of self-transformation. In the transformation of self the subject becomes different while remaining the same subject because something of the subject's network of associations interacts with something of the other's network of associations. The interaction is so complete that one cannot separate out a 'prior' self from the 'changed' self—for if one could, the changed self would be a different self rather than a changed self. Moreover, the interaction is genuine *inter*action or, as Black argues, 'reciprocally' induced—the interaction works through both sets of associations. That is, the ideal self is not a static definition, but is dynamically understood, itself affected and developed in interaction with the actual self.

What is right, then, about Black's interaction account is that genuine metaphorical reconceptualization is not one-way—the components held in dynamic tension mutually affect each other. What is not right about Black's interaction account, however, is his assumption that such interaction implies that in metaphor there are *two* distinct subjects. Mutual interaction need not mean a symmetrical relationship between two distinct subjects. As Soskice makes clear in her critique of Black's account, there is only one subject in a metaphor.[51] That subject undergoes change, is spoken of in terms suggestive of another—but the metaphor does not contain two actual subjects. Similarly, in the case of the shift by which one adopts the world-view of the ethical or of subjectivity, one subject (as both Judge William and Climacus make clear) persists through the change. The change undergone is that the subject redescribes herself in terms of an 'other'—sees and thinks of herself in terms suggestive of another description, in another semantic domain, with another set of associations. The actual self and the ideal self are not symmetrical entities, for one sees one's (actual) self in terms suggestive of the other (ideal) self. Although there are mutually inter-acting sets of associations (that is, change is not one-way), there is only one subject.

The transition described by Judge William and Climacus can thus be seen as a metaphoric activity, a transformation in which there is a meta-phoric imaginative exercise. It is an activity in which imagination acts metaphorically—not simply to hold two perspectives simultaneously or to see one thing in terms suggestive of another, but to achieve an interac-tive or interanimative relation. The actual is put imaginatively in tension with the potential in another domain, and they interact so as to achieve a

---

[51] Soskice, *Metaphor and Religious Language*, 25, 86.

transfer—the self is carried through imaginative involvement with a potential self (with possibilities in a new definition) to achieve a new self-understanding. That change—which can only be achieved by imagination—is a metaphorical process.

The value of seeing the transitions of which Judge William and Climacus speak as metaphorical processes is that doing so makes clear the decisiveness of the reorientation which is achieved and its character as a cognitive advance; the parallel with a visual *Gestalt* shift does not make this clear. Kittay argues that the 'cognitive force of metaphor comes, not from providing new information about the world, but rather from a (re)conceptualization of information that is already available to us'.[52] She elaborates on the way 'the apposition of two semantic fields . . . makes us realize new connections':[53]

The detour through a semantic field that normally applies to another domain is the distinctive metaphorical move—the perspectival shift in which the projection of the structure of the vehicle field onto the topic domain can force a reconceptualization of the referent, or the subject (when there is no referent), of the metaphor. It is such a reconceptualization that makes metaphor, when it is cognitively significant, irreducibly so.[54]

But lest we confuse that reconceptualization with what occurs in the case of discerning a visual *Gestalt*, consider that it is crucial in the case of metaphor that an object is placed in two perspectives 'simultaneously': 'From this juxtaposition results a reconceptualization, sometimes permanent, more frequently transient, in which properties are made salient which may not previously have been regarded as salient and in which concepts are organized both to accommodate and to help shape experience'.[55]

In the case of metaphor, both perspectives remain held in tension in order to yield the single decisive reconceptualization—the juxtaposition cannot be superseded. Although the reconceptualization need not be permanent, the metaphorical achievement is decisive in the sense that it does not carry with it the same notion of freedom between the two perspectives as we find in the case of *Gestalt* shifts—the two perspectives are neither symmetrical nor able to be seen as equivalent options. It is precisely the notion of the cognitive advance possible to metaphor which precludes the freedom possible to a reversible visual *Gestalt* shift. Metaphor achieves a decisive reconceptualization in the sense that it is

---

[52] Kittay, *Metaphor*, 39.   [53] Ibid. 289.
[54] Ibid. 313–14.   [55] Ibid. 4.

not free to shift back and forth as in the case of *Gestalt*, but, ironically, its decisiveness is actually a function of maintaining or sustaining a *tension* between perspectives rather than in shifting from one perspective to another. The maintenance of tension and the notion of cognitive advance (or decisive cognitive reorientation) are crucial to distinguishing the perspectival shifts achieved in the case of metaphor from that of *Gestalt*, and it is primarily in these ways that the perspective of metaphor can complement and correct the perspective of visual *Gestalt* shift in illuminating the character of qualitative transitions.

IMAGINATION: INFINITELY FINITIZING AND INFINITELY INFINITIZING

In Kierkegaard's later writing Anti-Climacus also elaborates on the same paradoxical 'task of the self freely to become itself', and the connection between imagination and that task is implied in the claim that the imagination is the 'medium of the process of infinitizing'.[56] The development of the self, he explains, in *Sickness unto Death*, 'consists in moving away from oneself infinitely by the process of infinitizing oneself, and in returning to oneself infinitely by the process of finitizing'.[57]

This formulation of the paradoxical task of subjectivity highlights the dual movements of first infinitizing and then finitizing the self.[58] In the process of 'becoming', the self first 'reflects itself in the medium of imagination' so that 'the infinite possibility comes into view'.[59] One cannot 'become' anything without such vision of possibility, but the infinitizing potential of imagination is not enough, for one can be so carried by it 'out into the infinite that it merely carries him away from himself and therewith prevents him from returning to himself . . . he becomes in a way infinitized, but not in such a way that he becomes more and more himself, for he loses himself more and more'.[60] The danger is the 'tendency to run wild in possibility', for 'that the self looks so and so in the possibility of itself is only half-truth'; the antidote is that one must also be 'aware that the self he is, is a perfectly definite something'.[61] To

---

[56] *Sickness unto Death*, 168, 163.   [57] Ibid. 162–3.

[58] Gouwens provides an excellent analysis of the use of imagination in the twofold movement of the ethical (the abstracting and the practical, or the infinitizing and finitizing processes), in 'Kierkegaard on the Ethical Imagination', 206–14; also in *Kierkegaard's Dialectic of the Imagination*, 195–9.   [59] *Sickness unto Death*, 168.

[60] Ibid. 164.   [61] Ibid. 170, 169.

become itself, that is, the self cannot simply become another nor can it simply remain itself: it must finitize itself as well as infinitize itself.

It is clear that, as he says, imagination is the 'medium' or 'reflection of the process of infinitizing',[62] and that process by itself can simply dissipate one. The activity of imagination is, however, not restricted to the infinitizing movement, but is equally necessary for the process of finitizing as well, for in 'becoming' one is not only 'moving away from oneself *infinitely*', but also 'returning to oneself *infinitely*'—and I suggest that to finitize yourself *infinitely* requires as much imagination as to infinitize yourself infinitely, because only imagination can do anything *infinitely*. Moreover, it takes imagination to hold the finitized and infinitized selves in tension with each other.

The same evaluation of transparency as the mark of the ethical which is found in Judge William is also evident in Anti-Climacus's equation between self-development and transparency: 'certainly it is rare for a man to be so developed, so transparent to himself . . . '.[63] The importance of transparency both ethically and religiously is stressed repeatedly[64] and revealed in parallel references to the obverse 'obscurity' of understanding.[65] In effect, Anti-Climacus underlines the centrality of such vision and extends it from ethics to faith. Anti-Climacus indirectly highlights the role of imagination in such vision when he affirms that 'the decisive criterion of the self' is 'consciousness of self'—'the more consciousness, the more will'.[66] That is, consciousness is the criterion or determinant even of will. In particular, the emphasis on consciousness of self is at the same time an emphasis on imagination because the self, in order to fulfil its 'task'—namely, the subjective task 'freely to become itself'—'reflects itself in the medium of imagination'.[67] The ethical task is fulfilled, not through decision, but through reflection in the medium of imagination— and such reflection, as we saw above, 'itself is an action' which can constitute change.

The relation between intellect and will is, in general and in faith in particular, a genuine question for Anti-Climacus. He affirms 'the distinction between not being *able* to understand/and not being *willing* to understand',[68] but the role of will is importantly qualified by his claim that the 'Christian motto' is that 'As thou believest, so it comes to pass; or As thou believest, so art thou; to believe is to be'.[69] Clearly it is imagin-

---

[62] *Sickness unto Death*, 163, 163–4.   [63] Ibid. 232.
[64] Ibid. 147, 213, 255.   [65] Ibid. 181, 225.
[66] Ibid. 162.   [67] Ibid. 168.
[68] Ibid. 226.   [69] Ibid. 224.

ative vision, rather than deliberate decision, which is here said to effect change. Moreover, this is explicitly predicated of the Christian realm.

The way in which imagination is integral to choice or transition, which remains relatively undeveloped in Judge William's account, is thus elaborated by Climacus and clarified by Anti-Climacus's exposition of the infinitizing role of imagination.[70] Judge William's claim that in the transition to the ethical, in choice, 'He becomes himself . . . yet he becomes another' is followed immediately by the conclusion that 'Thus his finite personality is infinitized by the choice whereby he infinitely chooses himself'.[71] But, as Climacus and Anti-Climacus both make clear, it is precisely imagination which infinitizes the self—we cannot speak of choice infinitizing the self except in terms of imagination. Thus, the transforming choice in question is not simply preceded by imaginative exploration, but is constituted by it.

Consistent across several accounts of transition, then, we find that the centrality of categories of 'paradox', 'passion', and the 'infinite' entails the crucial importance of imaginative activity. Since imagination is what perceives paradox or elements in tension, and since passion is generated in the experience of the paradoxical, imagination and passion are correlative. Passion is the appropriation of paradox. Since 'passion is subjectivity'[72] (as opposed to objectivity), as well as the 'highest expression of subjectivity',[73] imagination could be called the activity of subjectivity. Passion is thus the exercise of imagination attaining subjectivity—in understanding oppositions together in the 'contradiction' of existence, in striving to unite finite and infinite, in becoming who we are.

We find, that is, that imaginative activity is integral to the very activity of choosing and repenting, accomplishing (at least in part) the transition to another sphere of existence (rather than being prolegomenon to choice). I suggest that such a reading of transition could be plausibly extrapolated to the transition to religiousness, including Christianity.

There are qualitative transitions at every stage—from aesthetic to ethical, from ethical to religiousness A, from religiousness A (or the ethico-religious) to religiousness B. If some of these can be seen as paradoxical choices constituted by qualitative shifts of perspective, qualitatively new and transforming realizations, then Climacus might see the transition to Christian faith as *formally* similar. That is, if, as I have

---

[70] Gouwens too sees 'a core of agreement among the pseudonyms, from Judge William to Anti-Climacus, on the features of the imagination as it functions properly in subjectivity' ('Kierkegaard on the Ethical Imagination', p. 205).   [71] *Either/Or*, ii. 227.
[72] *Postscript*, 117.   [73] Ibid. 178.

suggested, the 'perilous transition' to the ethical or subjectivity is a reorienting shift in perspective, then the transition to 'faith' might be a similar shift in perspective or realization or recognition (though admittedly the object—what is seen—is different).

After all, Climacus describes the 'breach' through which religiousness is achieved in terms of the 'irruption of inwardness', for 'only in the inwardness of self-activity, does he have his attention aroused, and is enabled to see God', and he writes that within us 'is a potentiality . . . which is awakened in inwardness to become a God-relationship, and then it becomes possible to see God everywhere'.[74] If the qualitative transition from the ethical to religiousness is a qualitatively new seeing (of God—through 'attention'),[75] then might the 'leap' or 'decision' of (Christian) 'faith' be a qualitatively new seeing of God (in Time)? Climacus does actually speak that way sometimes: he speaks of the 'condition' in terms of the ability to 'envision' God, and describes the Christian thought project as one in which 'the god gave the follower the condition to see it and opened for him the eyes of faith', for 'without the condition he would have seen nothing'.[76] In what follows I will explore positive support for an extrapolation to Christian faith of this reading of transitional choice in terms of a transforming shift in perspective which is both qualitative and free—a creative interpretation, a new seeing.[77]

---

[74] *Postscript*, 218, 220–1.
[75] I take my suggestion to be one way of reading the claim by C. Stephen Evans that the transition to religiousness A is one of *recognizing* guilt and absolute demand (*Subjectivity and Religious Belief* (Grand Rapids, Mich., 1978), 110, 112).
[76] *Fragments*, 63, 65.
[77] This, I take it, is the import of Evans's claim that the choice at each level is contoured by how much it makes sense of our humanness, and that the transition to faith can be seen as a 'culmination of a process of personal development, the attainment of an increased self-understanding' (*Subjectivity and Religious Belief*, 116).

4

Surrender and Paradox: Imagination in the Leap

'Faith', Climacus tells us, 'has in fact two tasks: to take care in every moment to discover the improbable, the paradox; and then to hold it fast with the passion of inwardness.'[1] Kierkegaard reinforces and extends this understanding when in his journals he connects faith, passion, and possibility: 'Faith is essentially this—to hold fast to possibility'.[2] These descriptions not only point to the active and passionate character of the act of faith; they also imply the importance of imagination to it, for it is imagination which appropriates paradox and which envisions or gives us access to 'possibility'. In this and the following chapter I want to explore a formulation of the transition to faith in which imaginative activity comes into its own. In particular, I want to explore ways in which imagination can be said to work to give us access to Christian possibility, and to argue that the Climacus account of the transition to faith is best understood on the model of an imaginative *surrender* composed of moments or aspects of imaginative *suspension* and imaginative *engagement*.

The model of surrender suggests itself in the following way. What occurs in a 'leap', as Climacus describes it in the *Fragments*, is a 'letting go'.[3] The parallel movement in faith occurs 'when the understanding steps aside' or 'is discharged', and these two claims are treated by Climacus as interchangeable with his claim that in faith the 'understanding surrender[s] itself'.[4] The notion of surrender is particularly suggestive because even at a common-sense level it embodies an inherent tension between active and passive which is similar to that revealed in our earlier considera-tion (Chapter 1) of the dual character of 'passion'. The maintenance of such tension, as we have seen in preceding chapters, requires imagination.

The role of imagination, however, in the 'happy passion' called 'faith'

---

[1] *Postscript*, 209.
[2] *Journals*, ii. IX A 311, n.d. [1848], 13; he puts it more strongly: it is 'the fight of *faith*, which fights madly (if one would so express it) for possibility' (*Sickness unto Death*, 171–2).   [3] *Fragments*, 43.
[4] Ibid. 59, 64, 54.

is even more central, I shall argue, for imagination is at work in the surrender not only in holding elements in tension but also in the engagement or involvement normally associated with passion. That is, the transition or transformation or transfiguring move is composed of moments of both suspension and engagement. The suspension and engagement are not separable in practice, but as two aspects of the unitary act of surrender they can be distinguished. In the following chapter I will develop an understanding of the role of imaginative engagement; in this chapter I will explore the imaginative suspension at work, including its relation to the imaginative achievement of unity (by way of comparison with a Coleridgean view of imagination) and the kind of suspension involved in imaginative revisioning (as expressed in various accounts of conversion).

SURRENDER AS IMAGINATIVE SUSPENSION

In *Christian Ethics and Imagination*, Philip S. Keane writes that 'One of the main functions of moral imagination is to help us suspend our standard moral judgments so that we can entertain and play with new images which might be more appropriate in a changed social context'.[5] In my preceding consideration of the structure of the task of subjectivity in various Kierkegaardian accounts, I emphasized how the need to hold elements in tension which is central to that task necessarily involves imaginative activity; the activity of holding elements in tension is, I suggest, precisely the suspension to which Keane calls our attention. Moreover, I suggest in what follows that the 'stepping aside' or 'letting go' or 'surrender' which, on Climacus's account, is what the understanding is said to do in the moment of faith can be seen as just such suspension. The tension between active and passive, which I will highlight in the transition to faith and which introduces the relevance of imagination, is particularly apparent in the notion of suspension, and I propose that a model of imaginative surrender, constituted in part by imaginative suspension, can usefully illuminate the 'stepping aside' and 'letting go' which constitute the leap of faith.

---

[5] *Christian Ethics and Imagination* (New York, 1984), 118. In a discussion of the role of imagination in the Ignatian spiritual exercises, Antonio T. De Nicolas likewise suggests that the exercise of imagining will 'desensitize subjects to their original unities and attachments while sensitizing them to fresh and new sensations' (*Powers of Imagining: Ignatius of Loyola* (Albany, NY, 1986), 43).

Captivity and Surrender

Climacus makes clear that the purely active dimension does not do justice to the character of the stepping aside in faith when he writes in the *Fragments* that just as in erotic love, self-love is 'not annihilated but is taken captive' and 'can come to life again', so too in faith the understanding is not annihilated but is taken captive.[6] This description suggests a state of suspension or, alternatively, of holding elements in tension. Although, on the one hand, the notion of being 'taken captive' implies passivity, on the other hand, this non-annihilation is connected later by him with the notion of activity and contrasted with an event which just happens (p. 50). The implication is that the understanding remains active and free—for without its active presence there could be no recognition of paradox, nothing in opposition to the understanding—yet its letting go is an experience of being 'taken captive'.

The relation between active and passive is explicitly recognized by Climacus as a complex one in his discussion of 'offence'. It is, as I noted in Chapter 1, always a case of saying active *yet* passive; they are not separable, although we can 'distinguish' between them. All offence is, he says, 'suffering', being 'wounded', yet we can 'distinguish between suffering offense and active offense'; we can distinguish them, yet suffering offence is always to some extent active and active offence is always to some extent weak or passively wounded (pp. 49–50). The notion of 'offence' is such that it can be spoken of both in terms of being offended and of taking offence (p. 50); the offence 'takes affront, therefore passively, even though so actively that it itself takes affront' (p. 50 n.). Calling attention as he does to this Janus-faced character of offence reveals his recognition that even though aspects of activity and passivity can be 'distinguished', some activities either hold them in tension or maintain them in such a way as to transcend a dichotomy between them. Surrender is, for Climacus, just such an activity—a surrender at the same time implies the passivity of being 'taken captive' (the aspect of being 'taken captive', which is included in 'surrender', suggests what goes on in being 'captivated', and 'captivation' is not something achievable by direct wilful decision) and the active character of something we do (an action rather than an event that just happens to us). In virtue of the captivity involved, surrender is a suspending of what 'can come to life again'. Suspension is, I think, exactly what is pointed to

---

[6] *Fragments*, 48. Further parenthetical page references will be to the *Fragments* as introduced in the text.

in this description of the tension in a state in which something is neither straightforwardly expressed nor annihilated.

Such surrender (letting go, stepping aside), which cannot be neatly put under either rubric of active or passive, could be seen as the obverse of offence. If 'offence' is the name for the 'unhappy' lack of 'mutual understanding' of the difference between the paradox and the understanding, and the 'happy passion' of faith is the transition achieved in the 'happy', 'mutual understanding', then what is true of offence is true of the converse letting go which constitutes embrace: 'The more deeply the expression of offense is couched in passion (acting or suffering), the more manifest is the extent to which the offense is indebted to the paradox' (p. 51). The letting go is an activity in which the dualism between active and passive is transcended, and both are held in tension; it is *not* to be understood on the model, then, of a one-sidedly active 'will-power' kind of 'leap'.

Suspension of the Understanding

This interpretation of the understanding's stepping aside or letting go in terms of captivity or suspension can be made clearer by reconsidering for a moment the presentation by Climacus of the relation between reason and faith. The paradox provides the occasion for the understanding to step aside, and it provides the condition which allows it do so.[7] In the *Postscript* Climacus elaborates the idea of willing the downfall of the understanding, its stepping aside or letting go, by his constant references to believing 'against the understanding' and the need to 'give up' the understanding or reason or 'break with' the understanding.[8] But what precisely is it for the understanding to do these things? There seem to be two possibilities, corresponding roughly to the claims that faith is against reason or that faith is beyond reason. The understanding can say that: (1) this is against my judgement, and it is in my legitimate domain of judgement, but I will accept it anyway (faith against reason), or (2) in so far as I am judge this is not understandable, but there may be more than I can judge of, so I accept what is not understandable (faith above or beyond reason).

The first option—that faith is *against* reason's legitimate judgement—

---

[7] Refer to my discussion of the sufficiency of 'the condition' in relation to faith, in 'Kierkegaardian Faith: "the Condition" and the Response', in the *International Journal for Philosophy of Religion*, 28 (Oct. 1990), 63–70.

[8] *Postscript*, 208–9, 384, 502–5; 159, 337, 502; 505.

is the only one which makes it plausible to speak of the 'absurd' in connection with faith,[9] but it seems difficult to call it a case in which the understanding sets itself aside. To claim that a given domain is its legitimate domain is to claim that it is the supreme arbiter in that domain, and that effectively precludes an acceptance of what contradicts its judgement in that domain. To accept what contradicts its judgement in that domain is to deny its supremacy in that domain (i.e., to give up the claim that it is in fact reason's legitimate domain). It is difficult to see what it would mean for the understanding to deny *itself* in what it continues to claim as its legitimate domain.

The second option, on the other hand, is a version of the Jamesian view that it is sometimes reasonable to accept what is not understandable. Indeed Climacus speaks of reason coming to its limits (the unknown). But this option seems to emphasize the reasonableness of affirming the paradox and thus to render vacuous or at least dilute the references to the 'crucifixion of the understanding'. 'Crucifixion' does not, for Climacus, mean 'annihilation'; nevertheless, it is not clear that the second option does justice to his intentions when he speaks of the 'absurd' or of 'madness'.[10]

This way of phrasing the options assumes, however, that the only alternatives are acceptance or denial by the understanding, and I want to suggest that this does not do justice to Climacus's presentation. The situation he describes in the *Fragments* is rather one in which a tension is maintained: 'the understanding has strong objections to it [the double paradox of the God-Man]; and yet, on the other hand, in its paradoxical passion the understanding does indeed will its own downfall' (p. 47). Climacus likewise writes that one 'must have it [understanding] in order to believe against understanding'.[11] I suggest that the notion of 'suspension' expresses this tension (as well as the idea of captivity) more than either the notion of acceptance or that of denial. The understanding must be at the same time abandoned and maintained—it must be active enough to continue to perceive a paradox and yet not so active as to

---

[9] John Wisdom, for example, suggests that the 'absurd' (as opposed to 'nonsense') cannot be beyond the scope of reason. He writes that a statement is absurd if it is 'against all reason'; a statement may have meaning and yet be 'absurd and *against* all reason and therefore *not* beyond the scope of reason' ('The Logic of God' (1950) in *Paradox and Discovery* (Berkeley, CA, 1970), 20).

[10] *Postscript*, 159, 381.

[11] Ibid. 503. C. Stephen Evans is especially sensitive to this, noting that submergence is not the same as suicide of the understanding, but the character of such submergence is left unexplained (*Subjectivity and Religious Belief*, 120).

reject it automatically as an offence to its standards.[12] That is, the understanding must both maintain its traditional associations (or it faces no paradox) and yet will their downfall (or it cannot step aside)—the condition is one of neither acceptance nor annihilation, but one of suspension.

The understanding must remain discriminating enough to face a genuine paradox, 'the' absurd. Kierkegaard writes in his journals that he tried to explain in the *Postscript* that 'not every absurdity is the absurd or the paradox. The activity of reason is to distinguish the paradox negatively—but no more.'[13] To know it negatively, however, requires the active presence in some form of the traditional associations or standards of the understanding. But in order that rejection not be inevitable, in order, that is, that embrace of the paradox be possible, the traditional associations or standards cannot be operative as usual.[14] In other words, only if the understanding is 'supreme' can it face a paradox, and yet if it is 'supreme' it can only reject the paradox. What is called for is not denial (or acceptance), but suspension; suspension seems to provide a way to understand the requisite ability 'to care and not to care', to maintain and not maintain at the same time.

The letting go or holding opposites in tension which I have analysed as suspension occurs in the face of paradox—more specifically, it occurs both in the perception and in the embrace of paradox. It takes imagination to *perceive* a paradox—a statement of two elements which, at least apparently, contradict each other— because it takes imagination to *perceive* elements in tension, to put 'differences together'.[15] But the paradox is not limited to what is propositionally formulatable; rather, the passion is itself paradoxical,[16] a practical rather than theoretical paradox, for embracing the paradox is at the same time a letting go and a maintaining of the standards of the understanding. That too is an

---

[12] In *Sickness Unto Death* Kierkegaard distinguishes three kinds of offence: indifference, negative/passive, negative/active (pp. 260–2).

[13] *Journals*, i. X^2 A 354, n.d. [1850], 4. Similarly, he writes: 'The absurd is not the absurd or absurdities without any distinction. . . . The absurd is a category, and the most developed thought is required to define the Christian absurd accurately and with conceptual correctness.' (i. X^6 B 79, n.d. [1850], 7.)

[14] I use the word 'embrace' deliberately since if the understanding is set aside it cannot strictly speaking be said that we either affirm or deny the paradox. The embrace or 'mutual understanding' may be simply a stand-off—not denying or rejecting a proposition but acting as if the proposition expressing the paradox were true (although one still needs to ask what it is to act according to a contradiction).

[15] *Postscript*, 449; see 473 where he refers to the 'requirement of existence: to *put things together*'.

[16] *Fragments*, 44, 47.

exercise of imagination. To perceive a paradox, therefore, is one use of imagination, but to embrace it is another use. That is, the perception of paradox can occur even when the understanding is not set aside (i.e., even when one rejects the paradox), so the setting aside of the understanding which occurs when a paradox is embraced employs the imagination in still another way.

Suspension and Union

What occurs in the letting go of the understanding is therefore a holding of opposites in tension, a maintaining and not maintaining at the same time, a *suspension* of, traditional standards; such a holding of opposites in tension is precisely the work of imagination, and it is precisely when passion is generated. Such holding of opposites in tension, however, is also spoken of by Climacus in terms of *union*: the Paradox, he writes, cannot be an object of knowledge precisely because it 'unites contradictories'[17]—any appropriation of it is then in some sense a unifying activity. In this respect it is like the realization of 'a unity of the infinite and the finite which transcends existence'[18]—both are realizations of unity which can only occur in the moment of passion, and both involve uniting opposites. It is important, then, to see how the role of imagination in holding opposites in tension is to be understood in terms of the union involved: what is the character of such union; how do the opposites relate? One way of becoming clearer about Climacus's understanding of opposites and unity is to compare it with a similar-sounding one proposed a generation before Kierkegaard by a well-known defender of imagination, namely, the romantic poet and critic, Samuel Taylor Coleridge (1772–1834).

Like others in the philosophical tradition before him, Coleridge considered imagination an 'intermediate' or 'mediating' or 'synthetic' faculty. Such mediation or synthesis, moreover, is in the service of the search for unity, for the 'manifold *One*',[19] and addresses itself to 'opposite or discordant qualities'. Consider some of his descriptions in detail.

Imagination, he writes, is the 'idealising Power, of symbols mediating

---

[17] *Fragments*, 61.   [18] *Postscript*, 176.

[19] October 1805, # 2705, *The Notebooks of Samuel Taylor Coleridge* (1804–1808), ii, ed. Kathleen Coburn (Princeton, NJ, 1961). See James S. Cutsinger's useful and detailed discussion of Coleridge's complex notion of 'unity' or varied senses of 'one' (*The Form of Transformed Vision: Coleridge and the Knowledge of God* (Macon, GA, 1987), esp. Part II.

between the Reason and Understanding'.[20] It is the 'reconciling and mediatory power, which incorporating the Reason in Images of the Sense, and organizing (as it were) the flux of the Senses by the permanence and self-circling energies of the Reason, gives birth to a system of symbols, harmonious in themselves, and consubstantial with the truths, of which they are the *conductors*'.[21] That reconciling power is also the 'synthetic and magical power' which 'blends, and (as it were) *fuses* [our faculties], each into each', and

reveals itself in the balance or reconcilement of opposite or discordant qualities: of sameness, with difference; of the general with the concrete; the idea with the image; the individual with the representative; the sense of novelty and freshness with old and familiar objects; a more than usual state of emotion with more than usual order; judgement ever awake and steady self-possession with enthusiasm and feeling profound or vehement; and while it blends and harmonizes the natural and the artificial, still subordinates art to nature. . . .[22]

Coleridge also provides a characterization of imagination with an eye to its philosophical definition when, as a *not* 'unapt emblem of the mind's self-experience in the act of thinking', he suggests the 'pulses of active and passive motion' by which a water insect resists the current and then yields to obtain a fulcrum for further propulsion. He explains: 'There are evidently two powers at work, which relatively to each other are active and passive; and this is not possible without an intermediate faculty, which is at once both active and passive. In philosophical language, we must denominate this intermediate faculty in all its degrees and determinations, the IMAGINATION.'[23] Interestingly, this description of imagination occurs in the conclusion of a consideration of 'what we do when we leap'. I shall return shortly to this intriguing Coleridgean association between imagination and leap.

The 'synthetic' power of imagination, for Coleridge, seeks unity through mediation, fusion, blending, and balance, and does so in a manner 'at once both active and passive'. In such varied descriptions and definitions, however, we find significantly different emphases and implications. In what follows I will explore these, suggesting how

[20] *Coleridge's Miscellaneous Criticism*, ed. Thomas Middleton Raysor (Cambridge, Mass., 1936, reprint edn., Folcroft, Pa., 1969), 286.

[21] *Statesman's Manual* (1816), in *Lay Sermons*, *The Collected Works of Samuel Taylor Coleridge*, vi, ed. R. J. White (Princeton, NJ, 1972), 29.

[22] *Biographia Literaria*, Everyman's Library (London, 1906), 151–2. Reference to Imagination as 'the fusing power' is made in #4066, April 1811, in *The Notebooks*, iii.

[23] *Biographia Literaria*, ch. 7, 60.

Climacus's view of the role of imagination in maintaining tension in unity is illuminated by comparison and contrast with Coleridge's views.

One kind of emphasis in the Coleridge view of imagination is illustrated in the references to it as a faculty which is 'at once both active and passive', and to the role of 'balance' of opposite qualities. This sounds at first hearing like a reference to the role of imagination in maintaining elements in tension which I have described as 'suspension' and found to be an important role for imagination in the Climacus account. These descriptions, then, indicate a way in which imagination is understood to transcend a dichotomy between active and passive and to sustain a genuine tension. At other times, however, a quite different emphasis can be detected in Coleridge's thought—namely, an emphasis on imagination as that faculty which 'fuses' and 'blends'. In fact, Coleridge echoes a Hegelian notion of synthesis when he writes of the reconciliation of opposites as achieved when 'the two component counterpowers actually interpenetrate each other, and generate a higher third including both the former, "*ita tamen ut sit alia et major*"'.[24]

That the goal is unity or synthesis in both of these kinds of Coleridgean description is unquestionable—but the implications of the two contrasting ways of understanding the achievement of unity are remarkably different. In so far as Coleridge's thought on the imagination emphasizes the 'balance' of elements in unity, it expresses the role of imagination in maintaining a genuine tension or suspension between 'opposite or discordant qualities', and an activity which is 'at once both active and passive'. On the other hand, in so far as it assumes the second emphasis—on fusion and blending and the generation of a 'higher third'—it belies the descriptions which suggest a genuine 'balance'. An interpenetration to 'generate a higher third', through fusion and blending, suggests a unifying understood as resolution of tension in a higher synthesis—fusion or blending does not reflect a maintained tension, but rather a resolved tension, which on that account ceases to be a tension.

The suggestion that the 'higher third' *includes* the former two components might be thought to be sufficient to maintain their integrity in tension, but that integrity is rendered problematical by an example of synthesis—namely, the compound H_2O—which Coleridge uses repeatedly. He contrasts the 'mere juxta-position of Corpuscles' with 'Synthesis',

---

[24] MS note printed by A. D. Snyder, 'Coleridge's "Theory of Life"', *Modern Language Notes*, 47 (1932), 301, cited in James V. Baker, *The Sacred River: Coleridge's Theory of Imagination* (Baton Rouge, La., 1957), 200.

for 'Water is neither Oxygen nor Hydrogen, nor yet is it a commixture of both; but the Synthesis or Indifference of the Two'.[25] Such an example of the sought-after union is clearly at odds with any genuine notion of balance or tension between elements in their integrity.

Climacus's view of the paradox parallels his view of the task of subjectivity, for the task, we saw, consists of 'uniting opposites in existence'. This involves, as much as does Coleridge's philosophy, a prescriptive quest for unity. The locus of disagreement and/or agreement between the Climacus and Coleridge views of the synthetic role of imagination can be brought out more clearly by focusing on Climacus's rejection of Hegelian synthesis and 'mediation' and distinguishing between two meanings of 'both-and' which are part of his account. One of these meanings comes up when Climacus explicitly argues against a Hegelian notion of synthesis and 'the both-and of the principle of mediation'.[26] In general his diatribes against Hegelian 'mediation' and synthesis issue in the counter-proposal of an 'either/or'. [27] Yet in the context of the Climacus account it is clear that he nevertheless does actually require a 'both-and' of a certain sort: that is, his account of existence in which discordant elements are 'put together', lived together, exhibits a 'both-and' character. Although it is not a Hegelian kind of 'both-and' (and is certainly incapable of resolution into a higher unity) it is still not a case of alternatives of 'either/or', for there is no choice required between the contradictory elements that constitute existence: the task is to 'remain' in the 'tremendous contradiction'.[28] We cannot choose one element or the other, we must hold them in tension: *both* finite *and* infinite, *both* positive *and* negative, *both* comic *and* tragic. We must strive to understand, perceive, see, and think 'the greatest oppositions together';[29] the task, for example, is 'to think one [thought] and simultaneously have the opposite in mind, uniting these opposites in existence'.[30] But the meaning of 'uniting these opposites in existence' is that we understand them 'together', as 'both-and'—not in a higher synthesis, but not as an 'either/or'. The alternative to the Hegelian 'both-

[25] Essay 13, *The Friend, The Collected Works of Samuel Taylor Coleridge*, i, ed. Barbara E. Rooke (London, 1969), 94 n. Basil Willey illustrates the contrast between Coleridgean 'Fancy' and 'Imagination' with examples which make my point: 'mechanical mixtures (as of salt with iron filings)' as opposed to 'chemical compounds (say, of sodium and chlorine)' (*Nineteenth Century Studies: Coleridge to Matthew Arnold* (New York, 1949), 16).

[26] *Postscript*, 358–9.

[27] Ibid. 270–1; the either/or of subjectivity/objectivity, 23, and the either/or expressed in both volumes of *Either/Or*.   [28] *Postscript*, 313.

[29] Ibid. 316.   [30] Ibid. 317.

and' is not here an 'either/or' but rather the 'both-and' which constitutes paradox.

Although they share much in their appreciation of imagination in its role of 'uniting opposites in existence', Climacus's understanding of the unifying function of imagination is thus quite different from that strand in Coleridge which emphasizes fusion and blending and which calls to mind Hegelian synthesis and 'mediation'. The unity of contradictories which I have described in the Paradox as well as in the constitution of 'existence' is clearly not simply two elements side by side, or one contained in the other, but it is just as clearly not the kind of fusion exemplified in the synthesis of the compound water. That fusion is one which precludes the kind of integrity of elements which is necessary for a genuine tension or 'balance'—in so far as they fail to maintain their integrity they cease to be in tension. Such a version of the romantic quest for unity would seem to Kierkegaard just as existentially inadequate as Hegel's strategy of *Aufheben*: on the one hand, Climacus's quest for unity seeks more (for it does not simply reconcile in thought) and, on the other hand, less (for it does not preclude the mutual integrity which allows for genuine tension). One could, then, argue that by emphasizing the maintenance of a genuine tension Climacus's account actually does more justice to Coleridge's insight that imagination, 'at once both active and passive', exhibits and achieves 'balance' than does much of Coleridge's own discussion.[31]

One could, however, equally well turn the matter on its head and argue that Climacus's account of maintaining elements in tension sheds light on the resources within Coleridge's own account to avoid the criticism levelled at Hegelian 'mediation' and thus to bring the two accounts of unity and imagination closer. Climacus's account can do this by encouraging us to look again, long and hard, at Coleridge's thought for an account of 'interpenetration' (fusion or blending) generating a 'higher third' which does not empty of content the suggestions of balance and genuine tension. One possible account is found in the *Biographia*

---

[31] Baker in the *Sacred River* argues that 'Coleridge's whole theory of imagination, then, rests on a sharp distinction between active and passive powers' which Coleridge sometimes confusingly expresses by the contrast between 'imagination' and 'fancy' (pp. 128–9). Baker's own discussion is confusing, however, because he goes on to claim that Coleridge expresses a 'supreme insight into the alliance of active and passive in the creative act' (p. 228) and an appreciation of the 'collaboration' and 'coalition' of both powers (pp. 179, 191), but nevertheless concludes that Coleridge was right 'to sharply oppose' active and passive powers (p. 248); moreover, quoting on p. 135 the passage from the *Biographia Literaria* he leaves out (without providing ellipses!) the very sentence in which Coleridge claims that imagination is 'at once both active and passive'.

Literaria, chapter 13, in the discussion which precedes the famous definitions of primary and secondary imagination and fancy. This discussion is taken up with an attempt to relate the Kantian insight about 'real' opposites to the '*tertium aliquid*' achieved in the generation of 'an inter-penetration of the counteracting powers, partaking of both'.[32] His initial example of 'real' opposites is that of the 'motory force of a body in one direction, and an equal force of the same body in an opposite direction', for these are 'not incompatible, and the result, namely, rest, is real and representable'.[33] In the 'process of our own self-consciousness', likewise, 'two inherent indestructible yet counteracting forces' operate in 'one power'.[34] The reference to two equally indestructible forces in one power suggests the polarity exhibited in the phenomenon of magnet-ism—and this is explicitly affirmed in the concluding Chapter 24, when he speaks of how the 'two poles of the magnet manifest the being and unity of the one power by relative opposites'.[35] Such an appreciation of polarity invokes a notion of genuine tension which dispels the crude notion of fusion and blending sometimes found in Coleridge's account, and allows a *rapprochement* of the existentialist and romantic under-standings of imaginative synthesis and tension.

LETTING GO, CONVERSION, AND IMAGINATIVE REVISIONING

The 'letting go' in faith in terms of the suspension involved in embracing opposites (a paradox, 'the absurd') is one expression of the 'leap', but another expression for it is suggested by those journal entries, noted earlier, where Kierkegaard repeatedly refers to 'the leap of inference in induction and analogy', claiming that in such cases 'the conclusion can be reached only by a LEAP' and 'all other conclusions are essentially tautological'.[36] This leap is a letting go in the face of what is not logically or demonstrably compelling, and the surrender in such a case focuses on the generic gap between non-compelling evidence and a conclusion. This way of considering a letting go or a leap also implies imaginative activity, although here it is not a case of the imaginative suspension of *opposites*.

---

[32] Coleridge, *Biographia Literaria*, 143.
[33] Ibid. 142.   [34] Ibid.
[35] Ibid. 297. John Coulson's discussion of Coleridge focuses exclusively on this strand of his thought on unity and tension, ignoring those elements less congenial to his thesis about polarity (*Religion and Imagination: 'in aid of a grammar of assent'*, 135; also 113–14, 132).
[36] *Journals*, iii. V C 7, n.d. [1844]; V A 74, n.d. [1844], 19 and 16.

Rather, it is a case of the suspension (or holding in tension) involved in imaginative revisioning, and the suspension implied in the imaginative synthesis and extension through which we achieve the unity of a new seeing.

Such imaginative revisioning is another name for what I have already been considering as the shift in perspective which constitutes the transition to faith. The role of imagination in embracing the Paradox—in appropriating a uniting of contradictories, in holding elements in tension—also informs this revisioning because there is a relation between embracing the Paradox and embracing a new way of looking at the world (and self). That relation can be seen as follows. Climacus makes it clear in the *Fragments* that to accept the Paradox is not to accept a set of teachings or propositions: it is to accept a person, the 'Teacher'.[37] There is a message, nevertheless, which is thereby embraced, for the 'Teacher' exemplifies or embodies a paradoxical message (the message of unlikeness and likeness, of 'absolute difference' and 'absolute equality'[38]) and embracing the 'Teacher' is effectively embracing a new self-understanding and a concomitant new way of looking at the world. The uniting of contradictories in the 'Teacher' is echoed back into the new paradoxical self-understanding—in ways which recall the paradoxical self-understanding achieved in striving for subjectivity. In fact, the deeper subjectivity (subjectivity thrust back into itself in the face of the Paradox) is precisely what sin-consciousness is supposed to consist in, and it is significant that this new self-understanding is termed by Kierkegaard, we saw earlier, 'the leap of sin-consciousness'.[39]

The notion of imaginative revisioning which I am introducing is one of synthetic activity, yet one in which tension is not eliminated—what we see and embrace is a world (and self) in which tension is maintained. The new seeing is not a resolution of the tension, but the affirmation or active recognition of it; the imaginative synthesis which achieves revisioning will involve suspension. It will no more result in a resolution or elimination of tension than did the suspension considered earlier. What is achieved is a kind of unified vision, inclusive of tension.

That new understanding, as we saw with Coleridge, is a form of unity in which we imaginatively, creatively put things together. But we learn something else from Coleridge about this imaginative revisioning, for, as I noted in passing, he speaks of the activity of imagination in the course of considering 'what we do when we leap'. A brief exploration of this

---

[37] *Fragments*, 62. [38] Ibid. 47.
[39] *Journals*, iii. V C 7, n.d. [1844], 19.

suggestive connection between imagination and leap will be a useful preliminary to the examination of autobiographical accounts of conversion in the latter part of this chapter.

Coleridge and James: Leaps and Volitions

In chapter 7 of his *Biographia Literaria* Coleridge considers 'what we do when we leap' in a non-religious context. He begins by addressing the question of 'voluntary' movement: 'In every voluntary movement we first counteract gravitation, in order to avail ourselves of it. It must exist, that there may be a something to be counteracted, and which, by its re-action, may aid the force that is exerted to resist it.'[40] He then refers to the particular movement of interest to us:

> Let us consider what we do when we leap. We first resist the gravitating power by an act purely voluntary, and then by another act, voluntary in part, we yield to it in order to alight on the spot, which we had previously proposed to ourselves. Now let a man watch his mind . . . while he is trying to recollect a name; and he will find the process completely analogous.

Coleridge's indication that the character of a leap is illuminated by reference to the process of trying to recollect a name suggests that it will be useful to turn for a moment to his own description, elsewhere, of that frustrating activity. We go through the alphabet 'in vain', he writes, then the name all 'at once' starts up, 'perfectly insulated, without any the dimmest antecedent connection, as far as my consciousness extended'; the recollection occurs suddenly, 'by-act-of-will-unaided'.[41] The explanation, Coleridge continues, depends on a 'full sharp distinction of Mind from Consciousness—the Consciousness being the narrow *Neck* of the Bottle':

> The name, Daniel, must have been a living *Atom*-thought in my mind, whose uneasy motions were the craving to recollect it—but the very craving led the mind to a reach where each successive disappointment (= a tiny pain) tended to contract the orifice or *outlet* into Consciousness. Well—it is given up—and all is quiet—the Nerves are asleep, or off their guard—and then the Name pops up, makes its way, and there it is!—not assisted by an association, but the very contrary—by the suspension and *sedation* of all associations.

---

[40] *Biographia Literaria*, 60.

[41] *Inquiring Spirit: A Coleridge Reader*, ed. Kathleen Coburn (Minerva Press, 1951), 30–1. My attention was called to this passage by James S. Cutsinger's study, *The Form of Transformed Vision: Coleridge and the Knowledge of God*, 23.

This activity, remember, he claims is 'analogous' to what occurs in a 'leap'.

In the conclusion of his consideration of 'what we do when we leap' he elaborates the dual aspect of the leap and ties it to imagination. He describes how an animal, in parallel fashion to 'what we do when we leap', 'wins its way up against the stream, by alternate pulses of active and passive motion, now resisting the current, and now yielding to it in order to gather strength and a momentary *fulcrum* for a further propulsion'.[42] This description, he immediately continues, is 'no unapt emblem of the mind's self-experience in the act of thinking', and his explanation of this is striking:

There are evidently two powers at work, which relatively to each other are active and passive; and this is not possible without an intermediate faculty, which is at once both active and passive. In philosophical language, we must denominate this intermediate faculty in all its degrees and determinations, the IMAGINATION.

We can glean from these passages the following interesting suggestions about 'what we do when we leap'. First, the leap is said to be a single 'voluntary movement' composed of 'an act purely voluntary' and then 'another act, voluntary in part'. The former is later referred to an 'active' power, the latter to a 'passive' power—hence even the expression of the 'passive' power (or yielding) is, at least in part, a 'voluntary' exercise. Second, the combination of 'two powers at work' is exercised through 'an intermediate faculty', 'the IMAGINATION', 'which is at once both active and passive'. Third, the passive, yielding act (which itself is 'voluntary in part') is paralleled with the frustrating recollection of a name, which recollection is, he says, 'by act-of-will-unaided'. Fourth, that yielding only occurs in virtue of the 'suspension and *sedation* of all associations'. In sum, then, Coleridge views the leap as (1) a 'voluntary movement', of which one act is a 'voluntary in part' yet 'by-act-of-will-unaided' activity. That is, the discrete moment of the 'recollection' is considered to be preceded by straightforwardly voluntary activity, to be itself 'voluntary in part' and yet 'by act-of-will-unaided'. The transition, then, is not simply involuntary, though it is not intentional or 'on purpose'. Moreover, the leap (2) requires the exercise of a faculty— Imagination—'which is at once both active and passive', and (3) is constituted as much by a yielding as by an exercise of active power—a yielding illuminated by reference to the 'suspension and sedation of associations'.

[42] *Biographia Literaria*, 60.

The element of yielding in the leap and the idea of the suspension and sedation of associations are particularly intriguing in that they call to mind some considerations put forth by a thinker very different from Coleridge—namely, the American psychologist and pragmatist philosopher, William James (1842–1910). In particular, they call to mind aspects of James's discussion of 'volition'. The parallel between the two accounts can be instructive. In his *Principles of Psychology* James describes a case—an account of a decision to get out of bed on a cold morning—which seems to him 'to contain in miniature form the data for an entire psychology of volition'.[43] Consider someone saying 'I *must* get up' but not doing it—the 'resolution faints away and postpones itself again and again just as it seemed on the verge of bursting the resistance and passing over into the decisive act' (p. 524). How, then, does one get up? His answer:

If I may generalize from my own experience, we more often than not get up without any struggle or decision at all. We suddenly find that we *have* got up. A fortunate lapse of consciousness occurs; we forget both the warmth and the cold; we fall into some revery connected with the day's life, in the course of which the idea flashes across us, 'Hollo, I must lie here no longer'—an idea which at that lucky instant awakens no contradictory or paralyzing suggestions, and consequently produces immediately its appropriate motor effects. It was our acute consciousness of both the warmth and the cold during the period of struggle which paralyzed our activity then and kept our idea of rising in the condition of *wish* and not of *will*. (pp. 524–5)

In all of this James is wanting to argue, he explains, against the 'common prejudice that voluntary action without "exertion of will-power" is Hamlet with the prince's part left out' (p. 526). Here he echoes Coleridge's claim that 'voluntary' action may yet be 'by-act-of-will-unaided'.[44]

For James, it is not a question of 'will-power'—rather, we 'find that we *have* got up'. It is not a 'decision', he says, but rather 'a fortunate lapse of consciousness' which accounts for our getting out of bed; what is responsible is not the idea 'I must lie here no longer', but rather (what Coleridge calls) the suspension and sedation of those associations which could provide 'contradictory or paralyzing suggestions'. Admittedly, James's observations are addressed to the question of the 'mechanism of

---

[43] ii. 525. Further parenthetical references in this section will be to this work unless otherwise noted.

[44] Gilbert Ryle likewise distinguishes between 'voluntary' and 'intentional' in *The Concept of Mind*, 70 ff.

production' of 'voluntary [bodily] movements', which are the 'only *direct* outward effects of our will'; his topic is whether movement requires an 'express fiat' preceding it. But his discussion ultimately includes various types of decision-making in relation to such a 'fiat', because 'our higher thought is full' of the parallel phenomenon of 'blocking and its release' which is found in cases of bodily movement (p. 527). His example, therefore, has wider implications.

Examining 'voluntary action', James writes that an 'express fiat, or act of mental consent to the movement, comes in when the neutralization of the antagonistic and inhibitory idea is required', but is not needed 'when the conditions are simple'—in such cases voluntary action can occur 'with no fiat or express resolve' (p. 526). We are less likely to think that 'exertion of will-power' is required in all cases if we realize that 'consciousness is *in its very nature impulsive*. (Is this perhaps parallel to the impulse to will its own downfall which Climacus sees as the very nature of thought?) Presumably, what is required in such cases is simply a lapse or suspension, not a positive effort of will.

The 'popular notion' that activity 'must result from some superadded "will-force"' is, he writes, 'a very natural inference from those special cases in which we think of an act for an indefinite length of time without the action taking place'. Such cases, however,

are not the norm; they are cases of inhibition by antagonistic thoughts. When the blocking is released we feel as if an inward spring were let loose, and this is the additional impulse or *fiat* upon which the act effectively succeeds. We shall study anon the blocking and its release. Our higher thought is full of it. But where there is no blocking, there is naturally no hiatus between the thought-process and the motor discharge. (pp. 526–7)

Even this 'additional impulse or *fiat*' achieved by 'release' is not to be understood as 'some superadded "will-force,"' however, for when we examine what James argues we do when 'we are said to *decide*' we can see that the appeal is not to decision as directly constituted by will-power. The category of 'deliberate action' or 'action after deliberation' is explained by him in terms of cases in which an extremely complex set of 'motives and their conflict', ideas in antagonistic or reinforcing relations, is present to our consciousness—'when finally the original suggestion either prevails and makes the movement take place, or gets definitively quenched by its antagonists, we are said to *decide*, or to *utter our voluntary fiat* in favor of one or the other course' (p. 528). That prevailing or quenching occurs against a background in which, while we realize 'the totality' of the ideas 'more or less dimly all the while, certain parts stand out more or less sharply at one moment in the foreground, and at another moment other parts, in consequence of the oscillations of our attention, and of the "associative" flow of our ideas' (pp. 528–9). What we call 'decision' occurs, that is, 'in consequence of the oscillations of our attention'. It is for this reason that James's elaboration of his initial claim that 'will consists in nothing but a manner of attending to certain objects, or consenting to their stable presence before the mind' (p. 320) later yields the crucial suggestion that *'effort of attention is thus the essential phenomenon of will'* (p. 562). In particular, and all the emphases remain James's, *'The essential achievement of the will, in short, when it is most "voluntary", is to* ATTEND *to a difficult object and hold it fast before the mind'* (p. 561).

Two points need to be made here. First, such 'effort of attention' is not the 'superadded "will-force"' whose universal relevance James is concerned to argue against. The 'decision' to focus my attention is not the 'decision' whose origin is being sought. The decision (or decisive movement) which occurs in virtue of the oscillations of our attention is not subject to 'will-force' in the way in which the effort of attention preliminary to that decision may be. We cannot will to recognize something in the same way that we can will to focus on what may help us to recognize it.

But second, James's reference to the phenomenon of attention fits in with Coleridge's reference to imagination for the following reason. Imagination is not only the paradigmatic synthesizing ability—it is also required for the 'effort of attention' or focusing to which James points. To focus ourselves, to 'attend', is an activity of imagination because it requires a separating off, a creative and hypothetical restructuring. James's understanding of 'attention' reminds us how indispensable such focusing (or hypothetical restructuring) is, given the constant flux before us; the way in which imagination allows us to 'attend' is parallel, I suggest, to the way imagination, for Coleridge, is the power 'that *fixing* unfixes'.[45]

In order to illustrate the lack of 'will-power' in most fiats, James discusses 'four chief types' of decision or ways of ending deliberation. In what he calls a 'reasonable' type of decision the arguments before us leave 'a clear balance in favour of one alternative, which alternative we then adopt without effort or constraint' (p. 531). In such a case we have

---

[45] April 1811, #4066, emphasis mine, *The Notebooks of Samuel Taylor Coleridge* (1808–1819), iii, ed. Kathleen Coburn (Princeton, 1973).

'a perfect sense of being *free*, in that we are devoid of any feeling of coercion' even though 'the reasons which decide us' appear to 'owe nothing to our will'. In cases where no 'paramount or authoritative reason for either course' is apparent, however, 'our feeling is to a certain extent that of letting ourselves drift' in a direction 'accidentally determined' either from without or from within; these determinations constitute the second and third type of decision.

The fourth form of decision is described in ways which seem especially relevant to our concern with conversion, for they are 'changes of heart, awakenings of conscience, etc., which make new men of so many of us' (p. 533). They come, James says,

when, in consequence of some outer experience or some inexplicable inward change, *we suddenly pass from the easy and careless to the sober and strenuous mood*, or possibly the other way. The whole scale of values of our motives and impulses then undergoes a change like that which a change of the observer's level produces on a view. ... The character abruptly rises to another 'level', and deliberation comes to an immediate end. (p. 533)

In some cases, then, decision is constituted by something like a 'change of the observer's level' or an abrupt rise 'to another "level"'. These phrases call to mind the phenomenon of a *Gestalt* shift in perspective and James's claim is that deliberation ends in virtue of such a shift.

What distinctively characterizes a fifth type of decision and separates it subjectively or phenomenally from the others is the 'slow dead heave of the will that is felt', the *feeling of effort*', 'the sense of *inward effort*' (p. 534). In this case, whether 'reason has balanced the books' or not, James writes:

We feel, in deciding, as if we ourselves by our own wilful act inclined the beam; in the former case by adding our living effort to the weight of the logical reason which, taken alone, seems powerless to make the act discharge; in the latter by a kind of creative contribution of something instead of a reason which does a reason's work. (p. 534)

What misleads us into thinking such effort usually accompanies decision is 'the fact that *during deliberation* we so often have a feeling of how great an effort it would take to make a decision *now*. Later, after the decision has made itself with ease, we recollect this and erroneously suppose the effort also to have been made then' (p. 535). But in contrast to this 'peculiar sort of mental phenomenon', he concludes, 'the immense majority of human decisions are decisions without effort'.

Now, although James does not, like Coleridge, explicitly refer to imagination in the processes he describes, in so far as his account of decision attempts, as it does, to disabuse us of the notion that a 'super-added "will-force"' is necessary to cause movement or end deliberation, it leaves room for the activity of imagination. It has been argued, as I noted earlier, that the *suspension* of traditional associations is precisely the task of imagination,[46] and the role of 'lapse' and 'release' in James's account suggest the element of suspension involved, an element which is reinforced by his own very Coleridgean reference, in his own discussion of 'conversion', to 'how it is when you try to recollect a forgotten name' (namely, how you need to 'give up the effort entirely').[47] In this respect we can see James's account as implying a role for imagination.[48] Moreover, there is a (Kierkegaardian-sounding) explicit reference to imagination in his discussion of 'self-surrender' conversion (as opposed to 'volitional' conversion), for one of the 'two things in the mind of the candidate for conversion' is the (albeit dim) 'imagination of . . . [a] positive ideal we can aim at'; in this 'ripening' process of 'rearrangement' it is not the 'exercise of personal will' at work, but rather an 'act of yielding', and 'it is more probably the better self *in posse* which directs the operation'.[49] James also, as we have seen above, provides some specification of this locus of imaginative activity when, qualifying a crude notion of the effort of will involved in decisions, he highlights the importance: (a) of a shift in perspective, (b) of 'finding' ourselves in the situation of having *already* made the decisive transition, and (c) of the phenomenon of 'attention'.

Independently of the question of the adequacy of these accounts by Coleridge and James of leap and volition, both accounts are suggestive and provide what, I think, can be a fruitful vantage-point for assessing accounts of religious conversion. At the very least, their emphasis on notions of yielding, suspension, sedation, and of action which is active and passive at the same time, counteracts a one-sidedly active account of leaping or volition. Second, they suggest (Coleridge directly and James

[46] See n. 5 above.

[47] *The Varieties of Religious Experience* (New York, 1982), 205.

[48] Rollo May argues that, although James succeeds in showing the bankruptcy of the Victorian notion of 'will-power', he nevertheless fails to do justice to the category of willing because he ignores the element of 'imaginative participation' which constitutes the positive movement which is effective within the context of a suspension of contradictory associations (*Love and Will*, 220). I suggest that James leaves room for that 'imaginative participation'.

[49] *The Varieties of Religious Experience*, 209–10.

indirectly) an important role for imagination in their enriched notion of the activity of leaping or volition.

Faith, Unfaith, and Transforming Vision

I turn now to some accounts of conversion, or paradigmatic 'leaps' of faith, to see what these accounts might look like, both from the vantage-point of the suggestions by Coleridge and James as well as from the perspective of one sensitized by Kierkegaard (as we were in Chapter 3) to the phenomenon of paradoxical change, transparency, and transforming transitions. I suggest that we will discover in them, even in those speci-fically addressed to Christian faith, warrant for reading the leap or decision in terms of an imaginative revisioning.

Consider the following self-description given by someone who, after serious inquiry into Christianity, judged herself to have 'done it', to have made a 'leap' of faith. She wrote:

Today, crossing from one side of the room to the other, I lumped together all I am, all I fear, hate, love, hope, and well, DID it. I committed all my ways to God in Christ.[50]

It is easy to see why the idiom of will or decision sounds appropriate—namely, to emphasize the active, free, and qualitative character of the transition. In light of the preceding, however, we can now ask how this account relates to those given by Coleridge and James: in what way might this be seen as an activity exercised through imagination; does this activity exhibit a 'yielding' dimension; is it voluntary yet without exertion of 'will-power'; does anything in the account correspond to 'attention' and to the 'suspension and sedation of association'?

The following interpretation of this account of conversion along those lines suggests itself: namely, that the lumping together of hopes and fears and loves and hates is an imaginative activity—an imaginative gathering, a synthesis and extension by imagination—which effects a reorienting shift of perspective. What the agent *did*, that is, could be understood as an imaginative gathering together of her self in which a decisive reorientation is accomplished. What she *did* was to experience a change in her 'observer's level', to see something new come into focus. The act of committing herself could be understood, not as a decision which followed upon the lumping together of her hopes and fears and loves, but

---

[50] Jean Davis Vanauken, as cited by Sheldon Vanauken in *A Severe Mercy* (San Francisco, 1977), pp. 95–6.

rather as an active recognition or affirmation of the attraction and alignment which she saw in her newly gathered self.

In Coleridge's terms, what she did was an imaginative gathering, an
active and free lumping things together in a new way which came after
disciplined, desiring inquiry (propulsion)—lumping them together in
such as way as to *see* it differently (yielding) and be changed by it.[51] In
both Coleridge's and James's terms, what she did just *was* a letting go of
hitherto accepted associations—a shift in perspective, an abrupt rise to
another level of observation, a transition which is not achievable by fiat,
but rather by imaginative synthesis and extension. The synthesis and
extension which constitute a revisioning of life are activities of imagination and can be read, not as prolegomena to a change, but as constituting
the change which alters her whole life. In other words, the description of
her 'leap' could be explained as the achievement of a new imaginative
revisioning: it is a recognition of what is implied in the perception of the
self as gathered together in this way, a reorienting shift in perspective.

On such a reading the coming to faith is the surrender of an old vision
in the activity of seeing a new way in which things can be together. Such a
seeing things together in a new way is an imaginative suspension because
it assumes an imaginative positing of counter-factuals and hypothet-
icals—for example, it involves assuming a hypothetical place (or many
such places) from which to assess what stands before us. It is not a simple
cumulative endeavour, putting together a mosaic of things already there,
the whole of which is equal to the sum of its parts. Neither, however, is it
the resolution into a higher unity, the fusion, or reduction of multitude
into unity, which, as we noted earlier, is sometimes suggested by
Coleridge's examples of imaginative synthesis. The reorganization which
takes place is a re-creation, a creative perception, which brings to mind
Coleridge's other remarks on this 'shaping spirit'.[52] For example, while it
is not a synthesis into a higher unity, it is a re-creation, a 'shaping', which
assumes the kind of suspension alluded to in Coleridge's description of
'secondary Imagination' as a power which actively 'dissolves, diffuses,
dissipates, in order to re-create'.[53] This description re-emphasizes the

---

[51] Note that the model of vision invoked here need not imply the passive and confronta-
tional ocular model of knowing which contemporary philosophers (Richard Rorty and
others) criticize; reference to 'vision' need not, as Iris Murdoch notes, imply reference to
(rightly discredited) 'inner or private psychological phenomena, open to inspection'
('Vision and Choice in Morality', in *Christian Ethics and Contemporary Philosophy*, ed. Ian
T. Ramsey (New York, 1966), 200).

[52] *Biographia Literaria*, ch. 10, 76 (esemplastic: 'shape into one'); 'Dejection: An Ode'
(1802): 'My shaping spirit of Imagination'.

[53] *Biographia Literaria*, ch. 13, 146.

role of imagination in suspending associations—sedating associations and yielding—which we saw earlier in his description of imagination as the intermediate faculty which is 'at once both active and passive'.

The letting go or surrender assumes an imaginative suspension because it is a paradoxical seeing of what is both not yet there and already there, for sometimes it is only by putting-together imaginatively what could be there that we are able to recognize what is in some sense already there. The synthesis it achieves is not the discovering of a unity which underlies all, or a reduction of multitude into unity, or a resolution of tension in a 'higher third'—but rather a putting-together-imaginatively. Moreover, such a shift in perspective arising from imaginative activity—a seeing things together differently—would be a free, qualitative transition or leap as much as any deliberate, self-conscious decision would.

The plausibility of this kind of interpretation of a description of a 'leap of faith' is supported by other autobiographical accounts of conversion. Writing movingly of his decision to leave the Anglican Church for that of Rome, one author tells how, having been 'on the brink' for a year and a half, he responds to a friend's question by a realization:

Then it came to me that perhaps I could go on drifting, but, if I faced up to decision, I could not *reject* Holy Mother Church—just as, long years before, I had realized that I could not reject Jesus. . . . if I *cannot* reject the Church—if only one way is possible—I *have* decided, haven't I?[54]

The suggestion is that the moment of choice is, as James suggested, really one of coming to see that we have already decided—that is, we *realize* that we have already become engaged with a possibility in a reorienting, hence 'decisive', way. What one calls the 'decision' is the *realization* of our decisive engagement with a possibility, the realization of how real it is for us. That we can stifle or undermine its impact on us, its power to engage us, does not show that we can or must deliberately decide to feel that power.

A similar appeal to the non-volitionalist dimension of such change is found in the various accounts of conversion experiences recorded by a very well-known convert, C. S. Lewis. In his autobiography, *Surprised by Joy*, Lewis describes a succession of 'conversions' of differing kinds. His description of one early transition is clearly in terms of a shift in perspective, a new seeing of old-yet-new: he writes that what was now

---

[54] Sheldon Vanauken, *Under the Mercy* (Nashville, Tenn., 1985), 238.

seen was in some sense exactly like the old, yet 'all was changed'.[55] Moreover, his was a sense that something was 'out of reach not because of something I could not do but because of something I could not stop doing'—more precisely, 'If I could only leave off, let go, unmake myself, it would be there'.[56] Such an affirmation of the role of letting go or yielding informs his conclusion that 'all this was given to me without asking, even without consent'.[57]

Although Lewis's account of his later and distinctively religious conversion is framed in the idiom of 'choice', his actual explication of the character of the choice reinforces the sense of it as a realization or new seeing or a shift in perspective. For example, when he writes that 'I felt myself being, there and then, given a free choice', he qualifies this significantly—'I say, "I chose", yet it did not really seem possible to do the opposite'.[58] He continues to explain: 'People talk about "man's search for God". To me, as I then was, they might as well have talked about the mouse's search for the cat.'[59] Even more dramatically, he suggests that 'it was more like when a man, after long sleep, still lying motionless in bed, becomes aware that he is now awake.'[60]

Lewis's own retrospective look, in a later interview, at his earlier descriptions also repeatedly qualifies the ordinary sense of 'decision'. To the interviewer's question, 'Do you feel that you made a decision at the time of your conversion?' Lewis responds

I would not put it that way. What I wrote in *Surprised by Joy* was that 'before God closed in on me, I was in fact offered what now appears a moment of wholly free choice'. But I feel my decision was not so important. I was the object rather than the subject in this affair. I was decided upon.[61]

The interviewer's rejoinder—'That sounds to me as if you came to a very definite point of decision'—is met by Lewis's explanation:

Well, I would say that the most deeply compelled action is also the freest action. By that I mean, no part of you is outside the action. It is a paradox. I expressed it in *Surprised by Joy* by saying that I chose, yet it really did not seem possible to do the opposite.[62]

---

[55] *Surprised by Joy* (London, 1955), 145.   [56] Ibid.
[57] Ibid. 146.   [58] Ibid. 179.
[59] Ibid. 182. Note the striking similarity of this thought to Simone Weil's suggestion that 'We do not have to search for him, we only have to change the direction in which we are looking. It is for him to search for us' (*Waiting for God*, 216).
[60] Ibid. 189.
[61] Interview 7 May, 1963, in *The Grand Miracle and Other Essays*, ed. Walter Hooper (New York, 1970), 154.   [62] Ibid.

Lewis obviously wants to preclude an understanding of the conversion as a purely passive happening, and his reference to the exercise of an activity which is at the same time compelled yet free, hence passive yet active, recalls Coleridge's view of imagination. What occurs in 'the choice' is imaginative because it is an admittedly paradoxical holding together of opposites. 'The choice' is, in sum, an abrupt shift in the 'observer's level', in and through a yielding which is voluntary and free, yet without a 'superadded "will-force"'

The conviction, expressed in the second account of conversion noted earlier, that 'only one way is possible' is surely not meant to deny the undeniable—namely, that other ways are in some sense also possible, for they are actually exemplified in the lives of others we know; it is not an expression of a compulsion which renders us unfree, but rather an expression of the way in which one possibility has decisively become 'real' for us. We cannot immediately effect that engagement by a decision by fiat. Flannery O'Connor makes the same point indirectly when she writes to a correspondent: 'I hope you'll find the experience you need to make the leap toward Christianity seem the only one to you'.[63] But a leap which 'seem[s] the only one' is surely an imaginative crystallization, a decisive engagement, rather than a selection among perceived alternatives; its seeming to be 'the only one' is thus not a denial of the possibility of other ways or of our freedom, but rather an indication of the constraint compatible with a free recognition. This, I take it, is what C. S. Lewis meant when he wrote that 'I say, "I chose"', yet it did not really seem possible to do the opposite', and commenting on that, explained that 'the most deeply compelled action is also the freest action'.[64] It is also what I take Judge William to mean when he writes that if, driven by the recognition of the contradiction in the aesthetic, we 'contemplate existence under ethical categories', we 'will see that *only* then does existence become beautiful, that *only* in this way can a man succeed in saving his soul and gaining the whole world . . .'.[65]

The model of *Gestalt* shift is relevant here because in such a case the shift in perspective occurs only when a 'critical threshold' has been reached. Initially we perceive only one option, only one is 'real' to us. Although we can be told of and admit the possibility of another option, at the critical moment of transition there is no set of equally real

[63] Flannery O'Connor, 25 July 1962, in *The Habit of Being*, letters ed. Sally Fitzgerald (New York, 1979), 485.

[64] *Surprised by Joy*, 179; *The Grand Miracle*, 154.

[65] *Either/Or*, ii. 182, emphasis mine.

alternatives which we recognize from among which to choose—the moment of transition is rather the point at which what has been an abstract possibility (one we have been assured is there) suddenly comes into focus for us, the point at which it is so real that it seems to be the only way to see it (though, of course, we can try to revive the earlier picture by an effort of refocusing). The examples I have considered suggest that this point or 'critical threshold' is what in the description of faith is often called 'the decision'.

Such a shift in perspective is, I suggest, what Iris Murdoch (attempting in ethics to replace a model of will by a model of vision) describes as a 'piecemeal' effort working up to moments where 'most of the business of choosing is already over', rather than a leap of will at a crucial moment.[66] Stanley Hauerwas, following Murdoch in affirming 'the significance of vision for the moral life', suggests that the free activity integral to moral development is neither a 'sudden leap the isolated will makes' nor an 'efficacious' assertion of will.[67] He explains his alternative in terms of a 'disciplined overcoming of the self that allows for the clarification of our vision'—he emphasizes not an act of will, but 'attention' and 'reorientation' of vision.[68] Appropriating the theme of 'attention', Hauerwas notes Murdoch's direct indebtedness to Simone Weil's thought on 'attention', but, as we noted earlier, William James too saw '*effort of attention*' as '*the essential phenomenon of will*'.[69]

Murdoch's suggestion of a 'piecemeal' effort is not contrary to the qualitative *Gestalt* shift I have been using as an analogy—this shift in perspective occurs only when a 'critical threshold' has been reached, but it cannot occur unless preliminary material is registered or processed. In this sense the shift is able to be spoken of as both continuous and discontinuous. The decision which seems necessary turns out to be the recognition or realization that we have already decided. On the one hand, it is the result of a 'piecemeal' effort without being the cumulative issue of a quantitative process and, on the other hand, the qualitatively different character of the realization is achieved without being the direct result of a momentary act of will.

[66] 'The Idea of Perfection' (1964), in *The Sovereignty of Good* (New York, 1971), 37.

[67] 'The Significance of Vision: Towards an Aesthetic Ethic', in *Vision and Virtue: Essays in Christian Theological Reflection* (Notre Dame, Ind., 1974), 36, 41.

[68] Ibid. 42.

[69] *Principles of Psychology*, ii. 562. Simone Weil's treatment of the relevant 'act of attention' is often in terms of 'looking' or changing 'the direction in which we are looking'; 'religion', she concludes, 'is nothing else but a looking' and 'looking is what saves us' (*Waiting for God*, 193, 212, 216, 199, 192).

A variety of ordinary intentional decisions may be necessary to the final realization of faith (disciplined inquiry may need to be deliberately undertaken, deliberate decisions may be necessary to put oneself in a place conducive to the shift in perspective, to focus on this rather than that), but the shift itself is an activity of imaginative revisioning. It is not a case of seeing before you leap, or leaping before you see—the new seeing *is* the leap in understanding. On such a reading the new seeing would constitute the letting go of an old seeing. I repeat, some deliberate decisions may be a necessary preliminary to the new seeing, or seem appropriate as a response to the new seeing, but it is the new seeing itself which is effectively the leap or qualitative transition. In sum, such a qualitative shift in perspective is an example of a qualitative transition which is distinguishable from a quantitative process as well as from a momentary, separable, act of will which fills a gap. In particular, the category of a 'critical threshold' seems especially suited to illuminate this kind of transition (which is not reached by degrees, yet cannot occur unless preliminary material is registered and processed) and to show why one wants to say of it both that it is continuous and discontinuous.[70]

An understanding of willing in these terms is consonant with and reinforced by the non-deliberate character of the leap found in accounts of a converse 'leap of unfaith'. One of the most famous is Tolstoy's description of a man's loss of faith. It was *not*, he insists,

because he had resolved something in his heart, but simply because this comment of his brother ['Do you still do that?' in response to his kneeling to pray] was like a finger being pushed against a wall that was on the verge of collapsing from its own weight. *These words indicated that the place where he had thought faith to be had long been empty* and that the words he spoke, the signs of the cross and genuflections he made in prayer, were essentially meaningless actions. *Having recognized their meaninglessness he could no longer continue doing them.*[71]

Similarly, in a contemporary autobiography the author not only tells us how, after reading some Catholic literature, he first 'saw the world in a new way, saw explanations where there had been frustrating mysteries and alluring mysteries where there had been unsatisfying explanations'[72]

[70] I take my position to be an elaboration which is consonant with the suggestion of both continuity and discontinuity in faith put forth by John W. Elrod in *Being and Existence in Kierkegaard's Pseudonymous Works* (Princeton, NJ, 1975), esp. 232–4. I suggest that it is also compatible with the position espoused by C. Stephen Evans in *Subjectivity and Religious Belief*, especially the conclusions on 116, 120, 123.

[71] 'A Confession' (1879), from *A Confession and Other Religious Writings*, trans. Jane Kentish (New York, 1987), 20–1, emphasis mine.

[72] Richard Gilman, *Faith, Sex, Mystery: A Memoir* (New York, 1986), 56.

(and these, unfortunately, one cannot simply choose to do), but also details the non-volitional process of the decay of that faith. Working with metaphors of faith's slipping away and dissolving, he writes of the process in which his earlier stance 'started to seem irrelevant':

> Particular beliefs became obscure, grew faint and at last vanished; urgencies melted and crumbled; attachments loosened and became undone. The world I had been inhabiting shifted and rearranged itself along a new axis.[73]

We cannot deliberately choose to make something seem irrelevant, or to make an urgency melt. Such accounts suggest, then, that in either direction, coming to or turning from faith, the qualitative transition is a new, active, and free *seeing* rather than the direct achievement of an intentional, self-conscious decision.

These accounts of conversion and these contemporary suggestions reinterpreting decision in terms of attention and reorientation illustrate the reading I have been developing of the transition to faith in the Climacus account. The discussion in Chapter 3 of choice and transparency as paradoxical transition assumed that his presentation of the qualitative difference or leap to the ethical or subjectivity can bear illuminatingly on the character of the other qualitative transitions of which he speaks, including the transition to Christian faith. The warrant there for reading his radical emphasis on choice in terms of imaginative vision is at the same time prima-facie warrant for reading his notion of the transition to faith in the same way. As I noted earlier, Climacus himself speaks of a transition to the religious in terms of both 'attention' and vision: 'only in the inwardness of self-activity, does he have his attention aroused, and is enabled to see God'.[74] Moreover, this applies to religiousness B, for the emphasis on seeing is found as well in the *Fragments*'s description of the thought experiment of Christianity and its 'condition': 'if the learner could envision the god by himself, then he himself would possess the condition', and 'the god gave the follower the condition to see it and opened for him the eyes of faith', for 'without the condition he would have seen nothing'.[75] On such a reading the surrender in faith is the surrender of an old vision in the activity of seeing a new way in which things can be together; the qualitative transition would likewise be a clarification of our vision through the disciplined effort of 'attention', a qualitative shift in perspective arising from imaginative activity.

---

[73] Gilman, *Faith, Sex, Mystery,* 228, 227.
[74] *Postscript,* 218.   [75] *Fragments,* 63, 65.

I have tried to show how the correlative attribution of 'passion' to the concept of faith highlights the role of imagination in the 'decision' and coincides with independent suggestions about the necessity of imagination for subjectivity; it also reminds us that the 'leap' need not be seen as a deliberate decision in order to guarantee its character as a free and qualitative transition. Kierkegaard's concept of a 'leap' or 'decision' can be understood in terms of at least two expressions of imaginative activity: it is both (1) a letting go in the sense of captivity or suspension of the understanding through imaginatively holding opposites in tension, and (2) a shift in perspective through the imaginative synthesis and extension (presupposing suspension) which constitutes the imaginative revisioning. A letting go can be a surrender embodying a tension between active and passive; it can be a 'recognition' that something is the case, a qualitative shift in perspective effected through an imaginative suspension in which opposites are held in tension or an imaginative suspension in which a synthesis and extension issues in a revisioning of the self and world.

5

Engagement and the Passionate Imagination

The centrality of imagination to the task of subjectivity depends, as we have seen, on the need to maintain a tension between finite and infinite in their various expressions. That tension, on Climacus's account, is the locus of passion in an existing individual and reveals passion as an instance of imaginative activity: 'it is only momentarily that the particular individual is able to realize existentially a unity of the infinite and the finite which transcends existence. This unity is realized in the moment of passion'.[1] Although no existing person can 'be in two places at the same time' (for 'he cannot be an identity of subject and object'[2]), passion is precisely what occurs when a person comes closest to that state in the experience of holding or being two elements in tension: 'When he is nearest to being in two places at the same time he is in passion; but passion is momentary, and passion is also the highest expression of subjectivity'.[3] Imagination is the central activity of subjectivity precisely because passion is 'the highest expression of subjectivity'.

What needs to be stressed at this point is that Climacus's well-known category of the 'how' (in contrast to the 'what'), although apparently less extreme than the passion which is only momentary, also emphasizes passion, and through it, imagination. The 'how' refers to passionate appropriation; it is the 'passion of the infinite' which constitutes the decisiveness of the 'how' for truth. It is, I suggest, in this emphasis on the 'how' that it becomes clear that passion is expressed, not merely in the experience of elements in imaginative tension, but in imaginative surrender through *engagement*. I shall argue in what follows that the concept of passion qualifies (and illuminates) the concept of the 'decision' or 'leap' of faith by emphasizing the way in which engagement and 'interest', which I suggest are imaginative activities, play a role in the acquisition of, or surrender in, faith. I want to examine that

---

[1] *Postscript*, 176.
[2] Ibid. 178.   [3] Ibid.

emphasis on engagement: (1) to see precisely how it qualifies the characterization of the 'decision' or role of the will in faith, and (2) to see whether it allows a way in which faith as passion and leap need not imply (as they have often been taken to imply) immunity to criticism.

PASSION AS ENGAGEMENT

In the second volume of *Either/Or*, Kierkegaard foreshadows the distinction between the 'how' and the 'what' which appears later in his writings. The representative of the ethical, Judge William, there explains the character of ethical choice: 'If you will understand me right, I should like to say that in making a choice it is not so much a question of choosing the right as of the energy, the earnestness, the pathos with which one chooses'.[4] The importance of the manner of choosing—the 'how'—is emphasized repeatedly by Climacus in the *Concluding Unscientific Postscript*. The importance of the 'how' is dramatically affirmed, for example, when he writes:

The objective accent falls on WHAT is said, the subjective accent on HOW it is said. . . . Only in subjectivity is there decisiveness, to seek objectivity is to be in error. It is the passion of the infinite that is the decisive factor and not its content, for its content is precisely itself. In this manner subjectivity and the subjective 'how' constitute the truth.[5]

The radical decisiveness of the 'how' in faith is revealed in his journal claim that 'God himself is this: *how* one involves himself with Him', for 'In respect to God, the *how* is *what*'.[6]

His justification for the decisiveness of the 'how' is suggested when he reflects in his journals that Climacus's achievement was to point out 'that the remarkable thing is that there is a How with the characteristic that when the How is scrupulously rendered the What is also given, that this is the How of "faith" '.[7] Indeed, the *Postscript* several times claims that there is a unique fit between the 'true' manner of appropriation and its object.[8] Whether or not this radical claim can be sustained, however, a less controversial and more defensible expression of his point about appropriation or engagement is found in his claim that 'objective indifference' sometimes precludes learning: 'In the case of a kind of

[4] *Either/Or*, ii. 171.
[6] *Journals*, ii. X^2 A 644, n.d. [1850], 123.
[7] Ibid. iv. X^2 A 299, n.d. [1849], 351.
[5] *Postscript*, 181.
[8] *Postscript*, 174 n., 542 n.

observation where it is requisite that the observer should be in a specific condition, it naturally follows that if he is not in this condition, he will observe nothing'.[9] The 'condition' to which he refers, without which one 'will observe nothing', is a condition of engagement, involvement, interestedness.

The importance of such engagement is expressed graphically when Kierkegaard berates so-called 'swimmers' who think that 'to leap into the water would be dreadful presumption'; he writes:

In the New Testament a Christian is understood to be a swimmer who in order to express the divine requirement proclaimed to him leaps out into the depths—that is, right out into the middle of actuality, so that he may then find out whether or not he has faith, and so that he may practice learning to be a Christian.[10]

God will not, he continues, have anything to do with 'someone who does not leap out into the deep'. Knowing how to make the movements is a far cry from actually making them in the appropriate context.[11] Moreover, one cannot wait for a guarantee or certainty of the pleasure or value of swimming as the warrant for undertaking the activity, for it can only come in the experience.

The analogy with swimming is striking, for it makes clear the indispensability of engagement to certain ways of knowing or to certain knowledge achievements. It does not, however, settle the question whether such engagement is the direct result of a one sidedly active decision to engage oneself, or is, instead, a finding-oneself-engaged, an activity which embodies a tension between passive and active. Lest we assume that the required leap must be a separable decision to engage (in swimming, for example), I want to look at examples of engagement in which it is not so easy to think of it as explicitly or deliberately willed or chosen.

Engagement as Surrender: The Role of Imagination

C. S. Lewis illustrates the non-volitional character of engagement with art. He writes, in *An Experiment in Criticism*, that 'The first demand any

---

[9] *Postscript*, 51; see also 249.

[10] *Journals*, iv. XI² A 50, n.d. [1854], 607; see also i. X¹ A 185, n.d. [1849], 314.

[11] Johannes De Silentio writes that 'I can presumably describe the movements of faith, but I cannot make them. In learning to go through the motions of swimming, one can be suspended from the ceiling in a harness and then presumably describe the movements, but one is not swimming' (*Fear and Trembling*, ed. and trans. Howard V. Hong and Edna H. Hong (Princeton, NJ, 1983), 37–8).

work of art makes upon us is surrender', insisting that 'there is no good asking first whether the book before you deserves such a surrender, for until you have surrendered you cannot possibly find out'.[12] The surrender here is a surrender *to* the work which cannot be achieved by fiat. The tension between active and passive embodied in the concept of surrender expresses itself in response which as such is both our action and dependent on the power or attraction of something outside us. The surrender is an engagement, a finding-oneself-engaged, and while it may be preceded by a deliberate decision to try to be open, it cannot be directly willed. In this it is more like an active 'recognition', than either an unconstrained choice or a passive impression made on us. Such a finding-oneself-engaged, maintaining an intrinsic tension between active and passive, is arguably an exercise of imaginative involvement.

Such engagement is also an imaginative exercise because it holds both possibility and actuality in tension. To become engaged with something is to become involved with what is both already there and not yet there; engagement with a work of art, for example, is an imaginative develop-ment of a possibility, an imaginative positing of a particular kind of relation between the object and the self. It is, in other words, the creation of a relation rather than the discovery of an antecedently existing one.

The importance of engagement and its non-volitional character are revealed even more clearly in Kierkegaard's repeated use of the analogy between faith and the passion of love. Anti-Climacus's stark and unqualified claim in *The Sickness unto Death* that 'A believer is surely a lover, yea, of all lovers the most in love' is affirmed by Climacus when he explicitly uses erotic love analogically (or metaphorically) to tell us important things about the passion he calls 'faith'.[13] Although he qualifies the analogy here and elsewhere (the metaphor is 'imperfect', 'every analogy is a fallacy', and there is no 'perfect earthly analogy' for the relationship between God and human),[14] its repeated use shows it to be a crucial pedagogical tool. Its character as passion can importantly contour an understanding of the import of the passion (and the 'decision') of faith, for love, I suggest, is constituted by a surrender through engagement which is not the result of a deliberate decision— although it may be cultivated or stifled by deliberate decision.

---

[12] Cambridge, 1961, 19.
[13] *Sickness unto Death*, 234; *Fragments*, 30, 48–9; *Postscript*, 35–6, 52, 205, 371, 407–8, 454.
[14] *Fragments*, 48; *Postscript*, 529; *Fragments*, 25. The disanalogies are pointed out in *Postscript*, 51, 407 n., 454–5, 511, 542 n.

The passion of love is both constituted by, and embedded in a context of, surrender. The openness without which love cannot occur is not itself part of love, but a necessary condition of it. Love itself involves an initial surrender—coming to love someone is a becoming-engaged-with or a being-attracted-by which is already a leaping or letting go. Because one can stifle or resist this surrender or engagement, however, the continuance in love involves a further surrender, a deliberate affirmation and celebration of the initial surrender—in other words, a deliberate commitment to the experienced love. This too is a leap, a risk-taking. It is constrained though not compelled by the initial surrender in the sense that the latter depends on the quality of the former—one surrenders to the initial surrender. Both kinds of surrender, then, involve a leap, a risking, but the role of the 'will' in each, the kind of action in each, is not the same—the second surrender is a 'decision' in a way that the first is not. There is an important asymmetry in the roles of the will before, in, and after, the initial surrender—one can deliberately prepare for, stifle, or cultivate what one cannot deliberately create.

This suggestion can be refined by reference to Margaret A. Farley's analysis of love and interpersonal commitment.[15] On Farley's model there are both active and passive dimensions to the 'emotion' of love—which emotion I have called the initial, non-deliberate surrender. The active aspect is the 'affirming and unifying', which is what we *do* when we love; the passive is the aspect of response.[16] 'My loving affirmation of you', she writes, 'is, then, a *responding* as well as a *uniting affirmation*. . . . Love, therefore, is simultaneously passion and action, receiving and giving.'[17] But this combination of passion and action is still part of the 'spontaneous response to what is perceived as lovable'—it is, she insists, *not* a 'matter of free choice'.[18] That is, the non-deliberate commitment has both passive and active dimensions; even though it is not merely passive, it is not a deliberate selection among alternatives either. The activity of free choice, the deliberate selection, is a different kind of activity and comes into play in a variety of ways: for example, before we love we can choose to attend to particular possibilities for love; moreover, 'once a love exists' we can choose to affirm it or 'take responsibility' for it, and then choose to 'cultivate' and 'discipline' the love to which we have committed ourselves.[19]

Robert Solomon's more recent analysis of romantic love illustrates the

---

[15] *Personal Commitments: Beginning, Keeping, Changing* (San Francisco, 1986).
[16] Ibid. 31.   [17] Ibid. 32.
[18] Ibid.   [19] Ibid. 32–3.

difficulty of doing justice to the complexity of the active and passive dimensions of the emotion.[20] His work reacts (as we noted in Chapter 1) against a one-sidedly passive view of love, and his descriptions are meant to remind us how much we are actively responsible for with respect to what we call 'falling in love'. It is especially relevant to the question at hand, because his counter-proposal is, in a nutshell, that 'Love is a leap rather than a fall' (p. 125).

The love which Solomon is delineating is 'romantic love', and the 'decision' he refers to is also spoken of as 'personal *choice*'; such 'choice' is both central in and 'definitive' of romantic love (pp. 44, 46). His dissatisfaction with the metaphor of 'falling' in love derives, he says, from the way that metaphor can suggest that love is 'a misstep or a lucky accident'; the metaphor of 'falling', Solomon argues, distorts and obscures an understanding of the phenomenon in two ways: first, it ignores 'the extent to which love turns on a decision (or several decisions)', and second, it ignores the 'extensive preparation for this sudden experience' (p. 125). I suggest, however, that while it is certainly a mistake worthy of correction to see coming to love as 'a misstep or a lucky accident', the corrective to such a view is not necessarily found in the contrasting metaphor of a leap, for that calls to mind a number of equally misleading pictures. It calls to mind, for example, the sort of 'will-power' leap described and ridiculed by Climacus—the kind of activity where we shut our eyes, hold our breath, grab ourselves by the neck, and . . . behold ourselves on the other side.[21] That is, the metaphor in Solomon's counter-proposal—that love is a 'leap' rather than a 'fall'—can equally distort and obscure. I suggest that we need to avoid both sorts of misunderstanding in judging the role of decision and will in love, and ultimately, in faith.

What is insightful about Solomon's analysis can best be retrieved by considering in detail both the sorts of thing he sees at stake in arguing for the centrality of decision or choice, and the sorts of description he gives of love. His characterization of the feature of 'choice' or 'decision' which, in addition to sexuality and equality, is distinctive of such love includes the following information. It means, at the very least, that such love is 'spontaneous and voluntary, a matter of will and not just circumstances' (p. 43). Spontaneity, he reminds us, 'does not mean passivity', for 'it is always our choice' (p. 47). Moreover, since it is an emotion (as opposed to a 'feeling'), 'love, like all emotions, is a product of the will' (p. 78).

---

[20] *About Love: Reinventing Romance for Our Times*; further parenthetical page references in this section will be to this work.
[21] *Postscript*, 91.

The kind of activity involved, however, and the content of being a 'matter of will' and a 'product of the will', are importantly contoured by a variety of recognitions also included in his characterization. Love is, whatever else it may be, an 'emotion', and as such it is, presumably, only as much and in the same way a 'product of the will' as are other emotions like anger or fear. What he means by the claim that it is a 'product of the will' must also be reconcilable with his own admission that it can appear 'unannounced, suddenly' (p. 46). Moreover, such love, he says, is a 'form of intelligence, a set of judgements, a way of seeing the world' (p. 78); it is 'first of all a new way of looking at the world' (p. 126). All of these qualify the sense of 'choice' or 'decision' involved.

His claim that it is a way of seeing is a particularly important qualification, and one not always duly appreciated by Solomon. For example, he follows the claim that 'falling in love is a decision' with the explication that: 'Sometimes it is a gradual series of decisions—the decision to stick around till the end of the party, the decision to stay in town for another six months, the decision to "give it a try" for a year or two. Sometimes, at its most spectacular, falling in love is a mutual, explicit decision' (p. 127). The sense of 'decision' in 'the decision to stick around till the end of the party' is quite straightforward, and there is no question that falling in love may depend on that kind of decision, or many of them— but that kind of decision (whether a gradual series of them or a single striking one) does not account in the same way for our seeing the world in a new way. We can decide to stay longer at a party in a way that we cannot decide to see the world differently. So Solomon is entirely correct in arguing that when we choose to interpret our relationship 'in terms of an endless future instead of for the time being' we are actively and freely doing something, rather than passively and without deliberate preparation. But to call 'falling in love' and 'deciding to stay later at a party' equally a 'decision' is to mislead, for we do not do the same kind of thing in the two cases. Choosing to see our relationship in a particular way is better understood on the model of actively (and attentively) coming to see ourselves and the world differently, than on the model of deciding by fiat to see something in a particular new way. And if we take away the qualification 'by fiat' and emphasize the preparation and cultivation which precede the experience of the emotion, we have shifted away from the direct, discrete activity which characterizes a decision like the one to stay later at a party.

In sum, what is correct and important in Solomon's understanding of the role of 'decision' in the emotion of love is misrepresented because—

presumably to emphasize the fact that they are both active—he uses the same word for quite different kinds of activity. His claim, however, that the emotion of love is a 'decision' or 'product of the will' only obscures our understanding when he does not even attempt to distinguish between different loci of decision, or different senses of decision.

Another example of how Solomon does not sufficiently appreciate the import of his claim that love is a way of seeing the world is found in the following comment. With the general aim of showing the responsible active 'choice' involved, Solomon writes that 'we *look* for romantic love, or it "finds us" in the most unexpected of places' (p. 44). In the light of the claim that love is a set of judgements or way of seeing the world, this sentence can reveal something important about Solomon's analysis. The effect of the two purported characterizations of the emotion is subtly manipulated: the use of scare quotation-marks for 'finds us' mitigates or qualifies its force; the phrase '*look* for' is in bold face and without scare quotation-marks and so is apparently put forth, by contrast, straight-forwardly. What is misleading about the sentence is that at the same time as the disjunctive 'or' gives the appearance of two equivalent or alter-native expressions, a significant asymmetry is proposed, and the emphasis and validity are located on the side of active choice. But what 'finds us' is a very apt and straightforward expression for what is implied in his own claim that love is 'first of all a new way of looking at the world' (p. 126), and if one emphasizes that instead one gets a different sense of how 'looking for' love fits into the picture. That is, what we do in *looking for* a new way of looking at the world may well be different from what we do when we come to see it newly. Looking *for* something is a 'product of will' in a different sense than is coming to see something in a new way. We can choose to look *for* what we cannot choose to see; looking *at* the world in a new way cannot be achieved by the same kind of decision which effects a looking *for* a new way of seeing.[22]

In other words, although we can make ourselves look, we cannot make ourselves see. We can choose to attend carefully, hopefully, and then we may come to see something differently, a new vision may 'find us'—the two activities are not equivalents or alternatives, but successive activities. We can, of course, choose to try to see something as X, to 'look for' X (where we presently only see Y), and maybe with enough effort and attention we will come to see it as X. But we can't choose to see X or

---

[22] It is important to distinguish here between Solomon's concept of 'looking for' and that 'looking' advocated by Simone Weil; Weil specifically contrasts her view of attentive looking with an act of will (*Waiting for God*, 193–5).

to see something as X (if we now see only Y) the way we can choose to stay later at a party or to 'give it a try for a year or two', and it is surely a mistake to conflate the two senses of decision.

Any attempt to do justice to the importance of the cultivation and preparation without which one usually would not fall in love must also account for the fact that the preparation does not automatically result in the desired emotion—no matter how intense the preparation, the experience of the emotion cannot be guaranteed. Solomon wants to highlight, rightly, not only our active choice in the preparation for falling in love, but also our responsible activity in the very shift from seeing ourselves as, say, a couple of sexual companions to seeing ourselves as lovers. The way to do that, however, is not to make that shift identical to a decision of the sort one makes when one decides to stay later at a party. We simply do not have the same kind of direct control over the occurrence of the shift as we have over the preparation. The shift that occurs in love is crucially like the transition (as imaginative revisioning) Kierkegaard is at pains to elucidate—in both cases I suggest that the continuity and discontinuity which are inherent in the notion of a critical threshold can do justice both to the importance of our active preparation for the transition and its free and qualitative non-volitional character as a shift in perspective.

Moreover, Solomon's analysis contains an element which significantly supports my account of different loci and senses of decision—namely, his position on the role and relevance of imagination. He rightly recognizes that love involves a 'redefinition of personal identity in terms of the other person' (p. 193), and that 'finding the other attractive . . . has much to do with the way we envision—or would like to envision—ourselves' (p. 150). 'Falling in love', he suggests, 'is almost entirely a matter of looking forward, of envisioning the future, of becoming rather than being'; the importance of such a 'lavish use of the imagination' explains why 'the most imaginative people love the best' (pp. 160–1). The mutual discovery of the other and of the self at the same time, of which he makes much (p. 148), is effectively a description of the activity of imaginative exploration. An appreciation of the role of imaginative activity in interpreting a relationship differently or seeing the world (and self) in a new way makes it clear that such interpretation (however much it is an activity for which we are responsible) is not a 'product of will' in the same way as is the decision to stay later at a party.

This consideration of Solomon's account reveals that the way in which an emotion like love is a 'product of the will' is a complex one. I have been suggesting that Kierkegaard's dual attribution of 'leap' and 'passion' to faith (with its implied mutual correction) is an attempt to do justice to an analogous complexity. Solomon's preference for the metaphor of 'leaping' to the metaphor of 'falling' assumes a contrast between leap and fall which is thus challenged by Kierkegaard. An explicit challenge is posed by a remark in his journals, where in the context of a series of thoughts on motion and transition, he writes: 'Here is the leap. Therefore, man's walking is a falling'.[23] It is relevant to note, by the way, that in the *Fragments* a similar reference to the scientifically validated fact that 'the human act of walking . . . is a continuous falling' is used to illustrate how habit can obscure things—that is, just as we do not see that we are really falling when we are walking, so we do not notice and fully appreciate the passion of thought seeking its own downfall because it is so 'fundamentally present everywhere in thought'.[24] His reference to scientists in this passage suggests that the falling in question is the effect of the gravitational pull, the falling is the unimpeded following of a natural impulse—we, like thought, seek our downfall. But it is interesting that in his journals he connects this falling to the leap. And what he does *not* say is also revealing—that is, he does not say that walking is a striving against falling or that walking is an active effort not to fall or that walking is the antidote to falling. He says that the walking *is* the falling, and implies that the falling *is* the walking. The implication is that once again a dichotomy between active and passive is transcended, and I am reminded of Coleridge's description of 'what we do when we leap'—for Coleridge too, as we saw in Chapter 4, highlights the yielding involved, and claims that the active and passive motions are mediated by a faculty (namely, Imagination) which is 'at once both active and passive'.

There are two levels of surrender or leap in love (or faith), then, and it is a misunderstanding to read the former as if it were the latter. One should, instead, speak of a non-deliberate commitment followed by a deliberate one or of a spontaneous surrender followed by a deliberate one. The spontaneous surrender or non-deliberate commitment is not entirely passive (as is a feeling); it is an imaginative engagement rather than a passive impression made on us. The passion, in other words, is not purely passive, but neither should it be spoken of as a 'decision' on the model of the deliberate activity directed to influencing the experienced love or committing oneself to it. That Kierkegaard speaks of faith as both passion and leap is an indication of the mutually correcting character of

---

[23] *Journals*, iii. V C 6, n.d. [1844], 18.
[24] *Fragments*, 37.

the concepts—an indication that the spontaneous, non-deliberate surrender is nevertheless active and free.

Like the initial falling in love, a renewal of love is to be distinguished
from a deliberate commitment to the love. Renewal of love too can be
seen in terms of imaginative engagement. In the face of a loss, or the
threat of loss, of the original vision, Farley explains, 'the way to keep our
love alive is to try to keep seeing', to ' "attend" more carefully, more
consistently—as we heighten our capacity to see'.[25]

The importance of 'attention' or 'attending' is pointed to not only in
the writings of Simone Weil, as many have noted, but also, as noted in
chapters 2 and 4, in the psychological studies by William James. In his
Principles of Psychology (1890) he writes that 'effort of attention' is the
'essential phenomenon of will'.[26] Arguing against the 'common prejudice
that voluntary action without "exertion of will-power" is Hamlet with
the prince's part left out',[27] and stressing the relevance of attending,
James effectively supports Farley's conclusion that remaining faithful to
a love involves decision, but that 'decision in this sense is not just an
appeal within me to my "will-power" '; rather, she insists, 'the key is
more in my imagination than in my will'.[28]

'Remembering', Farley continues, 'is a way of growing into vision and
love'—remembering nourishes commitments.[29] In an essay on 'passion',
Roberto Unger gives expression to a similar understanding of the
renewal of love by reference to its converse. He writes: 'Indifference is the
waning of the power to imagine the other: the giving up of the added
effort, of the heightened availability, required to recognize his originality'.[30] A passion like love must be renewed, but renewing a passion is
not achievable by fiat. A marriage can be maintained by a decision,
commitment to the structure and acts of love can be maintained by a
decision, but the love cannot be directly renewed by fiat. The meaning-
fulness of any such 'duty' which we assume by the vows of marriage can
only refer to being enjoined to make such efforts at 'growing into vision
and love'.

Kierkegaard's discussion of faith in the *Postscript* in terms of
'decision' and its renewal[31] is understandable in terms of initial surrender
and the renewing of love which he speaks of earlier in the same work.

---

[25] *Personal Commitments*, 54. Although Solomon too is sensitive to the importance of
'attention', he seems to see the ability to choose to attend as equivalent to the ability to
choose to see—I have argued they are not identical.

[26] *Principles of Psychology*, ii. 562.　　　　　　　　　　　　　　　[27] Ibid. 526.

[28] *Personal Commitments*, 48.　　　　　　　　　　　　　　　　　[29] Ibid. 57.

[30] *Passion: An Essay on Personality*, 232.　　　　　　　　　　[31] *Postscript*, 277.

Inwardness, Climacus writes, 'consists in loving one and the same woman, and yet being constantly renewed in the same love, making it always new in the luxuriant flowering of the mood'.[32] The role of imagination—imaginative cultivation and 'seeing-as'—in such 'making it always new' seems clear, and although we can certainly try to be more imaginative, we do not always succeed, and when we do succeed it is never directly achieved by fiat.

In sum, even though deliberate decision can be said to be involved before, during, and after the transition to love, the transition itself is more a matter of imaginative engagement than of 'will-power'. The importance to Kierkegaard of the analogy with love, along with the claim that faith *is* a passion, suggest that he saw the leap in faith as more a matter of a transition through imaginative engagement than of 'will-power'. Deliberate decision can play a role first in terms of setting up preliminary conditions, or putting oneself in a suitable context, doing whatever is necessary to allow the imaginative shift to occur. Second, deliberate choice can be used to stifle those things that would prevent the occurrence of the imaginative shift. Third, it can play a subsequent role, in terms of a deliberate commitment to the non-deliberate imaginative engagement or surrender (love or faith) after its occurrence, in part by choosing to stifle what militates against the commitment. (One could, of course, also deliberately choose to cultivate what militates against the experienced surrender.) Deliberate decision, then, can be said to play a role in the acquisition of faith (and this emphasizes the freedom, responsibility, and activity involved), but what occurs at the moment of acceptance is not a volition, but rather a shift in perspective, an engagement or surrender, which is the achievement of imagination.

Interest and Decision

Such an understanding of transition ('will' or 'decision') in terms of engagement is, I suggest, supported by the way in which the concept of 'interest' functions in various Kierkegaardian accounts of subjectivity. The Climacus account of the importance of 'interest' applies in general: one's 'interest in his existence constitutes his reality'; subjectivity is being 'infinitely interested'.[33] The entire contrast between subjectivity and objectivity in the *Postscript* revolves around 'interest' (what I have been speaking of above as engagement)—abstract thought and reflection are

---

[32] Ibid. 232.   [33] Ibid. 279, 55.

both described as 'disinterested'.[34] Moreover, the centrality of interest applies *a fortiori* to Christian faith—'faith itself is the infinite interest in Christianity'.[35] While the connection between 'passion' and 'interest' is obvious, I want to suggest in addition that the concept of 'interest' can illuminate the relation between imagination and will in decision. This means showing first that the concept of 'interest' is tied to imaginative activity, and second that the concept of 'interest' is related to that of will in such a way that it (rather than deliberate volition) is intended by reference to the will. A reference to decision, choice, or will, would, on this account, be a way of referring to 'interested' appropriation or 'decisive interest'.

Choice or decision cannot be understood apart from interests, and what we are interested in is what we have become engaged with or attracted by. But as we saw earlier, such engagement is an imaginative exercise. What interests us is not what is absolutely other, but what is *inter-esse*, between us, or more precisely, what is *seen-as* between us.[36] Any relation, as such, is constituted imaginatively: elements are put into relation; the relation is given by imagination in the activity of holding elements in tension. Interest is passionate precisely because of that tension between possibility and reality—'knowledge' and 'abstract thought' are 'disinterested' precisely because the tension has been removed, with reality being turned one sidedly into possibility.[37] Choice or decision, then, cannot be understood apart from interest, but even more strongly, we could say that choice may just be the decisive engagement or attraction—the one that wins out by decisively engaging or attracting us—and thus be understood in terms of the activity of imagination.

Judge William's understanding of choice assumes that there is no such thing as a neutral 'instant of deliberation'—we are always 'already interested'[38] or attracted. There is no moment in which one fails to stand in a relationship to the things between which one is to choose: 'to think that for an instant one can keep one's personality a blank, or that strictly speaking one can break off and bring to a halt the course of the personal life, is a delusion'.[39] It is a 'delusion', he continues, because 'the per-

---

[34] *Postscript*, 302, 350; he writes that 'Reflection is *disinterested*', contrasting it with 'consciousness' which 'is the relation and thereby is interest' (*Johannes Climacus*, 170).

[35] *Postscript*, 23.   [36] Ibid., 279.

[37] Ibid. See also *Concept of Anxiety*, where he notes that 'Constantin Constantius . . . point[ed] out that immanence runs aground upon 'interest'. With this concept, actuality for the first time properly comes into view' (21 n.).

[38] *Either/Or*, ii. 167, 168.   [39] Ibid. 168.

sonality is already interested in the choice before one chooses'[40]—this conclusion exhibits the recognition that the possibilities which reveal themselves to us are in part constituted by our prior investment of the world with particular values. Climacus likewise speaks of the way in which possibilities are not merely neutral—there is a 'twilight' area between thought and action such that we can have a 'possibility in which the interest of action and of reality already reflects itself' because 'reality and responsibility reach out to lay hold of' and disturb the 'disinterested-ness' of thought.[41]

Such an understanding is elaborated by Iris Murdoch's emphasis on the 'slow and delicate processes of imagination and will' which inform our world with value, so that 'when moments of decision arrive we see and are attracted by the world we have already (partly) made'.[42] When the moment of choice arrives, what is called for is not an extrinsic decision, but a realization of what we have been attracted to, that is, what we have been deciding. Her understanding of the role of imagination in informing our world with values prior to the moment of decision and her rejection of the possibility of 'pure' (uncontextualized) willing in 'decision' thus echo Judge William's and Climacus's characterization and qualification of 'choice'.

Judge William writes that 'through the choice the personality immerses itself in the thing chosen'.[43] This can be read in two ways— either the immersion is seen as the subsequent result of a prior and separable choice or the immersion is seen as what constitutes the choice. Choice, on this latter view, just is becoming decisively interested. It is allowing one interest or attraction to win out, to take precedence, i.e., to engage us decisively. But to say that will can be understood in terms of *letting* an attraction win out, of affirming or validating that particular attraction rather than another, is to say that its activity is one of *affirmation or active recognition* rather than a selection through 'will-power' from what are perceived as equally real alternatives.

This implication of being already attracted or being already interested is what I take Margaret A. Farley to refer to when she writes that in free choice 'we already see the reasons and are already leaning into the desires before we choose . . . Choice is, therefore, my *ratification* of one desire (rather than its alternative), my allowing *this* desire (rather than its opposing alternatives) to issue in action'.[44] She explains: in free choice

---

[40] Ibid.   [41] *Postscript*, 302.
[42] 'The Darkness of Practical Reason', 49–50; 49.
[43] *Either/Or*, ii. 167.   [44] *Personal Commitments*, 27.

there is an 'internal "action" of our mind and heart' in which 'I, so to speak, "identify" with one desire and the action which is its object, and I "let go of", the others . . .'.[45] Climacus carries on the theme of imaginative engagement with a possibility when he speaks similarly of 'real action' in terms of an 'internal decision in which the individual puts an end to the mere possibility and identifies himself with the content of his thought in order to exist in it'.[46] The notion of 'identification with' a desire or thought content calls to mind the idea of imaginative activity more than it calls to mind the idea of deliberate volition: we talk of identifying with a person when we are so attracted by something about them that we feel 'one' with them or when we sympathetically imagine ourselves in their place. Such 'identification with' someone is an imaginative extension, or an imaginative transcending of 'otherness', which is not capable of being effected by fiat. We find ourselves identifying with a person or a cause; we cannot simply choose to 'identify with' them in any but a most external sense. That is, we can deliberately identify ourselves as attracted to or sympathetic with them (we can announce our allegiance or put our name on a membership roster), but we do that only *because* we have already identified with (become attracted or interested by, engaged with) their goals, desires, values, etc. Thus, seeing choice or decision in terms of 'identification with' would both emphasize the role of imagination in human activity and preclude a radical separation or contrast between will and imagination. This would go far towards explaining why Kierkegaard could, as we saw earlier, without explanation or apology, put 'imagination' in the place which he sometimes fills with 'will'.

This difficulty in radically contrasting will and imagination would also explain why Murdoch could write that once we admit the active character of imagination as 'exploring', it is 'difficult not to see this as an exercise of will'.[47] It would explain why Farley could write that the 'radical decision' involved in choosing to remain faithful to a love is 'not just an appeal within me to my "will-power". It is the recognition that there are certain ways I cannot allow myself to *think*. The key is more in my imagination than in my will'.[48]

Kierkegaard's understanding of the concept of 'imagination' implies a development in the understanding of the concept of 'will' similar to what

---

[45] *Personal Commitments*, 27.
[46] *Postscript*, 302.
[47] Murdoch, 'The Darkness of Practical Reason', 48.
[48] *Personal Commitments*, 48.

Josef Pieper describes as an 'enlarged concept of will'.[49] Here an act of will is not seen as a decision to act; a volition does not mean merely a will to act. Willing is not seen simply as the faculty of bringing about what does not yet exist—a causal faculty of bringing objects into existence—but rather willing is seen in terms of wanting, affirming, loving something that already exists.[50] In this sense will returns to its more classical sense of being the faculty of desire. Will is seen, as for Aristotle and Aquinas, as rational appetite or desire. Such affirmation or loving is another way of speaking about the engagement, attraction, interestedness which I have been suggesting is integral to an understanding of decision and willing.

ENGAGEMENT AND CRITICAL APPRAISAL

Having examined how imagination can function in the surrender through engagement that constitutes faith, I want to address the question whether such a notion implies immunity to critical appraisal. The criticism of Kierkegaard that there is about him 'something of the conviction that it is more important to be sincere and authentic than right'[51] is a commonly echoed one. More often than not, it is a response to claims in the Climacus writings about the indispensability and decisive relevance of 'passion'. The inference often drawn from his well-known emphasis on the 'how' (in contrast to the 'what') is that passion is a sufficient criterion of truth, and since 'faith' is, he says, a 'passion', a 'happy passion', the conclusion is that faith is, on this account, immune to criticism. My question, then, is whether the emphasis on passion precludes (or is necessarily meant to preclude) the possibility of critical appraisal.

Passion and the Possibility of Criticism

Even though Kierkegaard makes the strong claim at times that the 'how' constitutes the truth,[52] the importance of the 'how' is nevertheless crucially qualified in his works. That the 'how' is not in opposition to the 'what' is clear from the *Postscript*'s assertion that both are necessary: 'Precisely as important as the truth, and if one of the two is to be emphasized, still more important, is the manner in which the truth is

---

[49] *Belief and Faith* (New York, 1963), 30.
[50] Simone Weil likewise suggests that religion 'corresponds to desire, and it is desire that saves' (*Waiting for God*, 195).
[51] Lynch, *Images of Faith: An Exploration of the Ironic Imagination*, 81.
[52] *Postscript*, 181.

accepted'.[53] Given his audience, it is obvious which of the two he feels the need to emphasize. Nevertheless, each is 'precisely as important' as the other; the passionate 'how' is not a sufficient criterion of truth.

The common criticism noted above that for Kierkegaard 'it is more important to be sincere and authentic than right', so often supported by reference to the *Postscript*, thus loses its force when we recognize the *Postscript*'s attribution of equal importance to 'the truth' and 'the manner in which the truth is accepted.' This criticism is also belied by Kierkegaard's non-pseudonymous commitment to the ideal unity of the two—for example, in his 1850 journal he explains: 'The difficulty of my task is that I do indeed say: On the whole, the doctrine as it is taught is entirely sound. Consequently that is not what I am contending for. My contention is that something should be done with it'.[54] Here too Kierkegaard seems well aware of the crucial difference between a necessary and a sufficient condition.

From a different direction light is shed on the relevance of passion to critical appraisal in Judge William's account of choice and commitment. In a passage noted earlier, he crucially qualifies his claim about the import of the manner of choosing: 'If you will understand me aright, I should like to say that in making a choice it is not so much a question of choosing the right as of the energy, the earnestness, the pathos with which one chooses.' That is, he cautions that his claim must be understood 'aright', and the right understanding is suggested in a crucial sentence often ignored by readers who either glory in or deplore the emphasis on the 'how'; in that sentence Judge William tells us that because in the manner of choice 'the personality announces its inner infinity' and is 'consolidated', so the manner of choice has implicit critical potential: 'Therefore, even if a man were to choose the wrong, he will nevertheless discover, precisely by reason of the energy with which he chose, that he had chosen the wrong'.[55]

Note not only the reference to recognizing we have chosen 'the wrong', but also the phrase 'precisely by reason of the energy with which he chose'. It makes the eminently plausible suggestion that the more

---

[53] *Postscript*, 221.

[54] *Journals*, vi. X^3 A 635, n.d. [1850], 362. It is interesting to note here how Ludwig Wittgenstein's allusions to Kierkegaard distort him in some respects; in a series of comments ending with an explicit reference to Kierkegaard, Wittgenstein writes: 'I believe that one of the things Christianity says is that sound doctrines are all useless. That you have to change your *life*' (*Culture and Value*, ed. G. H. Von Wright, trans. Peter Winch (Oxford, 1980), 53e). Kierkegaard's emphasis on practice clearly does not imply that 'sound doctrines are all useless'.   [55] *Either/Or*, ii. 171.

wholeheartedly one chooses, or is engaged in the choice, the more likely one is to discover that one is wrong, *if* one is wrong. The reason, presumably, is that the more earnestly one follows through on one's choice, the more one is engaged with potential sources of disconfirmation as well as confirmation. Passionate adherence is not treated here as a quicksand from which no escape is possible—one can discover that one is in error. Lack of partiality does not require disinterestedness; interestedness does not preclude modifying one's position. Just as one misunderstands the judge if one thinks that his emphasis on the 'energy' or 'earnestness' of the choice implies that the content of the choice is irrelevant or that the choice is immune to critical appraisal, so too one misunderstands the relevance of the 'how' if one thinks that one should opt for the 'how' rather than the 'what', or that the 'how' is sufficient.

The importance, therefore, of the 'how' is in part to preclude a continued commitment to a wrong choice. That faith is a passion thus need not imply its uncriticizability. Just as surrender to a work of art is necessary if we are to be fair in our appraisal of it, so too surrender might be necessary in the case of a belief, if we are to be able to appreciate what might be correct or incorrect in it. In the discussion by C. S. Lewis referred to earlier, we saw that his critical injunction—'We must use our eyes. We must look, and go on looking till we have certainly seen exactly what is there'—is followed by the reminder that '[t]he first demand any work of art makes upon us is surrender'.[56] He insists, as we saw earlier, that only such surrender allows the possibility of honest or fair criticism: 'There is no good asking first whether the book before you deserves such a surrender, for until you have surrendered you cannot possibly find out'.[57] He makes Kierkegaard's point when he writes that, for example, we can only honestly find a book 'bad' by imaginatively surrendering to it: 'If you already distrust the man you are going to meet, everything he says or does will seem to confirm your suspicions. We can find a book bad only by reading it as if it might, after all, be very good'.[58] Kierkegaard had similarly suggested through Judge William that we can only find out we are wrong if we plunge in wholeheartedly.

The point that lukewarm, tentative holding at arm's length means we shall never learn, or learn only much later than necessary, whether we are 'wrong' is made as well in *Sickness Unto Death* where the self-correcting potential within venturing is affirmed: 'by not venturing, it is so dreadfully easy to lose that which it would be difficult to lose in even the most

---

[56] *An Experiment in Criticism*, 18–19.
[57] Ibid. 19.   [58] Ibid. 116.

venturesome venture. . . . For if I have ventured amiss—very well, then life helps me by its punishment. But if I have not ventured at all—who then helps me?'[59] To hold back, to choose half heartedly, to be too cautious to risk the full choice, makes it more difficult (if not impossible) to discover one's error, that one has 'ventured amiss'. In a variety of ways, and through different authorial voices, Kierkegaard makes the radical suggestion that half-way engagement is, for this reason, intellectually dishonest. It clouds the issue, preventing genuine confrontation and hence preventing genuine resolution: as with Christianity in general, 'the half has the very opposite effect of the whole'.[60]

It should be clear, then, that, contrary to popular (mis)readings of Kierkegaard's recommendation of whole-hearted engagement, it need not be meant to guarantee that one will continue in the choice no matter what—rather, it may be meant to guarantee that one will be able to experience fully what is implied by the choice (i.e., genuinely confronting the experience in question with other experiences) and that one will find out sooner whether the choice was right or wrong. In this sense then, imaginative engagement provides the critical potential for corroboration and disconfirmation.

None of this is meant to downplay or disregard Kierkegaard's own very adamant cautions about the relation of understanding to faith. The suggestion that passionate surrender will help you to find out if you are wrong implies the possibility of critical appraisal. It takes very seriously, nevertheless, Kierkegaard's firm denial that faith issues from understanding. It takes seriously too his warning against considering Christian faith a 'provisional function', like those faiths which are necessary if we are finally to understand a given theory.[61]

These strictures being duly noted, however, my proposal concerning the limits of the bearing and import of the 'how' seems necessary to make sense of his talk about 'right' and 'wrong'; if passion were a sufficient criterion of truth, such references would be meaningless. We have seen Climacus's awareness of the distinction between necessary and sufficient conditions, and his affirmation of the ideal unity of the 'how' and the 'what'—it would seem the wiser hermeneutical procedure to take his references to 'right' and 'wrong' at face value and reinterpret in the light of them his references to the lack of 'reasons' for choice.[62] Moreover, the

---

[59] *Sickness unto Death*, 167.

[60] *Journals*, iii. XI² A 385, n.d. [1854–5], 178.

[61] *Postscript*, 539, also 209.

[62] Alasdair MacIntyre adopts a perverse hermeneutical procedure when he criticizes Kierkegaard for inconsistency in this respect: 'The choices made by the individual confront-

claim that we can, while passionately believing, discover that we have 'chosen the wrong' not only fits with references to finding 'the right', it is what one would expect to follow from the claim that the understanding is 'not annihilated'.[63] Let us consider now ways in which the understanding plays a role.

In general we can say that although he clearly rejects the notion of 'faith seeking understanding' in the sense of seeing imaginative suspension and engagement as stepping-stones to an ultimate understanding or explanation of the paradox, he would certainly agree that we can come to a deeper appreciation of the character of our religious commitment. This is the point, I think, of his contrast in the *Point of View* between the scorned 'impulse to go farther *than* becoming a Christian' and the legitimate 'impulse to go farther *in* becoming a Christian'.[64] Moreover, Haufniensis's reminder about different kinds or levels of understanding—namely, that 'to understand and to understand are two things'[65]—seems to inform such a view; 'inwardness', he affirms, 'is an understanding, but *in concreto*, the important thing is how this understanding is to be understood', for 'to understand a speech is one thing, and to understand what it refers to, namely, the person, is something else'.[66] The paradox can never be understood in the sense of being 'explained' or resolved in any objective sense,[67] but on the other hand, Kierkegaard speaks of explanation in quite a different tone when, in the *Point of View*, he contrasts 'misunderstanding' and 'an over-hasty explanation' with 'the true explanation [which] is at hand and ready to be found by him who honestly [and with the 'requisite seriousness'] seeks it'.[68] In this sense, at least, the understanding is 'not annihilated'.

But Climacus even more explicitly affirms the illegitimacy of a rejection of the understanding when he writes:

It is easy enough to leap away from the toilsome task of developing and sharpening the understanding . . . and to defend oneself against every accusation

ing the alternatives of the ethical and the aesthetic, or the ethical and the religious, are, according to Kierkegaard, criterionless. But if this were genuinely so, how could it be right to choose one rather than the other?' (*A Short History of Ethics* (New York, 1966), 218). I suspect that given his recent conclusions about the 'imaginative conceptual innovation' and imaginative extension which occur in transitions to new frameworks (*Whose Justice? Which Rationality?* (Notre Dame, Ind., 1988), 362, 394–5), he might well retract this view of the implications of 'criterionless' transition.

[63] 'He who deeply and sincerely is in doubt of it on his own behalf will surely find the right', *Either/Or*, ii. 173; *Fragments*, 48.

[64] *The Point of View for My Work as an Author*, 98.

[65] *Concept of Anxiety*, 142.   [66] Ibid.

[67] *Postscript*, 196.   [68] *Point of View*, 16, 17.

by remarking that it is a higher understanding. So the believing Christian not only possesses but uses his understanding, respects the universal-human, . . . but in relation to Christianity he believes against the understanding and in this case also uses understanding . . . [69]

At the very least, then, he uses understanding 'to make sure that he believes against the understanding' and to keep him from believing 'nonsense', for 'precisely the understanding will discern that it is nonsense and will prevent him from believing it'.[70]

Referring to Hugo de St Victor's 'correct thesis' that, although 'reason does not comprehend what faith believes', there is nevertheless 'something here by which reason becomes determined or is conditioned to honor the faith which it still does not perfectly succeed in grasping', he reminds us that he has already made the point in the *Postscript* that 'not every absurdity is the absurd'.[71] The understanding still has definite roles to fulfil: 'the most developed thought is required to define the Christian absurd accurately and with conceptual correctness'.[72] My conclusion that critical potential is not incompatible with the decisive importance of the 'how' fits with this rejection of arbitrary and indiscriminate transitions.

Kierkegaard follows his recognition that 'not every absurdity is the absurd' with the claim that 'the activity of reason is to distinguish the paradox negatively—but no more'. There is, however, more allowed by him than this negative use—or perhaps it is more appropriate to say that this negative determination implies a positive exploration. There are a multitude of references to 'reflection' and 'dialectic' which express a positive evaluation of understanding or reasoning in relation to faith. The question is not whether reflection is relevant, but how it is. He always recognizes the dual potential of reflection. There is a 'reflection [by which] a man is taken out of immediate relation to God', and there is also 'another movement of reflection which takes the man *so far out* that governance can get hold of him'.[73] (Here we cannot help but be reminded of his other descriptions of imagination performing this latter function, and his claim that 'imagination is the possibility of all reflection'.[74])

[69] *Postscript*, 504.   [70] Ibid.
[71] *Journals*, i. X² A 354, n.d. [1850], 4.
[72] Ibid. i. X⁶ B 79, n.d. [1850], 7.
[73] Ibid. iii. X¹ A 330, n.d. [1849], 718.
[74] Ibid. ii. XI¹ A 288, 1854, 313–14; *Sickness unto Death*, 164. For a somewhat different approach to the question of Kierkegaard's view of imagination in relation to the justification of belief, see my discussion of what the limits of imagination are thought to 'prove' in 'The Faith/History Problem, and Kierkegaard's *A Priori* "Proof"', *Religious Studies*, 23 (Sept. 1987), 337–45.

Despite the negative potential, a commitment to its positive potential is unavoidable, for as we noted in our discussion of passion in Chapter 1, reflection is integral to passion. Robert C. Roberts elaborates on the importance of reflection in this respect:

Spirituality of the sort that Kierkegaard discusses and seeks to engender through his writing is essentially thought-determined, essentially conceptual, essentially reflective. And this reflection is directly related to passion . . . Passion as interest is thought-determined in that one must have some conception of what one is interested in, if one is to have a passion; and passion as emotion is thought-determined in that any emotional assessment that the subject makes of his situation must be in some terms of other.[75]

Moreover, Climacus affirms even more positive potential. The following passage is well known, and usually taken to show that he sees passion and reflection as mutually exclusive, but in it he makes important qualifications which cannot be ignored:

The psychologist generally regards it as a sure sign that a man is beginning to give up a passion when he wishes to treat the object of it objectively. Passion and reflection are *generally* exclusive of one another. Becoming objective in this way is always retrogression, for passion is man's perdition, but it is his exaltation as well. *In case dialectic and reflection are not used to intensify passion*, it is a retrogression to become objective . . . [76]

The implication is that reflection *can* be used to intensify passion, rather than diminish it.

His claim (marked by a double *nota bene*) that there is a 'God-fearing' use of the understanding in relation to faith, a reflection which is 'sanctified', also suggests how the understanding is not annihilated:

It has generally been thought that reflection is the natural enemy of Christianity and would destroy it. With God's help I hope to show that God-fearing reflection can tie knots again which a shallow, superficial reflection has toyed with so long. . . . the battle becomes a different one; up until now it has been between reflection and the immediate, simple Christianity—now it becomes a battle between reflection and simplicity armed with reflection. There is meaning in this, I believe. The task is not to comprehend Christianity but to comprehend that one cannot comprehend. This is the holy cause of faith, and reflection is therefore sanctified by being used in this way.[77]

---

[75] 'Some Remarks on the Concept of Passion' ('Passion and Reflection'), 91. The claim that 'Kierkegaard's complaint is not against reflection as such, but against reflection cut off from passion' is made by Merold Westphal ('Kierkegaard's Sociology', *International Kierkegaard Commentary: Two Ages*, 137, n. 9).

[76] *Postscript*, 540, emphasis mine.

[77] *Journals*, iii. IX A 248, n.d. [1848], 715–16.

'To comprehend that one cannot comprehend' is a 'task', something one works at: the expression of the achievement of this task is only legitimate at the end of the process, not at the beginning. It is legitimate only as a conclusion, not as a presupposition, because one comes to comprehend something positive when one comes to realize that one cannot comprehend.[78]

This is borne out in a passage where, although he acknowledges that 'worship itself is not dialectics', he nevertheless speaks approvingly of a limited use of dialectics:

For dialectics is in its truth a benevolent helper, which discovers and assists in finding where the absolute object of faith and worship is—there, namely, where the difference between knowledge and ignorance collapses in absolute worship with a consciousness of ignorance, there where the resistance of an objective uncertainty tortures forth the passionate certainty of faith, there where the conflict of right and wrong collapses in absolute worship with absolute subjection. Dialectics itself does not see the absolute, but it leads, as it were, the individual up to it, and says: 'Here it must be, that I guarantee; when you worship here, you worship God'.[79]

Even though dialectics cannot show us 'the absolute', the process of leading us to the altar of what is worthy of worship is at the same time a process of leading us away from other altars, other objects. When it leads

---

[78] Mary Warnock's work on imagination indirectly provides a suggestive approach to the question of paradox and reflection. Taking up her earlier discussion of Kant's view of aesthetic judgements (*Imagination* (London, 1976), 41–65), she reintroduces Kant's thought on the sublime as a way of understanding how religious ideas, including the idea of God, can function ('Religious Imagination', 144–5). When imagination presents us with an object as 'sublime' it 'invokes an indeterminate idea of reason' which cannot be imaged (*I*, pp. 55–6)—which is why the sublime, rather than the beautiful, is relevant to religious imagination and paradox. The object apprehended as sublime may, in Kant's words, ' "appear in point of form to contravene the ends of our powers of judgement, to be ill-adapted to our faculty of presentation and to be as it were an outrage on the imagination" ' ('RI', pp. 144–5). The finality or pattern cannot be sufficiently grasped to provide aesthetic satisfaction, but the imagination's frustration is itself significant: 'the role of imagination here is to lead us beyond what is present to our senses towards the realization that there is something *signified by* the things before us, something which we can grasp in a way, but cannot express'; 'we are in awe precisely of the human power to frame ideas which cannot be intuited' (*I*, p. 61; 58). An 'Aesthetic Idea', which is a 'counterpart' of an Idea of Reason, is, according to Kant, ' "a representation of the imagination which induces much thought; yet without the possibility of any definite thought whatever, i.e., concept, being adequate to it, and which language can never get quite on level terms with, or render completely intelligible" ' ('RI', p. 145). The notion of an imaginative representation which 'induces much thought' while it seems to 'contravene the ends of our powers of judgement' and to be 'an outrage on the imagination' may capture something of the Kierkegaardian notion of the paradoxical idea of the God/Man.

[79] *Postscript*, 438–9.

us to the certainty that 'when you worship here, you worship God', it is also, conversely, showing us what the places are like where 'God' is not worshipped. Dialectics then is used in a process of showing the inadequacies of other altars, other objects.

The 'ignorance' to which dialectics and reflection can lead one is qualitatively different from the ignorance from which one starts the process, for Kierkegaard speaks of faith as 'immediacy or spontaneity *after* reflection'.[80] The claim that we *should* use reason 'to distinguish the paradox negatively'—since 'not every absurdity is the absurd or the paradox'[81]—incorporates this positive evaluation of reflection. Reason is thus allowed to provide constraint even though it cannot provide compulsion. The possibility of critical appraisal is thus built into any attempt to 'distinguish the paradox negatively' or to 'comprehend that one cannot comprehend' because it is built into the exploring process of dialectics and reflection through which we come to see that we worship 'God' when we worship *here* rather than *there*.

The question remains, however, how we are to understand the relevance of reflection and dialectics in the face of the continued claim that one can in the end only 'comprehend that one cannot comprehend'. In other words, we have just seen that Kierkegaard speaks as if critical appraisal is possible, as if his emphasis on passion does not require him to claim that religious belief is self-authenticating simply in virtue of the passion with which it is held. But how could this be played out on his own terms? Conversely, is there something in his commitment to 'paradox' which precludes the exercise of such critical appraisal?

Passion, Paradox, and the Exercise of Criticism

Some light may be shed on this question by considering how John Coulson, in *Religion and Imagination: 'in aid of a grammar of assent'*, similarly affirms the importance of imagination in religious faith while suggesting that critical appraisal is possible. Distinguishing between 'the primary forms of religious faith (expressed in metaphor, symbol, and story)' and religious beliefs (explicit, conceptual, reflective formulations), Coulson's 'chief contention' is that 'religious belief originates in that activity we call imagination [because we are addressing 'polarity'[82]], and that its verification thus depends ... upon its first being made

---

[80] *Journals*, ii. VIII[1] A 649, 11 May, 1848, italics mine.
[81] Ibid. i. X[2] A 354, n.d. [1850], 4.
[82] *Religion and Imagination*, 63, 66, 90, 113, 132, 135.

credible to imagination'.[83] But while imaginative response is a necessary condition, without which verification is irrelevant, it is not sufficient— critical appraisal is, for Coulson, bound up with a 'social framework for imagination', a 'critical community'.[84] He leaves behind the simplistic positivist notion of verification by comparison with a totally un-problematic 'reality' and assumes a notion of authentication within the context of the tradition of a critical community. Individual imaginative response is clearly, for Coulson, not self-authenticating; the appeal to imagination does not result in immunity to criticism precisely because imaginative responsiveness is contoured by the 'negative curb' of authority embodied in the community's tradition. If the tradition of a community provides a 'negative curb' and allows conflict to express itself, beliefs can develop through a process of self-criticism.[85] More positively, 'religious explanation and act cohere within a community of acts', and it is '*praxis*, socially conceived' which explains the 'movement from imagination to belief'.[86] Such praxis thereby explains as well the possibility of critical development of beliefs. For Coulson, religious beliefs express attempts to grasp polarities, and in the end the question whether such beliefs are true or not 'can be resolved only within this framework of polarities and by the activity of the imagination thus engendered: what our beliefs profess must correspond to the forms presented by faith'.[87]

But if, on such a view, our beliefs are only accountable 'to the forms presented by faith', are we left with a fideistically insulated language-game account of religion, left only with assessments of coherence within the religious circle? Admittedly, even such a minimal account would invalidate the charge that religious beliefs are self-authenticating by virtue of the passion with which they are held, as well as the charge that religious beliefs are uncriticizable as such—and there seems no reason why Kierkegaard's account could not be elaborated along similar lines. But such an account would still seem open to the objection that religious beliefs are not accountable to anything outside the specifically religious experiences of the community, that they are, so to speak, self-authen-ticated in virtue of collective passion.

What prevents an emphasis on imagination or passion from issuing in an unhealthy individual relativism and absolute uncriticizability is the appeal to community, and Kierkegaard's account (in particular, his

---

[83] *Religion and Imagination*, 145, 46.
[84] Ibid. 72, 130, 137, 159.   [85] Ibid. 159.
[86] Ibid. 78.   [87] Ibid. 130.

account of the 'individual'), does not rule out this appeal.[88] Such community relativism need not constitute an insulated language-game account of religious belief as long as it is recognized that the community and its tradition are not in the end *simply* religious. That is, no community is only a religious community, with only a religious tradition— any community has various traditions with which a religious tradition necessarily relates. Religious beliefs either begin with or come to be included in a web of other beliefs—religious beliefs are involved in a network with other kinds of beliefs in such a way as to render it difficult (if not impossible) to avoid seeing them in the light of the others, to avoid having their adequacy judged with respect to their fit with the others. The relationships need not be one sided; there can be a mutual adjustment and reinterpretation. The critical community is one in which religious responses occur, but even the primary religious forms to which the beliefs must correspond are themselves mediated and contextualized—that is, the web of our beliefs as a whole contours the kinds of religious experience we can have. It would take a great effort even to try to compartmentalize the various elements of our world-view so as to immunize any set of beliefs (religious or otherwise) from critical appraisal, and there is much to suggest that Kierkegaard's understanding of transitions to alternative frameworks does not require that we try to do this.

In addition to the general argument that, in principle, the rejection of a 'natural theology' does not necessarily commit one to the position that beliefs are immune from criticism,[89] we can find explicit Kierkegaardian

---

[88] The entire collection of essays in the *International Kierkegaard Commentary: Two Ages* argues, according to the editor, that the 'myth' of the Kierkegaardian 'individual' as the 'bare particular,' 'stripped of his social relations . . . cannot be justified by a balanced and thorough reading of the whole authorship' (p. xiii). In this same volume Merold Westphal analyses 'the crowd' in terms of moral cowardice, escapism, and irresponsibility ('Kierkegaard's Sociology'); he considers the individual/social relationship too in *Kierkegaard's Critique of Reason and Society* (Macon, Ga., 1987). I have argued in defence of a non-individualistic Kierkegaardian ethic in 'Kierkegaardian Imagination and "the Feminine"', and I would add to that defence the *Point of View*'s contrast between loving 'the neighbor' and loving 'the crowd' (p. 118), as well as a comprehensive reading of *Works of Love: Some Christian Reflections in the Form of Discourses* (trans. Howard and Edna Hong (New York, 1962)), esp. Part One, IV.

[89] Challenges to theological accounts implying fideistically insulated religious beliefs have long been addressed to positions like those of Karl Barth (at least the early writings). Garrett Green provides a useful discussion of Barth's proposed alternative to natural theology (in which philosophy functions as the 'ground'); Green's interpretation of Barth can support my argument that Kierkegaard's similar rejection of natural theology need not imply fideistic insulation (*Imagining God: Theology & the Religious Imagination*, ch. 2). Louis Pojman offers a reading of the Abraham story which argues for the rationality of

warrant for a use of reflection which goes hand in hand with the possibility of criticism. I refer to his discussion of indirect communication or teaching in his *Point of View*. The question which preoccupies him here is 'the question of the use of reflection in Christendom'.[90] That we are speaking of transitions to Christianity in cases where people are under the illusion that they already know what Christianity is implies that the communication 'is qualified by reflection'; the problem of becoming a Christian when 'the situation is Christendom', 'when one is a Christian of a sort' (i.e., when one thinks that 'the aesthetic is Christianity') is a 'problem of reflection'.[91] 'To become a Christian in Christendom', he writes, 'means either to become what one is (the inwardness of reflection or to become inward through reflection), or it means that the first thing is to be disengaged from the toils of one's illusion, which again is a reflective modification'.[92] It is easy to see why he concludes that 'with me everything is reflection'.[93]

The question is not whether reflection can intensify rather than dissipate passion (for we saw earlier that he thinks it has that potential)—the question is whether it can be legitimately used in a way which carries with it the obverse risk of criticism. Such a legitimate use is introduced, I think, in his discussion of teaching. The *Concluding Unscientific Postscript*, he writes in the *Point of View*, 'concerns itself with and sets "the Problem" . . . of the whole authorship: how to become a Christian'.[94] But it not only sets the problem, it provides an answer, for Climacus (as he explicitly notes) fits his description of the teacher, the one who attempts to dispel the 'illusion' about Christian faith which interferes with the transition to such faith.[95] Since 'an illusion can never be destroyed directly', Climacus is an indirect communicator, realizing that 'one must approach from behind the person who is under an illusion', taking pains 'to find HIM where he is and begin there'—to this end Climacus is 'ready to declare that he is not a Christian at all'.[96] The teacher (who is thereby also a learner) thus attempts (through the 'caustic

---

Abraham's act (*The Logic of Subjectivity*, 84–6); Pojman, however, sees this as an alternative to the Kierkegaardian assessment—I wonder whether such an account might not, on the contrary, flesh out my reading of Abraham's religious stand as an interpretative one.

[90] *Point of View*, 41.

[91] Ibid. 42, 41, 43. This role of teaching is more generally applicable because the relevant aspect of the complicating situation of being 'in Christendom' applies not only to those who have been baptized, but to those who have heard of and think they know what Christian faith is.   [92] Ibid. 42–3.

[93] Ibid. 90.   [94] Ibid. 13.

[95] Ibid. 24 n.   [96] Ibid. 24–5, 27.

means' of 'negativity') to free the person from illusion, 'bringing to light a text which is hidden under another text'.[97] Climacus is the teacher who, though he cannot compel another, can persuade him—albeit 'indirectly'—concerning what it is to be a Christian, can 'compel him to take notice' of non-aesthetic categories in such a way that 'possibly he may come to his senses and realize what is implied in calling himself a Christian'.[98] The teacher, that is, is one who offers persuasive (tempting) redescriptions of the situation in which the student finds himself, redescriptions which can precipitate a collision which can jolt him out of the illusory picture he holds.[99]

What Kierkegaard affirms here is the potential of teaching for helping someone to come to a new interpretation of life, a new self-understanding. Moreover, the relevance of such teaching is perfectly consonant with the claims in the *Fragments*, for once the occasion and condition for faith are given, some teaching may still be necessary; as long as it is remembered that such teaching cannot communicate directly, one human being can occasion an 'ambiguity of awareness' in another, precipitating the crisis and helping to dispel an illusion so that the other may 'come to his senses'.[100]

The legitimacy of such teaching embodies an affirmation of reflection, and the consequent possibility of reflective considerations which can undermine that new interpretation or self-understanding. The role of reflection is specified: 'one does not reflect oneself into being a Christian,

[97] Ibid. 40.

[98] Ibid. 35, 37. This agrees with Stewart R. Sutherland's rejection of the view 'too recently assumed that Kierkegaard's occasional appeal to the metaphor of the leap of faith has put him unequivocally amongst those who affirm in a radical sense that until the lamp of faith has been lit by some form of divine encounter or experience, then all is darkness and understanding is impossible' (*Faith and Ambiguity* (London, 1984), 52).

[99] This understanding of the necessity of indirect communication and the pedagogy of dispelling illusions calls to mind some of Wittgenstein's comments on religion, which make clear the bearing of the goal of passionate appropriation on the necessity of indirect communication; for example, he writes that 'It strikes me that a religious belief could only be something like a passionate commitment to a system of reference. . . . It's passionately seizing hold of *this* interpretation. Instruction in a religious faith, therefore, would have to take the form of a portrayal, a description of that system of reference, while at the same time being an appeal to conscience. And this combination would have to result in the pupil himself, of his own accord, passionately taking hold of the system of reference. It would be as though someone were first to let me see the hopelessness of my situation and then show me the means of rescue until, of my own accord, or not at any rate led to it by my *instructor*, I ran to it and grasped it' (*Culture and Value*, 64e).

[100] *Fragments*, 103–4; also see 55. The role of teaching as presented in the *Point of View* does bear on the indirect communication which is legitimated in the *Fragments*—the complicating situation of being 'in Christendom' applies to all who think they know what Christian faith is.

but out of another thing in order to become a Christian . . . one must reflect oneself out of the semblance of being a Christian'.[101] But this contrast is not a simple one—even if one cannot reflect oneself into being a Christian, in the sense of justifying it as a conclusion which one must needs accept, one does not move into a vacuum. One is only freed of an illusory picture by being enamoured of another picture. The inadequacy of one altar is only apparent in relation to another possibility; the illumination through which one is freed of the captivation of one description involves being tempted by another. Thus, although one does not become a Christian 'by means of reflection', one can become a Christian 'in reflection', and the 'reflection is defined by the difficulty, which is greater just in proportion to the value of the thing left behind'.[102] He offers, not a rejection of reflection, but a reconceptualization of its role, and in the end he describes himself as having 'carried to completion the work of reflection, the task of translating completely into terms of reflection what Christianity is, what it means to become a Christian'.[103]

I have taken Coulson's appeal to a 'critical community' further than he explicitly did, in order to show how it could avoid the drawbacks of an insulated language-game account—in order, that is, to provide some real substance to the notion of critical appraisal, without falling prey to an untenable view of an absolute reality with which we can match our language. To decide whether or not a similar appeal can be used to give some substance to Kierkegaard's claims about discovering right and wrong would take a fuller investigation than I can undertake here, but in principle, at least, his view that reason cannot create faith or that one cannot explain the Paradox need not mean that formulations of our experience are insulated from criticism or immune to critical development.

It should be noted that if an emphasis on paradox implied ineffability such an emphasis would entail uncriticizability—but Kierkegaard's insistence on paradox is not an insistence on ineffability. He is not anti-doctrinal; indeed, he even claims, as we saw, that 'on the whole, the doctrine as it is taught is entirely sound'. His emphasis on paradox may thus represent a meta-level comment on the status of religious language, which allows first-order language to go on as it does in many other accounts considered to have a far more cognitive understanding of religious language. John Henry Newman is one example of a religious thinker whom many would take to have a more cognitivist view than

---

[101] *Point of View*, 96.
[102] Ibid.   [103] Ibid. 103.

Kierkegaard, yet Coulson points out that Newman appreciated the inescapability of contradiction and incompatibility in religious language. Coulson, however, contrasts Newman and Kierkegaard in an attempt to separate them in this respect: '[Newman] did not go so far as Kierkegaard, therefore, who in speaking of the inevitably paradoxical nature of religious discourse, claims that "the paradox is not a concession but a category, an ontological definition which expresses the relation between an existing cognitive spirit and eternal truth" '.[104]

Coulson intends a significant contrast here and his undisguised admiration for Newman throughout seems to imply that by not going 'so far as' Kierkegaard, Newman went as far as one should, while Kierkegaard went a bit too far. But Kierkegaard's claim that paradox is not a 'concession' seems to be just the right thing to say on Coulson's own terms, given his admission on the same page that 'ambiguity, polarity, even paradox are inseparable from our attempts at metaphysical or theological statement'. This admission implies not only that Kierkegaard did not go too far, but that the distance between Kierkegaard and Newman in this respect may not be as great as they appear to some to be.

Kierkegaard's emphasis on the meta-level paradoxical status of religious language highlights the limits of simplistic verificationist/falsificationist critiques of religious claims; it challenges positivistic notions not only of what it means to falsify or verify a claim, but also of what is to be falsified or verified.[105] If his emphasis on paradox reflects a meta-level perspective on religious language, it allows for a first-order language which, while inherently unable to express adequately the tension between incommensurables, nevertheless can express something worth expressing. Accordingly, Kierkegaard is not necessarily more subject to being faulted as a non-cognitivist (much less an irrationalist) than many of those in a long tradition which emphasizes the inadequacy of religious language. Whether or not it could be shown to require it, Kierkegaard's understanding of the ultimate paradoxicality of langugage about the transcendent, his recognition that even analogical language is ultimately paradoxical, at least leaves room for a critical (and fallible) development of first-order theological statements—and that room fits well with his claims about reflection and discovering right and wrong.

In the end, then, the charge that Kierkegaard (or Climacus) sees the

---

[104] Coulson, *Religion and Imagination*, 63.

[105] Soskice gives an account of a 'theological critical realism' which involves metaphorical 'reality-depiction'; such 'depiction' or 'reference' is possible, she argues, if we do not confuse 'reference' with either 'identifying description' or 'definition' (*Metaphor and Religious Language*, ch. 7, esp. 127 ff. and ch. 8).

leap as absolutely uncriticizable seems unwarranted. Kierkegaard's appreciation of the role of imagination in the transition to religious faith is a function of his appreciation of paradox (and incommensurability in general), for it is *that* which ultimately limits the relevance of disinterested theorizing and so generates the qualified attack on theory which he mounts. But neither the limits of objectivity nor the importance of engagement guarantee, nor are they intended to guarantee, immunity to criticism. Indeed, engagement can be seen as a condition which facilitates the possibility of critical appraisal.

6

Concluding Applications

The 'typical picture' of 'Kierkegaard's view of Christian faith', to which I referred at the outset of this study, is presented by C. Stephen Evans as follows:

It requires a 'leap of faith'. The leap is necessary because Christian faith requires belief in the reality of the incarnation, the absolute paradox, which the critic perceives as a logical contradiction. Assisted by divine grace, the believer manages, through an heroic act of will, to get himself to believe what he knows is absurd, for what is logically contradictory could not possibly occur.[1]

That picture, he suggests, 'is fundamentally flawed'. In the preceding chapters I have proposed a reading of the Kierkegaardian transition which, though it does not focus, as Evans does, on a rejection of the notion of logical contradiction, just as decisively finds this picture of the required heroic act of will 'fundamentally flawed'. Rejecting the need for such an 'heroic act of will', however, Evans seems to turn away (I shall suggest) from a role for human activity in the actual transition, restricting it instead to the prolegomenon to faith. My proposal, on the contrary, delineates an alternative reading of the human activity required in the actual transition; in particular, it reconceptualizes the categories of will and decision in terms of various dimensions of imaginative activity (suspension, engagement, synthesis, extension). In this concluding chapter I want to indicate at a general level ways in which such an understanding of Kierkegaard's Climacan 'leap of faith' reveals something of Kierkegaard's contribution to the study of human ethical and religious transitions. Before turning to these general themes, however, I want to suggest how my analysis and conclusions concerning the leap bear on a number of other typical pictures of Kierkegaardian faith; these pictures, even when they are inadequate or inaccurate, none the less are instructive both in terms of what they do rightly appreciate and what motivates their (as I see it) misreading.

---

[1] 'Does Kierkegaard Think Beliefs Can be Directly Willed?', 182.

Misreadings of the Climacus account of the transition to faith can occur even in those writers who show an exceeding sensitivity either to the role of imagination in religious faith or to the limits of volitionalist accounts of transitions to faith—for they can fail to recognize in the Climacus account the very thing whose absence they decry. An example of the first kind is found in the recent book, *Imagining God: Theology & the Religious Imagination*, where Garrett Green explores the thesis that religion is 'an activity of the human imagination'.[2] The suggestion itself, he concedes, is not novel; what is important to note, however, is that in addition to the obvious historical treatments in which it is explicitly claimed that religion is imagination (and consequently criticized as 'illusion'), the claim has also been made implicitly, as the 'positive correlate of the negative thesis that religion does not deliver theoretical truths about the supernatural world'.[3] His goal is to show that one can see religion as an imaginative activity without thereby having to 'expose theology to the anthropological reductionism' which has previously attended such a claim.[4] One can, that is, see the religious imagination as directed towards truth because there is a parallel role of imagination in the truth-seeking activity of science—namely, the role of imagination in the phenomenon of 'paradigm shifts' which modern philosophers of science have highlighted.[5] Indeed, he calls our attention to Whitehead's reference to a 'leap of imagination', arguing that 'the recurrence of the "leap" as a metaphor for paradigmatic change is a reminder that the similarities between science and religion have to do with the holistic grammar of both enterprises and therefore with the important role played by paradigms and paradigm changes in both'; moreover, he continues, 'there is a close relation between the role of paradigms and the imagination'.[6]

What I find most intriguing about his discussion, with which I am otherwise in almost whole-hearted agreement, is that his only reference to Kierkegaard with respect to a 'leap' implies that Kierkegaard did not

---

[2] *Imagining God: Theology & the Religious Imagination*, 27.
[3] Ibid. 13.   [4] Ibid. 40.
[5] I do not, however, mean by this to accept the use made by some writers of such parallels between science and religion; significant differences remain which must not be obscured. See my 'A Common Defense of Theistic Belief: Some Critical Considerations', *International Journal for Philosophy of Religion*, 14 (1983), 129–41.
[6] *Imagining God*, 59–60.

appreciate any of this, including the role of such change and the role of imagination in it—for, he writes in a note, 'despite a deeply held modern prejudice going back to Kierkegaard, such leaps are neither unique to religious experience nor irrational'.[7] Such an interpretation of Kierkegaard's understanding of the leap is itself, however, a 'deeply held modern prejudice'—one which I have done my best in this study to dispel.

In so far as incommensurability plays a role in Kierkegaard's understanding of ethical imagination, Green's interpretation of him is incorrect in this respect—Kierkegaard does not propose the 'leap' as 'unique' to the religious sphere, but suggests, on the contrary, that a 'leap' or 'transfiguring' move, which can only be understood properly in the light of his understanding of the role of imagination, is constitutive of *all* such qualitative transitions (whether to the ethical or to the religion of immanence or to Christianity). Moreover, the second element in Green's interpretation of the Kierkegaardian leap—the claim that it is 'irrational'—repeats a view that is as simplistic as it is long-standing. Given that Green, in his effort to rehabilitate the epistemic potential of imagination, allows that 'the philosophical discontinuity between competing paradigms can be accounted for rationally by examining the logical relations of wholes and parts' and rejects the assumption that rationality entails a 'cumulative or associative logic',[8] it is particularly difficult to understand why he would still level such a charge at Kierkegaard.

David Burrell, on the other hand, recognizes the limits of volitionalist accounts of faith in general and avoids impoverished notions of both freedom and rationality when he writes that religious 'assent' is free not 'because logical argument gives way to a willful leap, but because the relevant movements of the understanding cannot be displayed logically'.[9] Such an incommensurability between modes of appropriation is also what Coleridge points to when he explains that a '*metabasis eis allo genos*' (a term which Climacus himself uses to refer to the 'leap'[10]) exists when 'the faculty and forms of reasoning employed are inapplicable to the subject'.[11] Burrell, however, assumes that such a 'willful leap' accurately describes Climacus's account, going on to bemoan Kierkegaard's 'fate' in having his position identified with that of Climacus.[12]

---

[7] Ibid. 159, n. 28.   [8] Ibid. 56.
[9] *Analogy and Philosophical Language* (New Haven, CT, 1973), 134, 134 n.
[10] *Postscript*, 90.   [11] *Biographia Literaria*, 97 n.
[12] Burrell, *Analogy and Philosophical Language*, 134 n.

But it is just such an assumption that I have been challenging in the preceding study. It is clear, then, that even such perceptive writers can fall into the same misreadings of Kierkegaard as those who come to his thought with less nuanced views of either imagination or religious belief.

The preceding chapters thus serve to illustrate how even sensitive commentators on Kierkegaard have missed how he (or Climacus) actually does just what they think he should have done but failed to—for example, how his understanding of imagination offers an alternative to a simple notion of 'willful leap' (or, conversely, offers an enriched notion of willing) and how his heightened and very rich appreciation of the role of incommensurability (or paradox) expresses a sensitivity to the qualitative transitions which were later called *Gestalt* or paradigm shifts, as well as to the role of imagination in them. I have, in addition, argued that Kierkegaard's emphasis on the paradoxical *tension* involved adds to the contemporary discussion by suggesting ways in which a *Gestalt* or paradigm shift model needs to be qualified and complemented—for example, by a model of transition in terms of metaphorical reconceptualization.

Even the very finest commentary on Kierkegaard, among which I place Evans's writings, can be ambiguous as to the activity involved in the transition to faith. Evans's rejection of the 'typical picture' noted at the outset of this chapter is most specifically directed to the question of paradox and logical contradiction. Evans argues, here and elsewhere:[13]

> The paradox of the incarnation cannot be known to be a logical contradiction. It is at most an apparent contradiction, a reality which is so incongruous that human reason cannot understand it. . . . To know that the incarnation is a logical contradiction, we would have to have a clear grasp of what it means to be God and to be human. The message of Christianity, according to Kierkegaard, is that we lack any such knowledge.[14]

Evans's point is well taken. The context of his claim is an attack on volitionalist accounts of the Kierkegaardian act of faith; he argues against the view that for Kierkegaard 'beliefs are normally under direct, voluntary control', and he concludes that 'to say that belief is grounded in the will by no means implies that belief is always or even usually the result of a *conscious* act of willing'.[15] Indeed, much of my preceding study can be seen as an elaborated rejection of volitionalism, whether of

[13] 'Is Kierkegaard an Irrationalist: Reason, Paradox, and Faith', *Religious Studies*, 25 (Sept. 1989), 347–62.
[14] 'Does Kierkegaard Think Beliefs Can be Directly Willed?', 182.
[15] Ibid. 178.

belief in general or of Christian faith—my concern, however, is that while Evans's challenge is correct, his alternative picture can be somewhat misleading.

Evans's counter-picture is that 'This faith is not produced by an act of will on the part of the believer, but rather is an act of God. All that the believer can will to do is to be open to God's gift of grace.'[16] He continues, 'What is required in the leap of faith is not an immoral attempt to manipulate my beliefs so as to make myself believe what I know is untrue. Rather, I am asked to transform myself so that I can be open to an encounter with the truth which will totally transform my life'.[17] Evans's motivation—a rejection of volitionalism—is one with which I clearly agree, but whether he intends it or not, the implication appears to be that our activity is exercized only as a prolegomenon to God's gift. This could lead one to see the transition in terms of the dichotomy of which I spoke in Chapter 2—the false and unnecessary dichotomy between God's grace and our activity. This is quite a commonly assumed dichotomy,[18] and it is worth noting here the way in which it seems so often to attend critiques of volitionalism. What I have been arguing throughout this study is that alternatives to volitionalist accounts of the transition are not limited to accounts which stress 'God's gift' and our passivity once we have decided to 'be open' to it.[19] The moment of transition is as genuinely our activity as anything else we do, however much grace is necessary—that transition is *our* active, imaginative reconceptualization and reorientation, not something that simply happens (or may happen) to us willy-nilly once we have willed to 'be open'.

---

[16] Ibid. 182.

[17] Ibid. 183.

[18] Not only do Evans and Wisdo and Penelhum (as we saw in Chapter 2) assume this false dichotomy between grace and human activity, but David Gouwens assumes it when he writes that 'Grace is central to Kierkegaard's understanding of Christianity, *despite* his frequent remarks on the importance of the human will in faith' (*Kierkegaard's Dialectic of the Imagination*, 245, emphasis mine). Indeed, Terence Penelhum concludes that 'it is not really the man's, but an act of God's grace in the man', despite talk about 'a free recognition, a chosen leap', 'an act that only God can enable him to perform' (*God and Skepticism*, 83).

[19] Louis Pojman's volitionalist account of the *acceptance* of faith claims that faith itself 'is not an act of the will, but a gift' (*The Logic of Subjectivity*, 92). Even though elsewhere he recognizes a 'synergistic tension between grace and free will,' his understanding of Kierkegaard's appeal to stop at something we do 'with regard to becoming a believer'—his appeal to the regress of God's gift and our activity being 'stopped by the subjective'—is that the appeal is to an act of will ('Kierkegaard on Freedom and the Scala Paradisi', *International Journal for Philosophy of Religion*, 18 (1985), 146.

AN ENDURING HERITAGE: SOME KIERKEGAARDIAN THEMES

Having indicated some ways in which popular readings of Kierkegaard's (or Climacus's) leap of faith need to be remedied or qualified, I want now to indicate something of Kierkegaard's more general contribution. The three general themes I will focus on by way of summary to indicate that contribution are: (1) the theme of discontinuity/continuity, (2) the theme of the challenge to dualism, and (3) the theme of transforming vision.

Discontinuity and Continuity: The Ladder of Imagination

I have argued throughout that the 'leap' (including in the case of Christian faith) is presented by Kierkegaard from two perspectives—namely, in terms of paradox and in terms of analogical revisioning or reconceptualization—and that from both perspectives the leap is more fruitfully understood by appeal to imaginative activity than to a direct act of will. Such an appeal, I have argued, can satisfy the need for freedom which motivates talk of a leap, as well as account for the qualitative and passionate character of the transition; moreover, a proper appreciation of the epistemic relevance of imagination can obviate objections that such transitions are arbitrary.

In Chapter 5 I considered one of the questions which naturally arises about the Kierkegaardian understanding of the leap: namely, the question whether the emphasis on imagination and passion and paradox is meant to entail an immunity to criticism. A different question arises with respect to my interpretation of the leap as a revisioning or reconceptualization—namely, the question whether that interpretation of the leap fails to do justice to Kierkegaard by, in effect, reducing faith to a probabilistic conclusion. Whereas the earlier concern was with whether Kierkegaard's leap was irrational, this concern is with whether I have made it too rational (for Kierkegaard's intentions and other commitments).

That concern can be usefully expressed in relation to John Coulson's understanding of the leap in faith, for it has much in common with the understanding of leap as metaphorical reconceptualization which I have proposed. Coulson's main concern is with illuminating John Henry Newman's understanding of the transition to faith, suggesting that Newman avoids the simple resort to a 'leap', preferring instead to illustrate the mode of transition by the metaphor of an expanding polygon

inscribed within a circle.[20] However, in his discussion he compares Newman to Kierkegaard in a way which reinterprets the category of leap,
rather than rejects it, and it is such a comparison which can raise the
question whether my interpretation of the Kierkegaardian leap is 'too
rational' after all. Claiming that the reference to a leap expresses the fact
that we do not experience a 'simple chronology', he writes:

In religious assent, therefore, in one respect we 'leap'; but in retrospect we
experience that leap as precipitated by an accumulation of probabilities; and the
difference between Newman and Kierkegaard may well amount to no more than
that between retrospective and prospective ways of looking at the same fact: it is
spoken of as a 'leap' *before*, and is conceived as a polygon expanding into a circle
after.[21]

'Newman', he continues, highlights 'conditions which, socially, historic-
ally, and reflectively, enable us to be certain that our spontaneous leap of
faith is a rational act rather than a merely subjective feeling.' It should be
noted that Coulson has already reminded us that Newman admitted
contradictions and incompatibilities in religious discourse,[22] but since
Newman is none the less said to see the transition as a 'rational act', the
suggestion that there may be no substantive difference between Newman
and Kierkegaard is quite a challenging one.[23]

My interpretation of the leap as a reconceptualization process implies
(as does Coulson's) that there are considerations (perhaps reconstruct-
able in retrospect, if not at the time) which converge and can be taken so
as to yield a change in perspective; the question arises whether, if we
grant that, we have done justice to the intention behind Kierkegaard's
understanding of the leap. I suggest that the adequacy of my interpretation of the reconceptualizing or revisioning leap can be defended,
however, if we recognize the kind of incommensurability in reconceptualization which would justify the reference to a leap.

The reconceptualization or revisioning is a process in which pieces fall
into a *pattern*—it is a process through which we come to see that, along
the lines of Judge William's suggestion, 'only in this way does life become
... beautiful, meaningful, hopeful, etc.'. The notion of 'pattern' is
central, and Garrett Green has emphasized this in his definition of

---

[20] Coulson, *Religion and Imagination: 'in aid of a grammar of assent'*, 49, 69.
[21] Ibid. 71.   [22] Ibid. 63.
[23] Louis Pojman offers a suggestive reading of the 'arguments inherent in the Climacus
writings': arguments in which he is 'explicating and defending the Christian faith',
arguments for the existence of God, for the 'reasonableness of the leap of faith', all in all 'a
reasonable case for Christianity' (*The Logic of Subjectivity*, pp. x, xii, 15, and ch. 5 *passim*).

imagination 'not as the image-making faculty, but rather as the paradigmatic (pattern-making and pattern-recognizing) faculty'.[24] We discern a
pattern, for example, when we see perspective in a painting or recognize
a melody or see eternity in a grain of sand.

Green also points out another aspect of a pattern when he suggests,
'Something serves as a paradigm—that is, as an exemplar or ideal type—
because it shows forth a pattern, a coherent nexus of relations, in a
simple and straightforward manner'.[25] This feature of pattern-as-
exemplar is highlighted in Anti-Climacus's references to Christ the Pattern: it is 'the picture of His life, which is the pattern', and without 'the
Pattern to look upon', one could not 'dare to believe in love within himself'.[26] But for the Pattern to be one we can imitate, it must first fall into
place; we must recognize the Face (the life, that perspective on the world)
before we can follow it.

The relevance of the category of 'pattern' to our question about the
incommensurability (or leap) in the process of reconceptualizing is found
in the way that discerning a pattern involves a dimension of discontinuity
as well as of continuity. Green is correct in noting that discontinuity
exists even though the process may involve 'first getting "glimmers"' of a
different pattern; by going through periods of confusion; or by enter-
taining new possibilities without initially finding them persuasive'[27]—
that is, there is both discontinuity and continuity. But contrasting
discontinuity and continuity in terms of logical vs. psychological, as he
does, is unhelpful.[28] The model of *critical threshold* which I introduced
much earlier serves more fruitfully, I suggest, to illustrate how both
perspectives of discontinuity and continuity can be incorporated in the
process of revisioning. That process, like the process of reaching a critical
threshold, is such that, even when elements are gradually registered (i.e.,
continuity), it involves a conceptual leap (i.e., discontinuity).

The discontinuity is clear. Climacus's comments on Lessing make
clear that as long as there is any incommensurability, there is a leap; as
long as one cannot get there by quantitative progression, it is ludicrous to
quibble about the length of the leap, for a little is as much as a lot in such

---

[24] *Imagining God*, 94.   [25] Ibid. 53.
[26] *Training in Christianity*, 182–3, 195. The relevance of the 'Pattern' is recognized also
by Gouwens (*Kierkegaard's Dialectic of the Imagination*, 259) and James Collins (*The
Mind of Kierkegaard*, 237).   [27] *Imagining God*, 56.
[28] Following Wittgenstein, I would argue that an appreciation of the relation between
'prescriptive' (or 'normative') and 'descriptive' challenges that simplistic contrast between
'logical/psychological'—the discontinuity and continuity are both in the same category,
whichever way one wants to characterize it.

cases—'as if the least leap did not have the characteristic of making the chasm infinitely wide; as if it were not equally difficult for one who absolutely cannot leap whether the chasm is wide or narrow'.[29] The presence of a convergence of considerations would not in itself preclude the shift from being qualitative rather than quantitative, or free rather than compelled.[30] The incommensurability at the heart of religious belief guarantees, for Kierkegaard, that even if considerations are registered and make a difference, the conclusion is not rendered 'probable' in the sense which he is concerned to reject—i.e., what is affirmed remains intrinsically paradoxical and is not a mere quantitative extrapolation.

The relevance of the discontinuity should not, however, be misconstrued. I suggested in the Introduction that the metaphor of the 'leap' has caused the dimension of discontinuity to be emphasized, indeed overemphasized. But certainly one of Kierkegaard's contributions to the religious discussion consists in the ways he includes the dimension of continuity in the transition. The importance, for example, of interest and engagement to his account of the transition to faith (which is distinguishable from its importance in the prolonged struggle of the lived life of faith) is illuminated by the way in which the metaphor of the ladder embodies the perspective of continuity as well as that of qualitative change.

One way of understanding this is indicated in Gregor Malantschuk's emphasis on what I call the 'continuity' embodied in the notion of a 'transfiguring' move. Malantschuk writes that, for Kierkegaard, 'the content of the subject's previous experience is fully retained when a new factor enters or when a new stage begins, but each time the total content is seen in a new perspective'.[31] He not only refers to Kierkegaard's journal suggestions about the way in which a new element transforms what is already present, or, alternatively, what it is to hear the 'same' melody repeated in a new 'key', he suggests that, for Kierkegaard, Christianity 'reinforces' in a new way the insight into our inadequacy which we obtain 'on the human level'.[32]

Another way of understanding this continuity is suggested in Garrett

---

[29] *Postscript*, 90; this conviction is also expressed repeatedly in *Concept of Anxiety* as the irrelevance of the 'more' to the transition from quantitative to qualitative (pp. 38, 60, 72). Thus I disagree with Penelhum's understanding of the difference between leaps in terms of greater or lesser 'length' (*God and Skepticism*, 83, 84).

[30] This possibility is affirmed in terms of the relevance of 'an intermediate term' in passing from possibility to actuality—such a term can have a necessary bearing on the outcome without being thereby said to 'explain' or 'justify' it (*Concept of Anxiety*, 49).

[31] *Kierkegaard's Thought*, 136. [32] Ibid.

Green's discussion of Barth and contemporary theology. Although he does not refer to Kierkegaard in this connection, Green argues for the importance of the distinction between the content of revelation and the form of the human activity of imagination. With this distinction, he maintains, theology can do justice to both the irreducibility of grace and the human activity which is formally similar to other human experiences.[33] In this way we can say, he writes, that the revelatory point of contact 'depends wholly on the initiative of divine grace and nevertheless appears in the wholly human form of imagination'.[34] I clearly agree with Green's emphasis on the continuity with other human experience and on imagination as the relevant form of human activity involved. My proposed reading of Kierkegaardian transitions includes both emphases, and my suggestion is that an emphasis on imagination does more justice to the element of continuity than does a volitionalist account of the human activity of transition because imagination has a receptive (as well as active) dimension. Another way of putting that is to say that imagination is more closely tied to an understanding of will in terms of appetite and attraction rather than in terms of volition ('pull' rather than 'push', so to speak), and that the categories of 'interest' and 'concern' which inform that understanding of will *anchor* the Kierkegaardian transition in a more significant continuity with other human experience than does the category of 'volition'.

Imagination and the Challenge to Dualism

The way in which Kierkegaard highlights the importance of imagination challenges a variety of dualisms which infect a great many of the pictures of humanness given to us by philosophers. In particular, we have seen how it challenges a common dichotomy between passive and active (with its implied restrictive view of both 'will' and 'reason'). By highlighting the importance of both ethical and religious imaginative activity, Kierkegaard challenges all those philosophical or theological divisions of the self which ignore imagination or limit it to the ways in which imagination can be deceitful.

In her criticism of one such philosophical account of freedom and the structure of the self, Iris Murdoch indirectly sensitizes us to Kierkegaard's contribution. Stuart Hampshire's picture of the self, she writes, 'depends on a divorce between will and reason'[35]; he 'uses words such as

---

[33] *Imagining God*, 39–40.   [34] Ibid. 112.
[35] 'The Darkness of Practical Reason', 48.

"will", "desire", and "reason", and by-passes "imagination" because this word may be used to name an activity which is awkward for his theory'.[36] She explicitly challenges the limits of such a theory, suggesting that it 'depends on the purity of the two dualisms: active and passive, and (within the former) reason and will'.[37] In so doing she echoes the same sort of challenge I have been suggesting is found in Kierkegaard's thought.

Hampshire 'by-passes' the operation of imagination, Murdoch charges, because in his view freedom requires a strict dichotomy between reason and will: 'our freedom is said to consist in our ability to remove ourselves into a region where we can assess situations under no pressure from the will'.[38] Freedom, for Hampshire, requires 'pure' reason, reason uninfluenced by will—any activity on our part would pressure reason and thus taint its conclusions which should be a 'pure' response to the evidence.

To acknowledge imagination at all would, at the very least, complicate his theory if it does not fit neatly into either category, and it is Murdoch's view that it does not. As we saw earlier, she suggests that imagination is an activity which is neither simply active nor simply passive: it is, like seeing, and because it is a seeing, at the same time a kind of reflection and a kind of doing. Imagination is 'a type of reflection on people, events, etc., which builds detail, adds colour, conjures up possibilities in ways which go beyond what could be said to be strictly factual', and at the same time it is a 'doing'—a 'sort of personal exploring'.[39] Murdoch claims that Hampshire's acknowledgement of both dimensions is precluded by his assumption that freedom requires reasoning which is entirely independent of active influencing. Imagination, when it is recognized by him, must be restricted to a non-active role because to see it as active at all would make it 'difficult not to see this as an exercise of will'[40]—and, like other exercises of the will, it would, for Hampshire, be an illegitimate influence on reason. He 'relegates *imagination* to the passive side of the mind'[41] because in so far as imagination is admitted to be active, it is rendered illegitimate. Its legitimacy is salvaged only by ignoring its full character—that is, by refusing to acknowledge both active and passive dimensions. Thus Murdoch criticizes both descriptively and prescriptively Hampshire's account—and others which may do the same thing with more subtlety. She challenges not only their dualistic descriptions of the self in which functions are either simply

[36] Ibid.   [37] Ibid. 47.   [38] Ibid. 48.
[39] Ibid.   [40] Ibid.   [41] Ibid.

active or simply passive, but also the priority which gives one pole of the dualism (reason) a monopoly—sole and entire—on epistemological value.

I suggest that, like Murdoch, Kierkegaard understood imagination to mediate the active and passive in our perception and appropriation of the world. Despite the appearance at times of dualism—for example, the appearance of a stark and unmitigated contrast between objectivity and subjectivity[42]—Kierkegaard's recognition of the importance of tension (expressed in the variety of ways I have indicated throughout) precluded the need for him to posit a dualism or mutual exclusiveness between reason and will. One could, in fact, consider his reminder (by Anti-Climacus) that 'one may err, either by emphasizing knowledge merely, or merely the will'[43] to be a kind of leitmotiv of his thought in general. I have elaborated the implications of this reminder by arguing that his under-standing of 'choice' and 'will' (hence of 'leap') is effectively a rejection of the dualism implied in a purely volitional model of 'choice', and an affirmation of a descriptively more complex phenomenon. I have done this in part by arguing that the concepts of 'passion' and 'leap' are mutually correcting, and that illuminated and supported by his explicit affirmation of imaginative activity, they express the dual aspect of the shift in vision which constitutes faith, in much the same way as reflection and exploring are aspects of the seeing which is imagination at work.

Imagination and Transforming Vision

Just as Kierkegaard drew our attention (through Vigilius Haufniensis) to an important difference between kinds (or levels) of understanding when he noted that 'There is an old saying that to understand and to under-stand are two things, and so they are',[44] so too he points, in effect, to a parallel kind of difference between vision and vision. I have in my emphasis on seeing or revisioning (as a corrective to the standard emphasis on a heroic act of will-power) tried to avoid the error of redu-cing Kierkegaard's position to a mere intellectualism or neutral vision (in

[42] The *Postscript* at times presents subjectivity as an 'opposite direction' to objectivity (p. 55), as the stark either/or of infinite interest or objectivity (p. 23), but that dualism is mitigated because the general contrasts between subjectivity and objectivity as two modes of acceptance (p. 116) or two modes of reflection (p. 178), need to be understood in light of his claims that dialectics can intensify passion (p. 540) and that subjectivity and objectivity each represent a different 'accent' (p. 181) and that in our thinking one of the two is 'accentuated' at any given time (p. 85).

[43] *Sickness unto Death*, 181.   [44] *Concept of Anxiety*, 142.

Anti-Climacus's words, I have tried not to err by emphasizing 'knowledge merely'). But self-understanding and transparency are, as I have shown, indisputably central to his understanding of personal qualitative transitions. The relevance of this even for Christian faith is revealed in a variety of the formulations we have seen, up to and including his retrospective *Point of View for My Work as an Author*. He writes there, for example, in decidedly non-volitionalist terms of the co-extensive authorial/personal transition[45] he experienced, and it is worth looking at that briefly in closing.

His final description of the transition he experienced is given in terms of the 'factum' or 'collision' which occurred before his 'real activity as an author' began. He writes:

I became a poet; but with my predisposition for religion, or rather, I may say, with my decided religiousness, this *factum* was for me at the same time a religious awakening, so that I came to understand myself in the most decisive sense in the experience of religion, or in religiousness, to which, however, I had already put myself into relation as a possibility. The *factum* made me a poet. . . . But just because I was so religiously developed as I was, the *factum* took far deeper hold of me and, in a sense, nullified what I had become, namely, the poet. It nullified it, or at least I was led simultaneously to begin in the same moment at two points . . . [46]

He concludes: 'the religious awakening, though it was certainly not a thing I had experienced by means of myself, yet it was in accordance with myself, that is to say, in this thing of becoming a poet I did not recognize myself in a deeper sense, but rather in the religious awakening'.[47]

The emphasis on 'religious awakening' is striking—the awakening is a coming to understand oneself, to recognize oneself; it is what he refers to later on as the 'decision' (a 'momentous' one) to become a Christian.[48] The awakening is the decision: the decision is the decisive overcoming of one understanding by another; the decision is achieved in understanding oneself 'in the most decisive sense'.

Moreover, his initial description of the transition has much in common with my conclusions in Chapter 4 concerning reports of conversions. He writes:

When I began *Either/Or* . . . I was potentially as deeply under the influence of religion as ever I have been. I was so deeply shaken that I understood perfectly

---

[45] He writes that 'The movement from "the poet" to religious existence is substantially the movement of my whole activity as an author integrally understood', *Point of View*, 132 n.   [46] *Point of View*, 83–4.

[47] Ibid. 84.   [48] Ibid. 96.

well that . . . I had either to cast myself into perdition and sensuality, or to choose the religious absolutely as the only thing. . . . *That it was the second I would and must choose was at bottom already determined*: the eccentricity of the first movement was merely the expression for the intensity of the second; it expressed the fact that I had become thoroughly aware how impossible it would be for me to be religious only up to a certain point.[49]

Such an understanding of choice calls to mind those descriptions of transitions or conversions in which what occurred was that people realized that they were *already* decided. The moment of decision was actually a moment of realization, of becoming 'thoroughly aware' of what was already decided. Such a view of the transition is in accord with his description of the goal of the teacher who presents Christianity in its 'true form'—namely, that the teacher, 'bringing to light' the hidden text within the learner, may lead the learner to 'come to his senses' and 'realize' what is implied in having been baptized.[50]

Without such an emphasis on vision, we misunderstand the Kierke-gaardian transition by emphasizing 'will merely'. Although Kierkegaard is committed to a biblical notion of will (as revealed in obedience[51]), there is, nevertheless, mixed in with his criticism of the limits of the Socratic way of recollection enough expression of appreciation of the Greek tradition to suggest that Kierkegaard's was more a selective appropriation and qualification of Greek insights than a wholesale rejection of the Greek tradition as antithetical to the Christian altern-ative. For example, the injunction to 'choose oneself', we saw earlier, was said by Judge William to be equivalent to the Greek injunction to 'know oneself' as long as the latter was understood properly—that is, as referring to a knowing which was 'not a mere contemplation', but as engaging or efficacious, 'a reflection . . . which itself is an action'.[52] Moreover, the 'profundity' of Greek wisdom is affirmed across accounts.[53]

---

[49] *Point of View*, 18, emphasis mine.

[50] Ibid. 40, 37. *The Point of View* gives still another non-volitionalist account of the transition as a 'process' by which 'a poetic and philosophical nature is put aside in order to become a Christian': 'the unusual feature is that the two movements begin simultaneously, and hence this is a conscious process, one is able to perceive how it comes about, the second movement does not supervene after a series of years which separate it from the first. . . . The religious is present from the very first instant and has a decisive predominance, but for a while it waits patiently to give the poet leave to talk himself out . . . .' (pp. 73–4).

[51] See his reference to the New Testament connection between will and sin (*Journals*, ii. I A 36, 25 Nov. 1834, 3), and other examples in Chapter 2, above.

[52] *Either/Or*, ii. 263. The importance of the 'profundity' of this Greek saying is also affirmed in *Concept of Anxiety*, 79.

[53] *Concept of Anxiety*, 79; *Postscript*, 110–11, 187, 191.

Such a notion of efficacious reflection embodies the element of attraction or engagement which is central to my reading of the Climacus model of transition (for without it we have 'knowledge merely'[54]). What is at issue is the transformation of self, not the static revelation of self. The dichotomy between knowledge (reason) and will is thus transcended in an understanding of will which reinvests the concept of will with some of the richness of the classical Aristotelian heritage—where will, seen as the motive power of reason, is rational appetite, desire, attraction (*boulesis*).[55] The understanding of will in terms of appetite and attraction fits in easily with his emphases on 'interestedness' and the engagement of the 'how'.

Not only is it an error, however, to emphasize either side (knowledge or will) at the expense of the other in our understanding of transitions—the very dichotomy is unnecessary if will can be captivated or, conversely, if vision can be transforming. And it is imagination at work in either case, both because transitions involve a vision of possibility (which itself is an imaginative extension) and because that possibility can be imaginatively presented so as to be engaging (hence, demanding). *The Concept of Anxiety*'s assessment of possibility as 'the weightiest of all categories'—placing demands on us by educating us to our infinitude[56]—is reinforced not only by the thought of Climacus and Judge William, but also by Kierkegaard's expression of the positive role of imagination in his journal entry from 1854: 'Imagination is what providence uses to take men captive in actuality, in existence, in order to get them far enough out, or within, or down into actuality.'[57] Such a view of the potential for imagination to be a mechanism for a faith which is 'honest toward

[54] Wittgenstein's account of Kierkegaard emphasizes this: 'The point is that a sound doctrine need not *take hold* of you; you can follow it as you would a doctor's prescription. ... Wisdom is passionless. But faith by contrast is what Kierkegaard calls a *passion*' (*Culture and Value*, 53e).

[55] Albrecht Dihle's book-length study analyses in detail the development 'by the means and methods of Greek philosophy, [of] the clear-cut notion of will which was always implied in the Biblical image of God, man, and the universe, though utterly alien to Greek cosmology and ethics'; he also explores the relation between the Greek notion of *boulesis* (with overtones of 'desire, purpose, longing, or pleasure') and the contrasting volitionalist translations which downplay the intellectual activity preceding action (*The Theory of Will in Classical Antiquity*, 19). My view of Kierkegaard's agreement with the classical heritage is expressed in James Collins's claim that 'the will is regarded by Kierkegaard as a major natural passion', whose presence is expressed in the 'synthesis of psycho-physical powers, under the guiding discipline of what Aristotle and Aquinas called "rational desire" or "desiring reason"' (*The Mind of Kierkegaard*, 262).

[56] *Concept of Anxiety*, 156.

[57] *Journals*, ii. XI^1 A 288, n.d. [1854], 313–14.

possibility'[58] is reflected in the recognition, permeating the Kierke-gaardian writings, that imaginative vision can be demanding and trans-forming. Thus sensitized to Kierkegaard's challenge to dualistic assumptions about reason and will (and to the understandings of transition based on those assumptions), and to his appreciation of the roles of imagination in transitions, we can be more discriminating in our assessments of contemporary accounts of religious faith in general and of Kierkegaardian faith in particular.

[58] *Concept of Anxiety*, 157.

Selected Bibliography

PRIMARY KIERKEGAARD WORKS

The Concept of Anxiety, ed. and trans. Reidar Thomte (Princeton, NJ, 1980).
Concluding Unscientific Postscript, trans. David Swenson and Walter Lowrie (Princeton, NJ, 1968).
Either/Or, ii, trans. Walter Lowrie (Princeton, NJ, 1959).
Fear and Trembling, eds. and trans. Howard V. Hong and Edna H. Hong (Princeton, NJ, 1983).
Philosophical Fragments and *Johannes Climacus*, Kierkegaard's Writings, vii, eds. and trans. Howard V. Hong and Edna H. Hong (Princeton, NJ, 1985).
The Point of View for My Work as an Author, trans. Walter Lowrie and ed. Benjamin Nelson (New York, 1962).
Repetition: A Venture in Experimenting Psychology, Kierkegaard's Writings, vi, eds. and trans. Howard V. Hong and Edna H. Hong (Princeton, NJ, 1983).
Samlede Vaerker, vi, ix, x, eds. A. B. Drachmann, J. L. Heiberg, and H. O. Lange (Gyldendal, 1963).
The Sickness unto Death, trans. Walter Lowrie (Princeton, NJ, 1954).
Soren Kierkegaard's Journals and Papers, eds. and trans. Howard V. Hong and Edna H. Hong with the assistance of Gregor Malantschuk, 7 vols. (Bloomington, Ind. and London, 1967–78).
Training in Christianity and the Edifying Discourse which 'Accompanied' It, trans. Walter Lowrie (Princeton, NJ, 1944).
Works of Love: Some Christian Reflections in the Form of Discourses, trans. Howard and Edna Hong (New York, 1962).

OTHER WORKS

Alston, William P., 'The Elucidation of Religious Statement', in *Process and Divinity*, ed. William L. Reese and E. Freeman (LaSalle, Ill., 1964).
Aristotle, *The Rhetoric of Aristotle*, trans. Lane Cooper (Englewood Cliffs, NJ, 1932).
Baker, James V., *The Sacred River: Coleridge's Theory of the Imagination* (Baton Rouge, La., 1957).

Bonaventure, Saint, *The Works of Bonaventure: Cardinal, Seraphic Doctor, and Saint*, trans. José de Vinck, i, *Mystical Opuscula* (Paterson, NJ, 1960).

—— *Bonaventure*, Classics of Western Spirituality, trans. Ewert Cousins (New York, 1978).

Burrell, David, *Analogy and Philosophical Language* (New Haven, CT., 1973).

Coleridge, Samuel Taylor, *Biographia Literaria*, Everyman's Library (London, 1906).

—— *Inquiring Spirit: A Coleridge Reader*, ed. Kathleen Coburn (Minerva Press, 1951).

—— *Miscellaneous Criticism*, ed. Thomas Middleton Raysor (Cambridge, Mass., 1936; reprint edn. Folcroft, Pa., 1969).

—— *Collected Works*, i. *The Friend*, ed. Barbara E. Rooke (London, 1969); vi. *Lay Sermons*, ed. R. J. White (Princeton, NJ, 1972).

—— *The Notebooks of Samuel Taylor Coleridge*, ii (1804–1808); iii (1808–1819), ed. Kathleen Coburn (Princeton, NJ, 1961, 1973).

Collins, James, *The Mind of Kierkegaard* (Princeton, NJ, 1983).

Coulson, John, *Religion and Imagination: 'in aid of a grammar of assent'* (Oxford, 1981).

Cutsinger, James S., *The Form of Transformed Vision: Coleridge and the Knowledge of God* (Macon, Ga., 1987).

De Nicolas, Antonio T., *Powers of Imagining: Ignatius of Loyola* (Albany, NY, 1986).

Dihle, Albrecht, *The Theory of Will in Classical Antiquity*, Sather Classical Lectures, vol. 48 (Berkeley, CA., 1982).

Dupré, Louis, *A Dubious Heritage: Studies in the Philosophy of Religion After Kant* (New York, 1977).

Edwards, Steven A., 'Paradox in Context: Impasse and Passage'. Paper presented at the 1985 meeting of the American Academy of Religion (23–6 Nov. 1985, Anaheim, CA.).

—— 'Structure and Change in Aquinas's Religious Ethics', *Journal of the American Academy of Religion*, 54 (Summer 1986), 281–302.

Elrod, John W., *Being and Existence in Kierkegaard's Pseudonymous Works* (Princeton, NJ, 1975).

Evans, C. Stephen, *Subjectivity and Religious Belief* (Grand Rapids, Mich., 1978).

—— *Kierkegaard's Fragments and Postscript: The Religious Philosophy of Johannes Climacus* (Atlantic Highlands, NJ, 1983).

—— 'Does Kierkegaard Think Beliefs Can Be Directly Willed?', *International Journal for Philosophy of Religion*, 26 (Dec. 1989), 173–84.

—— 'Is Kierkegaard An Irrationalist: Reason, Paradox, and Faith', *Religious Studies*, 25 (Sept. 1989), 347–62.

Farley, Margaret A., *Personal Commitments: Beginning, Keeping, Changing* (San Francisco, CA., 1986).

Ferreira, M. Jamie, 'A Common Defense of Theistic Belief: Some Critical Considerations', *International Journal for Philosophy of Religion*, 14 (1983), 129–41.

—— 'The Faith/History Problem and Kierkegaard's *A Priori* "Proof"', *Religious Studies*, 23 (Sept. 1987), 337–45.

—— 'Repetition, Concreteness, and Imagination', *International Journal for Philosophy of Religion*, 25 (1989), 13–34.

—— 'Kierkegaardian Imagination and "the Feminine"'. Presidential Address, Society for Philosophy of Religion (2 March 1990, New Orleans, La.).

Fortenbaugh, William W., *Aristotle on Emotion* (New York, 1975).

Gilman, Richard, *Faith, Sex, Mystery: A Memoir* (New York, 1986).

Gouwens, David J., 'Kierkegaard on the Ethical Imagination', *Journal of Religious Ethics*, 10 (Fall 1982), 204–20.

—— *Kierkegaard's Dialectic of the Imagination* (New York, 1989).

Green, Garrett, *Imagining God: Theology & the Religious Imagination* (San Francisco, CA., 1989).

Hanson, N. R., *Patterns of Discovery* (Cambridge, 1969).

Hauerwas, Stanley, *Vision and Virtue: Essays in Christian Theological Reflection* (Notre Dame, Ind., 1974).

Ishiguro, Hidé, 'Imagination', Part II, *Proceedings of the Aristotelian Society*, Supplement XLI (1967), 37–56.

James, William, *Principles of Psychology*, ii (New York, 1950).

—— *The Varieties of Religious Experience* (New York, 1982).

Keane, Philip S., *Christian Ethics and Imagination* (New York, 1984).

Kearney, Richard, *The Wake of Imagination: Toward a Postmodern Culture* (Minneapolis, Minn., 1988).

Kittay, Eva F., *Metaphor: Its Cognitive Force and Linguistic Structure* (Oxford, 1987).

—— and Diana T. Meyers (eds.), *Women and Moral Theory* (Totowa, NJ, 1987).

Kuhn, Thomas S., *The Structure of Scientific Revolutions* (Chicago, 2nd edn. enlarged, 1970).

Kundera, Milan, *The Unbearable Lightness of Being*, trans. Michael Henry Heim (New York, 1984).

Lakoff, George and Mark Johnson, *Metaphors We Live By* (Chicago, 1980).

Lewis, C. S., *Surprised by Joy* (London, 1955).

—— *An Experiment in Criticism* (Cambridge, 1961).

—— *The Grand Miracle and Other Essays*, ed. Walter Hooper (New York, 1970).

Lynch, William F., *Images of Faith: An Exploration of the Ironic Imagination* (Notre Dame, Ind., 1973).

MacIntyre, Alasdair, *A Short History of Ethics* (New York, 1966).

—— *Whose Justice? Which Rationality?* (Notre Dame, Ind., 1988).

Malantshuk, Gregor, *Kierkegaard's Thought*, eds. and trans. Howard V. Hong and Edna H. Hong (Princeton, NJ, 1971).

May, Rollo, *Love and Will* (New York, 1969).

Murdoch, Iris, 'The Darkness of Practical Reason', *Encounter*, 27 (July 1966), 46–50.

—— 'Vision and Choice in Morality', in *Christian Ethics and Contemporary Philosophy*, ed. Ian T. Ramsey (New York, 1966).

—— *The Sovereignty of Good* (New York, 1971).

Nietzsche, Friedrich, *Untimely Meditations* (1873–6), trans. R. J. Hollingdale (Cambridge, 1983).

O'Connor, Flannery, *The Habit of Being*, ed. Sally Fitzgerald (New York, 1979).

Ortony, Andrew (ed.), *Metaphor and Thought* (Cambridge, 1979).

Pieper, Josef, *Belief and Faith* (New York, 1963).

Penelhum, Terence, *God and Skepticism: A Study in Skepticism and Fideism* (Dordrecht, 1983).

Perkins, Robert L. (ed.), *International Kierkegaard Commentary: Two Ages* (Macon, Ga., 1984).

Pojman, Louis, P., *The Logic of Subjectivity: Kierkegaard's Philosophy of Religion* (University, Ala., 1984).

—— 'Kierkegaard on Freedom and the Scala Paradisi', *International Journal for Philosophy of Religion*, 18 (1985), 141–8.

—— *Religious Belief and the Will* (London, 1986).

Ricoeur, Paul, *Interpretation Theory: Discourse and the Surplus of Meaning* (Fort Worth, TX., 1976).

Roberts, Robert C., 'Solomon on the Control of Emotions', *Philosophy and Phenomenological Research*, 44 (March 1984), 395–403.

—— 'Some Remarks on the Concept of Passion' ('Passion and Reflection'), in *International Kierkegaard Commentary: Two Ages*, ed. Robert L. Perkins (Macon, Ga., 1984).

—— 'What An Emotion Is: A Sketch', *The Philosophical Review*, 97 (April 1988), 183–209.

Rorty, Richard, Romanell Lectures, No. 1 (unpubl.), University of Virginia, Jan. 1988.

—— *Contingency, Irony, and Solidarity* (Cambridge, 1989).

Ryle, Gilbert, *The Concept of Mind* (New York, 1949).

Sacks, Sheldon (ed.), *On Metaphor* (Chicago, 1979).

Solomon, Robert C., *The Passions* (Notre Dame, Ind., 1983).

—— *Above Love: Reinventing Romance for Our Times* (New York, 1988).

Soskice, Janet M., *Metaphor and Religious Language* (Oxford, 1985).

Strawson, P. F., 'Imagination and Perception', in *Kant on Pure Reason*, ed. R. C. S. Walker (Oxford, 1982). First published in *Experience and Theory* (eds.) L. Foster and J. W. Swanson (Amherst, Mass. and London, 1971).

Sutherland, Stewart R., *Faith and Ambiguity* (London, 1984).

Tanner, Kathryn, *God and Creation in Christian Theology: Tyranny or Empowerment?* (Oxford, 1988).

Unger, Roberto M., *Passion: An Essay on Personality* (New York, 1985).

Vanauken, Sheldon, *A Severe Mercy* (San Francisco, 1977).

—— *Under the Mercy* (Nashville, Tenn., 1985).

Warnock, Mary, *Imagination* (London, 1976).

—— 'Religious Imagination', in *Religious Imagination*, ed. James P. Mackey (Edinburgh, 1986).

Warren, Robert Penn, *All the King's Men* (San Diego, CA., 1976).

Weil, Simone, *Waiting for God*, trans. Emma Craufurd (New York, 1951).

Westphal, Merold, *Kierkegaard's Critique of Reason and Society* (Macon, Ga., 1987).

—— 'Kierkegaard's Sociology', in *International Kierkegaard Commentary: Two Ages*, ed. Robert L. Perkins (Macon, Ga., 1984).

Wheelwright, Philip, *The Burning Fountain* (Bloomington, Ind., rev. edn. 1968).

Willey, Basil, *Nineteenth Century Studies: Coleridge to Matthew Arnold* (New York, 1949).

Wisdo, David, 'Kierkegaard on Belief, Faith, and Explanation', *International Journal for Philosophy of Religion*, 21 (1987), 95–114.

Wisdom, John, *Paradox and Discovery* (Berkeley, CA., 1970).

Wittgenstein, Ludwig, *Culture and Value*, ed. G. H. Von Wright and trans. Peter Winch (Oxford, 1980).

—— *Philosophical Investigation*, trans. G. E. M. Anscombe (New York, 3rd edn. 1958).

Wollheim, Richard and James Hopkins (eds.), *Philosophical Essays on Freud* (Cambridge, 1982).

Index

'This is a work of great originality and high quality. It challenges the simple but all-too-common picture of Kierkegaard's "leap of faith" and replaces it with a subtle, but clear and helpful, account in which imagination plays a central role in ethical and religious transformation. I learned a great deal from it.'

Professor C. Stephen Evans, Professor of Philosophy and Curator, Hong Kierkegaard Library

The metaphor of a 'leap of faith' is probably the element most widely recognized as a distinctive characteristic of a 'Kierkegaardian' account of the transition to religious faith. Both in popular and scholarly circles this 'leap' has usually been understood in terms of an act of 'willpower'. Challenging such a volitionist view (as well as some current alternatives to it which see instead only an ineffable 'miracle' of grace), Professor Ferreira argues that Kierkegaard's striking appreciation of a wide variety of roles of imagination supports a reconceptualization of the 'leap' or 'decision' in terms of a reorienting shift in perspective, an imaginative revisioning. Exploring the relation between passion and paradox in several of Kierkegaard's accounts of selfhood, and developing an account of transitional choice in which imagination is a constitutive element, Professor Ferreira elaborates an understanding of the faith-transition in terms of such imaginative activities as 'suspension', 'synthesis', and 'engagement'. The analysis of imaginative activity in these ethical and religious transitions has, moreover, implications which go beyond Kierkegaard scholarship, for it bears importantly not only on other 'conversion' accounts, but also on the question of transitions to alternative or 'incommensurable' conceptual frameworks in general.

M. Jamie Ferreira is Associate Professor of Religious Studies and of Philosophy in the University of Virginia at Charlottesville.